A Spectacular Failure

COSTERUS NEW SERIES 198

Series Editors:
C.C. Barfoot, László Sándor Chardonnens
and Theo D'haen

A Spectacular Failure

Robinson Crusoe I, II, III

Virginia La Grand

 Amsterdam-New York, NY 2012

Contents

Preface 1

Chapter One
Reading *Robinson Crusoe* 3

Chapter Two
Print Discourse in Defoe's Day 31

Chapter Three
A Long Battle over *The Shortest-Way* 59

Chapter Four
Pirating *Robinson Crusoe* 87

Chapter Five
Robinson Crusoe's Textual Neighbors 107

Chapter Six
What Defoe Lost to the Pirates 129

Chapter Seven
A World United by Trade 157

Chapter Eight
Serious Reflections 185

Chapter Nine
The End of the Debate 215

Bibliography 229

Index 239

Robinson Crusoe and Friday live today in children's literature and childhood games. Tales of being lost on an island and wilderness survival tests also entertain twenty-first century adults. When Defoe wrote his story he insisted that it was a serious book for adults. He acknowledged that there were parts that might be called "invention or parable"[1] but he insisted that his story tackled religious and philosophical questions that he and his readers must ponder: what is the religious value of solitude? How can one hear the voice of Providence?

The story of Robinson Crusoe is part of our story. As twenty-first century readers in the European and North American world, we have become aware that there are related but different stories told by the various cultures in our world. Our anthropological sophistication has prepared us to acknowledge that the account of what happened to Defoe's tale is also a chapter in our global autobiography. The story of Defoe's work and its reception shows how cultures choose and shape their own stories. The specific transformations of this tale reveal fault lines and crisis points in modern thinking.

Daniel Defoe wrote *The Life and Strange Surprizing Adventures of Robinson Crusoe* as the tale of a young man seeking his vocation as an international trader. When Crusoe's shipwreck and survival caught the imagination of the public, Defoe tried to continue the tale in a second volume, *The Farther Adventures of Robinson Crusoe*. When the public remained interested only in the island adventure, Defoe tried to explicate his parable in a third volume, *Serious Reflections during the Life and Surprising Adventures of Robinson Crusoe: With His View of the Angelick World*. He promoted the set as a three-volume series, rather than as a single-volume story of individual triumph.

---

[1] Daniel Defoe, *The Farther Adventures of Robinson Crusoe: Being the Second and Last Part of His Life, and of the Strange and Surprising Accounts of His Travels Roud Three Parts of the Globe. Written by himself.* London, 1719. This statement comes from the Preface to the second volume of the Robinson Crusoe series.

Public reception celebrated the first volume for its narrative suspense and engaging narrative voice. On the same grounds, the public rightly dismissed the sequels. They lack the focus on despair and escape that unifies most of the first volume. The story of the author's three-volume work is not about a man's survival on a deserted island, but it is another kind of struggle for survival. Defoe's first volume achieved its popular success only in an altered version. Readers neglected the second and third volumes, and critics treated Defoe as a storyteller whose sequels were thinly disguised profiteering.

The second and third volumes of Defoe's saga will never become popular reading, but their history is a story of the way Western individualistic capitalism shaped its own myths. New approaches to literature and new studies of Defoe illuminate Defoe's effort to control the interpretation of his text. Communications revolutions in contemporary life – from "blogs" to "zines" – encourage literary scholars to treat literature as discourse rather than as a special artistic use of language cut off from ordinary uses. Contemporary confusions over fake news published in the satiric paper *The Onion* and over the status of the 1967 *Report from Iron Mountain*[2] highlight interpretation and misinterpretation as contemporary concerns. We have come to see fiction, drama, and poetry as part of the way a culture creates its public dialogue. Our contemporary concern with interpretation enables us to read the whole story of Robinson Crusoe. More than a story of survival on a desert island, the saga of Defoe's volumes is a story of a failed Speech Act.

The use of Discourse Analysis to study the three volumes of *Robinson Crusoe* lets us consider the series as a three-stage dialogue with its readers. We can investigate the role readers themselves played in creating Defoe's most famous work. In reconsidering these volumes, readers can see them as landmarks in the construction of our public square.

---

[2] Leonard Lewin, "Report from Iron Mountain", The Guest Word, *New York Times Book Review*, 19 March 1972, 47. In this essay Lewin confesses, "I wrote the 'Report,' all of it .... What I intended was simply to pose the issues of war and peace in a *provocative* way." This ironic volume pretends to be a secret report to the United States government advocating a constant state of war as the means of economic security. Conspiracy-hunting groups still insist that this document is an authentic report.

CHAPTER ONE

READING *ROBINSON CRUSOE*

Everyone knows Robinson Crusoe, the man. Scholars call *Robinson Crusoe*, the tale, a classic because it is a *"work of literature that has left the book*; it has become a defining part of those people's minds to whom it is a classic".[1] Although the first volume is nearly three-hundred-years old, editions continue to be reprinted and read. It is one of the books adults assume every child can and should read; if they cannot read, their grandparents delight in telling the story out loud. The fictional hero, cast away alone on an island, is a character people enjoy imagining. They can use him in organizing their ideas, without referring to the specific details of Defoe's narration. The fictional character Robinson Crusoe functions as a symbol according to Engler's operational definition: *"What does the symbol do? .... It creates community."*[2] We see the enduring fascination of the theme and the power of the symbol in current pop culture: a Hollywood film, *Cast Away*, in 2000, a long-running American television series, *Lost*, and another television series called *Robinson*.

Most readers see Robison Crusoe as a simple character, although they have interpreted this simple man in radically different ways: he can be a hero, or he can be a villain. Often people refer to Defoe's character as "Crusoe" so it comes as a surprise to note that when he thought of himself, he called himself "Robin". The narrator of the story, can serve as the archetype of the heroic European colonist who transforms desert islands into productive farms, and cannibals into Christians. Alternatively, he can serve as the archetype of the

---

[1] Balz Engler, *Poetry and Community*, Tübingen, 1990, 55 (emphasis in the original).
[2] *Ibid.*, 31-32 (emphasis in the original).

villainous imperial exploiter who seizes lands and enslaves people. In more complex treatments by authors such as Michel Tournier in *Friday* (1967), Derek Walcott in *Pantomime* (1980), and J.M. Coetzee in *Foe* (1986), the story becomes an investigation of the relationship between Robin and Friday. For these authors it serves as a vehicle for their examination of colonialism.

The character Robinson Crusoe lives outside of Defoe's text, but twenty-first-century readers have become interested in looking behind the text. Dana Souhami's 2001 book *Selkirk's Island: The True and Strange Adventures of the Real Robinson Crusoe* does just that, and its popularity shows that the reading public wants to go behind Defoe's imagined hero to imagine the privateering culture of the day. Souhami recounts how Alexander Selkirk was marooned on the Pacific Island Juan Fernandez in 1704, rescued in 1709, and celebrated in London in 1713.[3] Defoe's story was not simply an elaboration of Selkirk's adventure, but a critique of its public account. By tracing the story of the Robinson Crusoe volumes we can see that current events also shaped the way his texts were read.

Defoe's story of an island castaway was immensely popular as soon as *The Life and Strange Surprising Adventures of Robinson Crusoe ...* appeared on 23 April 1719. Many editions and several pirated versions appeared even before the publication of the second volume on 17 August 1719. Modern editors count six editions published by William Taylor in 1719.[4] The immediate translation of the first volume into German and French and the production of German and French imitation Robinson Crusoes indicate the wide

---

[3] Dana Souhami's Introduction makes Alexander Selkirk's life the single source of Defoe's book. She says, "The Island on which Alexander Selkirk was marooned, for four solitary years, lies in the eastern Pacific Ocean at latitude 34 [degrees] south, three hundred and sixty miles west of the coast of Chile. In 1966 the Chilean government named it Robinson Crusoe Island, in tribute to Selkirk, the real Robinson Crusoe, who inspired Daniel Defoe to write his famous novel in 1719" (Dana Souhami, *Selkirk's Island*, New York, 2001, unpaged Introduction).

[4] Taylor labeled the reprint editions two, three, and four, but produced two distinct printings of the third and fourth editions. In the *Norton Critical Edition*, editor Michael Shinagel says, "In this Norton Critical Edition I have followed the more recent bibliographical findings and speak of the *six* editions published by William Taylor in 1719" (*Robinson Crusoe*, New York, 1994, 222; Shinagel's italics).

appeal of the story. Both German and French translations appeared in 1720, and imitation tales followed a generation later. [5]

Defoe's two sequel volumes faded quickly after their publication and are now virtually unknown. In *The Farther Adventures of Robinson Crusoe*, the second volume in the series, Robin returns to the island for a brief visit and then takes a ten-year trading expedition to the Spice Islands before returning to London through China, Mongolia, and Siberia. The third volume of the series, *Serious Reflections ... of Robinson Crusoe*, appeared in August 1720, a year after the second volume. This third volume is a book of essays, beginning with the essay "Of Solitude" – in which Robin offers to tell what he has learned from being alone on his island. It features a long chapter on listening to Providence. Defoe claimed that this volume of essays belonged with the story volumes. Readers did not agree.

The publication history of Defoe's initial volume shows what readers thought the book was about: the triumph of an individual. Abridgments preserved Robin's island adventure and cut down both the frame story and the analysis. The popularity of the abridgments shows Defoe losing control of his text. Defoe's unsuccessful second and third volumes show that he failed to regain control of the narrative as it became a popular story. Because research libraries still have exemplars of his originals as well as the abridgments and the contemporary pamphlet commentary on his work, we can observe the struggle from a distance of nearly three-hundred years. Defoe's futile attempts to regain control over the text provide us a unique window on the negotiation of authorial rights.

Defoe's failure to control the Robinson Crusoe story does not represent a loss of his ability to write for the British public of his day. The volumes that modern readers know as his novels are only an episode in his career as a writer. After writing the three volumes of *Robinson Crusoe*, he went on to write four more first-person life-

---

[5] Paul Dottin lists three "French family Robinsons .... *Les memoires de chevalier de Kilpar* by Gain de Montagnac appearing in 1768, Grivel's *L'ile inconnue, ou Memoirs du chevalier de Gastines*, in 1783, and *Lolotte et Fanfan* of Ducray-Duminil, in 1788". These followed the publication of Rousseau's *Emil* (1762), which "called attention to the great human lesson in one man's experience on a desert island". Dottin says that in German "there was a Robinson for every district and subdivision, for every layer of the social strata" (*The Life and Strange Surprising Adventures of Daniel Defoe*, London, 1929, 206-207).

stories before abandoning this mode. *The Complete English Tradesman* (1726) and *A Tour thro' the Whole Island of Great Britain* (1724-27) returned to the combination of story and analysis that Defoe had pioneered in his *Family Instructor* (1715 and 1718).

Defoe's instructions to his readers

Defoe and his publisher insisted that the three volumes were a series. Certainly the way these volumes are written ties them together. The character Robinson Crusoe narrates all three. In the third volume this narrator assumes that the readers remember his struggles and his travels in both previous volumes. Defoe creates several different speakers for the Prefaces, because the reading public soon realized that Robinson Crusoe was the creation of Daniel Defoe, the well-known journalist. In the first volume the Preface speaker pretends to be the editor of a true story. By the second volume, the Preface editor is defending the story and complaining about abridgments. A year later, in the third volume, Defoe has "Robinson Crusoe" himself speak the Preface. Each Preface prescribes how the text is to be read, but the tone and specific topics all reply to contemporary critics.

By telling readers how to interpret the story and by responding to his critics, Defoe makes the interpretation of his story into one theme of the three-volume series. His main concerns may come as a surprise to twenty-first-century novel readers. As he flounders in his attempt to claim moral standing, we realize that he does not have a label for realistic fiction. There is no genre category to which he can appeal. The first-person seafaring journal written by a ship's captain was a well-established genre in the early eighteenth-century range of possible texts.[6] In imaginative writing there were fables, allegories, and medieval romances, but Defoe himself is often considered the first writer of the realistic novel. The term "novel" was not applied to this work, because of the simple fact that it did not exist in the critical vocabulary of the day.

---

[6] Willard Hallam Bonner reports, "In the seventy years before Dampier, then, there were but three collections of voyages in English worthy of notice. In the fourteen years following Dampier's *New Voyage* [1697] no less than eight completely new collections appeared in London" (*Captain William Dampier, Buccaneer-Author*, Stanford: CA, 1934, 53).

In his Prefaces, Defoe returns obsessively to the relationship between fact and imagination. He is stung by the critics' objections to his having invented the story. The critic Charles Gildon went so far as to accuse him of lying,[7], and this charge seems to have angered Defoe. To defend himself, in the Preface to the third volume he has Robinson Crusoe list scenes from the first that are allegorical representations of someone's actual experiences. Ian Watt comments on this section:

> These remarks seem to employ a crazy logic. What is the value of setting an invented name to verify the literal truth of an invented story? .... Defoe certainly muddies counsel; but we are entitled to assume that there is some truth in Crusoe's assertion that there is a 'man alive, and well known too'; the man is Defoe himself, and he is in some sense the subject of *Robinson Crusoe.*[8]

Defoe's book is not autobiography; it is a novel. Paula Backscheider describes this kind of literary communication, familiar to modern readers:

> In writing of Crusoe's experiences, Defoe drew upon his own emotions and created symbolic parallels. The progression of emotions in Crusoe reflects the succession of emotions, recollected and imagined, in Defoe and is transmitted to the reader who recognizes the state of mind, supplies a personal analogy, and therefore, shares in the emotional experience.[9]

Although Defoe had not been isolated on a deserted island, he had suffered social isolation when he was cast into prison for libel by a hostile judge and jury who refused to acknowledge the irony in Defoe's pamphlet *The Shortest-Way with the Dissenters.*

Readers then and now identify Defoe with his hero, but readers then and now fail to hear self-irony in Robin's account. Defoe's contemporary opponent Charles Gildon called Robin – and Daniel

---

[7] Charles Gildon, *The Life and Strange Surprizing Adventures of Mr D..... De F..., of London, Hosier* ... (London, 1719), in Paul Dottin, *Robinson Crusoe Examin'd and Criticis'd*, London, 1923, 33.
[8] Ian Watt, *Myths of Modern Individualism: Faust, Don Quixote, Don Juan, Robinson Crusoe*, Cambridge, 1996, 149-50.
[9] Paula Backscheider, *Daniel Defoe, His Life*, Baltimore, 1989, 415.

Defoe – "a strange, whimsical, inconsistent Being" in his 1719 pamphlet response to *Robinson Crusoe*.[10] The twentieth-century critic Everett Zimmerman also identifies the two:

> Defoe is no more distant from the Crusoe who acts than is the Crusoe who narrates. They share both a sympathy for the creature of their story and a limited insight into his failure.[11]

These critical readers cannot find an ironic distance between Robin and his creator. Unlike the narrator of Swift's "A Modest Proposal" Robin does not drop out of character to distance himself from his erratic or foolish positions. Another modern critic, Laura Curtis, sees the issue as a technical problem: "An innovator, Defoe had no support from a tradition showing how to differentiate the author's point of view from that of his fictional protagonist."[12]

In the Prefaces and in the third volume Defoe states his intention to teach a moral lesson. Robin promises the reader that he will distinguish his allegorical storytelling from "the Sport of Lying"[13] – an issue that does not trouble modern readers at all. Modern readers have no difficulty understanding that, as Paula Backscheider explains: "Its autobiographical elements are states of mind, not events."[14]

Responding to his critics, Defoe has Robin demand justice:

> If any Man object here, that the preceding Volumes of this Work seem to be hereby condemn'd and the History which I have therein publish'd of my self, censur'd; I demand in Justice, such Objector stay his Censure, till he sees the End of the Scene, when all the Mystery shall discover itself, and I doubt not, but the Work shall abundantly justify the Design, and the Design abundantly justify the Work.[15]

---

[10] Gildon puts these accusations in the voice of his parody of Crusoe (Gildon, *Life of D.... De F..*, viii).

[11] Everett Zimmerman, "Defoe and Crusoe", *English Literary History*, XXXVIII/3 (September 1971) 396.

[12] Laura Curtis, *The Elusive Daniel Defoe*, London, 1984, 7.

[13] Defoe, *Serious Reflections During the Life and Surprising Adventures of Robinson Crusoe*, 118.

[14] Backscheider, *Daniel Defoe, His Life*, 414.

[15] Defoe, *Serious Reflections During the Life and Surprising Adventures of Robinson Crusoe*, 118.

The lesson Robin points to, however, is not the one picked up by most of his contemporary readers or by twenty-first-century readers. Robin points to his essay "On Listening to the Voice of Providence". At the end of the scene, Defoe pictures Robin struggling to learn how to listen, not how to act. For Defoe's first readers and modern readers of *The Life and Strange Surprising Adventures of Robinson Crusoe*, the story celebrates rational self-reliance.

The third volume, *Serious Reflections During the Life and Surprising Adventures of Robinson Crusoe*, was the least successful volume of the series by a large margin. It deserves that failure. It is not entertaining. It contains no new adventures, but doggedly revisits the story told in the first and second volumes. A thread of social criticism of contemporary England familiar to Defoe readers runs through these essays. The volume meanders into a dead end in a chapter that looks astoundingly like his early pamphlet *The Shortest-Way with the Dissenters* in its cold-blooded recommendation of violence against religious opponents. This essay, "Of the Proportion between the Christian and Pagan World", carries Defoe's criticism of Protestant England to its most extreme level.[16] This essay was not received as satire. How can such a success as Defoe's *Robinson Crusoe* be part of a series with these failed sequels?

If the three volumes are a series, is the popular reading of *The Life and Strange Surprising Adventures of Robinson Crusoe* mistaken? Defoe himself forces this question on the critical reader by Robin's assertion at the very beginning of the third volume:

> As the Design of every Thing is said to be first in the Intention and last in the Execution; so I come now to acknowledge to my reader, That the present Work is not merely the Product of the two first Volumes, but the two first Volumes may rather be called the Product of this: The Fable is always made for the Moral, not the Moral for the Fable.[17]

Is it possible that Defoe's perception of his story was radically different from that of his contemporary readers and from ours?

---

[16] Defoe, *Serious Reflections During the Life and Surprising Adventures of Robinson Crusoe*, Chapter 6, 217-49.

[17] *Ibid.*, "Robinson Crusoe's Preface", ix.

Nothing can reverse the failures of Defoe's second and third volumes. But a close look at the whole series can illuminate the roots of our self-made culture.

The limits of previous studies of *Robinson Crusoe*
Many critics have examined the first volume of the Robinson Crusoe series. Very few critics have worked with the second and third volumes. No one has treated the three volumes as a thematically linked series. Studies of Defoe's religious or economic views, such as Robert Stamm's *Der aufgeklärte Puritanismus Daniel Defoes* use the second and third volumes in their argument, but do not focus on the relation between the three volumes.[18] Paula Backscheider's definitive biography, *Daniel Defoe, His Life*, mentions incidents from the first two volumes in presenting Defoe's skillful mix of character, incident and didactic theme. Backscheider's summation of the third volume is that it "responds specifically to ridicule of the novel".[19] She does not examine how *Serious Reflections* picks up themes from *The Life and Strange Surprising Adventures of Robinson Crusoe*. This omission by critics from the beginning to the present time can be explained not only by the obscurity of the second and third volumes, but also by Defoe's ambiguous status in the canon of English literature. All three volumes have been printed in scholarly editions, but these copies have been available only in research libraries.[20]

One reason the second and third volumes could be ignored was that Defoe himself seems to be an example of accidental success. Moving from political pamphleteering to journalism to story-telling, and then how-to books and economic geography, he wrote fiction for only a few years of his career. Defoe's prose style with its long cumulative and paratactic sentences, its colloquial vocabulary, its eccentric punctuation, and its lack of political or literary allusions allows modern readers to feel that they are hearing the voice of an energetic,

---

[18] Rudolf Stamm, *Der aufgeklärte puritanismus Daniel Defoes*, Zurich, 1936.

[19] Backscheider, *Daniel Defoe, His Life*, 414.

[20] For example, Cambridge University Library and the British Library have copies of all three and copies of many early abridged versions. The Newberry Library in Chicago has copies of all three original volumes and copies of many early abridgments. Now these texts are available as electronic texts at many college libraries through the Gale collection *Eighteenth Century Collections Online*, 2005.

enthusiastic, simple businessman. The same features encouraged Defoe's contemporaries both to identify him as the speaker of this narrative and to disparage his writing as not having a structure worthy of analysis.

His peers did not respect him as an artist. In her study *The Elusive Daniel Defoe*, Laura Curtis reports on Defoe's reputation: "In the early eighteenth century Jonathan Swift anathematized Defoe as a stupid, illiterate fanatic, and Joseph Addison dismissed him as a false, prevaricating rogue."[21] Unlike Swift, Pope, and Dryden, he has not been given a place in the literary canon shaped by these same eighteenth-century classicists. Later critics, copying the dismissive attitude of his contemporary opponents, saw him as a facile writer willing to sell his pen to the highest bidder. For many critical readers Defoe stood as a symbol of writing as a commodity: valuable, powerful, and suspect. This suspicion led critics to suggest that *The Farther Adventures of Robinson Crusoe* and *Serious Reflections* were simply attempts to make a quick profit on a popular title. Even Ian Watt, the twentieth-century critic who champions Defoe as the inventor of the realistic novel, dismisses the second and third volumes of the series: "The truth seems to be that Defoe, as he finished the first volume, and knowing more Crusoe adventures would sell, thought of a second part; and then calculated that the odd scraps of writing from his desk could be turned to profit if they were attributed to Crusoe in a third."[22]

Defoe's opponents accused him of writing for money, not from conviction. While it is true that Defoe had not set out to be a writer, it is also true that before this period the kind of public writing by which he supported himself and his family was not a possible career. In fact, Defoe's career options were limited. The University, the Church, and the Military were barred to him because he was a Dissenter. The Dissenters pastors were "Presbyterians and Independents [who] had been introduced into church livings during the Commonwealth",[23] and they refused to comply with the 1662 Act of Uniformity, an Act that required exclusive adherence to the Book of Common Prayer and

---

[21] Curtis, *The Elusive Daniel Defoe*, 7.
[22] Watt, *Myths of Modern Individualism*, 147.
[23] Frederick A. Youngs, *The English Heritage*, 2nd edn, Arlington Heights: IL, 1988, 156.

outlawed non-Anglican worship services. Backscheider judges that "Almost every provision of the oaths either contradicted an earlier oath or violated the consciences of non-Anglicans".[24] Some 1,800 clergymen left the official English church at that time. Defoe's family followed their pastor, Samuel Annesly, out of the established church. The Act of Uniformity also required any office holder to take communion in the Anglican Church. The Act of Toleration that King William managed to pass in 1689 gave the Dissenters and other non-Anglican Protestants permission to assemble for worship, but even under the Act of Toleration "Public office, both in the central government and at the local level, was restricted to communicants of the Church of England".[25] The term "dissenter" gradually came to incorporate non-Anglican Protestants from various groups, since they all had the same political disadvantages.

Dissenters established excellent clandestine schools for their children, and Defoe attended one of these. The Newington Green Academy was set up by Charles Morton, an Oxford graduate whose teaching earned him harassment by the Bishop's court.[26] Defoe spent five years in Morton's Academy. Backscheider infers that he "must have begun the theological curriculum".[27] But Defoe did not become a Dissenting preacher. Instead he became a shopkeeper, a property developer, and a public-minded businessman. He was full of money-making schemes, but his business career was haunted by ambitious projects that he failed to control – including a ship at sea captured by French privateers when England and France went to war. When his creditors ran out of patience, Defoe was imprisoned for debt and

---

[24] Backscheider, *Daniel Defoe, His Life*, 7.

[25] Youngs, *The English Heritage*, 191.

[26] The treatment Defoe's teacher and his pastor received shows the atmosphere of religious persecution in which Defoe grew up: "Before he [Charles Morton] emigrated to America to accept Increase Mather's invitation to assume the presidency of Harvard College, he had been excommunicated, apprehended on a *capitas* [an arrest writ], repeatedly arrested, and, in his own words, 'infested with Processes from the Bishops Court.' He and Annesley had both been rounded up and imprisoned as 'disaffected and dangerous' men during the fear of a rebellion in October 1684" (Backscheider, *Daniel Defoe, His Life*, 14).

[27] Backscheider calculates that Defoe was one of the "theological students" at Morton's Academy. He was there for five years, and "lay students" only stayed there for three years. Backscheider also quotes Defoe's own memory of having once felt that he was "set a-part" to be a pastor (*ibid.*, 14-15).

declared bankrupt in 1692. Backscheider details all his failed projects, and delivers a summary judgment:

> Surely the war and Defoe's ambitious speculations contributed, but his bankruptcy was, at the core, boringly mundane. The greatest causes were his inattention to detail and his speculations, and his initial mistakes probably as basic as inexperience, investing in too much stock, and having too many of his debts due before he could collect money owed him.[28]

Defoe negotiated with his creditors and got out of debtors prison. Through friends he got a job as an accountant to the collector of duty on glassware. He came up with new entrepreneurial plans – land speculation, tile manufacture, building public housing, and writing. He wrote for the religious market – an elegy on his pastor Samuel Annesley. He wrote his *Essay on Projects* as a money making project of his own, and Backscheider judges, "It might have been expected to make money".[29] He proposed a new financial system involving a national bank. He proposed overseas ventures such as a colony on the Orinoco River in South America. He was part of the English commercial development that led to England's revolution of 1688, and he was one of the businessmen King William consulted.

Defoe began writing political pamphlets while he was a London businessman. He claimed the right to speak on political issues. Defoe was credited with an open letter to Parliament, *Legion's Memorial*, in 1701. The letter asserted his right as an Englishman to petition parliament. Writing anonymously, as was the custom for such pamphlets, he nevertheless set himself up for ridicule by his self-ironic use of Biblical allusion. Defoe closed his pamphlet with an echo of the demons Jesus cast out of a man and into a herd of swine (Mark 5.9): "Our name is LEGION, and we are many." For Defoe the allusion warned his opponents not to imagine that they were dealing with only

---

[28] Paula Backscheider, sees this early bankruptcy as a transformative experience for Defoe: "The attack on Defoe's self-image, the years of financial struggle, and the final financial collapse changes Defoe forever from a prominent joiner of respected groups to a solitary with secrets, and from a tradesman to a writer" (*ibid.*, 61).
[29] *Ibid.*, 68.

one troublesome spirit, but with a whole crowd. Defoe's opponents seized this allusion to caricature Defoe as a devil.[30]

After 1704 Defoe was paid by the government to write on public issues. He was part of Robert Harley's[31] public-opinion research and propaganda operation, but he resisted being labeled as a propagandist. In his own summary of his career as writer for the government, *An Appeal to Honour and Justice* (1715), Defoe protested that although he had been loyal to Harley, he had never been a blind follower and that he had never taken instructions on what to write. Backscheider evaluates Defoe's claim with sympathetic skepticism:

> Harley's and the secretaries of states' grants … usually came *after* the publication of useful or pleasing pamphlets …. If Defoe received his money in all or some of these ways, he was guilty of special pleading, not lying.[32]

Defoe's opponents charged that he had no consistent principles. They proved their charge by assigning him authorship of several contradictory anonymous pamphlets. Defoe protested that his opponents linked him with pamphlets he had not written:

> I do grant, had all the books which have been called by my name, been written by me, I must, of necessity, have exasperated every side; and, perhaps have deserved it. But I have the greatest injustice imaginable in this treatment, as I have [also] in the perverting [of] the design, of what really I have written. I bore infinite Reproaches from clamouring Pens, of being in the *French* Interest, being hir'd and brib'd to defend a bad Peace, and the like.[33]

Nineteenth-century critics generally accepted the accusations against Defoe. Many would-be biographers began their study by trying to establish a list of his works. They searched through the reams

---

[30] *Ibid.*, 82.

[31] Robert Harley, later the Earl of Oxford, was a supporter of King William in 1688. Under Queen Anne he was Speaker of the House from 1701 to 1705 and a principal secretary of State for the Northern Department 1704 to 1708. Out of office in 1708, he was back in the government as Chancellor of the Exchequer in 1710.

[32] Backscheider, *Daniel Defoe, His Life*, 358.

[33] Daniel Defoe, *An Appeal to Honour and Justice* (London, 1715), in *The Shortest-Way with the Dissenters and Other Pamphlets*, Oxford, 1974, 103.

of anonymous pamphlets preserved in libraries and in private collections. These biographers often let their personal feelings and moral judgments about Defoe influence their attributions, as P.N. Furbank and W.R. Owens show in their 1988 study *The Canonisation of Daniel Defoe.*[34] Furbank and Owens track the efforts of the major Defoe bibliographers, of whom there were many. Starting with George Chalmers in 1790, this list includes Walter Wilson (1830), William Lee (1869), James Crossley (1884), W.P. Trent (1912), and John Robert Moore (1961). These biographers' conviction that Defoe had written on almost any political or economic topic and that his style was conversational rather than ornamented led them to think they had discovered hitherto unknown works by Defoe in the welter of anonymous eighteenth-century pamphlets. They often had no more to go on than the topic and style of the pamphlet.

From the speculative 128 items in the Defoe canon suggested by George Chalmers ninety years after Defoe's death, the list grew to the 570 in John Robert Moore's 1960 *Checklist*.

Recent developments in studies of *Robinson Crusoe*
Recently scholars have begun to take Defoe seriously both as a thinker and as an artist. This change accompanies a re-evaluation of his whole body of writing, including the Robinson Crusoe series. The scholarly reappraisal of his canon led P.N. Furbank and W.R. Owens to question many of the attributions that have been added over the years. They say:

> The Defoe 'canon' is a remarkably strange and not very satisfactory construction. It contains, indeed, as odd and as great an assortment of texts as, perhaps, has ever been attributed to one author, and for the larger part these texts have been ascribed on internal evidence alone.

---

[34] P.N. Furbank and W.R. Owens began their 1988 study of the Defoe canon with a puzzle. Their investigation led to two more volumes – one in 1994 (*Defoe De-Attributions*) and one in 1998 (*A Critical Bibliography of Daniel Defoe*). Their initial concern was "a feeling, which seems to be shared in varying degrees by a number of scholars, that …. from the very beginning, something may have gone wrong – that some error crept in, begetting over the years a long series of further errors, or that the basic principles of attribution adopted have somehow been faulty" (*The Canonisation of Daniel Defoe*, New Haven: CT, 1988, 1).

Can they really all be by Defoe? It calls for most ingenious mental gymnastics to support this belief.[35]

Furbank and Owens narrow the list of writings attributed to Defoe by insisting on external as well as internal evidence for attribution. They also refuse to assume that Defoe was an unprincipled pen for hire, "a gratuitous and incorrigible hoaxer".[36] Their analysis of Defoe's work rests on their own hypothesis about who Defoe was and what he was doing. They imagine Defoe as:

> … an extremely clever (and in a sense rather solitary) man who felt he had good reason, intellectually speaking, to despise his adversaries – not without a lingering incredulity that they could be so crass. Indeed it is plain that he did despise them; for though his tone towards them is often plaintive and self-righteous, it is just as often airily and triumphantly mocking.[37]

In their 1994 *Defoe De-Attributions*, Furbank and Owens suggest the removal of 252 of Moore's 570 items.[38] *A Critical Bibliography of Daniel Defoe* (1998) completes their three-volume bibliographical project by giving a detailed description of the Defoe works that have survived their scrutiny.

The revised Defoe canon supports not only respect for Defoe's thinking, but also a new appreciation for Defoe's creative ability. This is the latest in a long series of reappraisals. In English-speaking culture, Defoe was always a well-known writer because of the enduring popularity of Robinson Crusoe abridgments. Defoe's standing as an artist, however, had nowhere to go but up. By the early twentieth century, Defoe was respected as the creator of a great story. It was generally assumed that he had invented all of the details in *Robinson Crusoe*. Arthur Wellesley Secord[39] reversed that approach

---

[35] Furbank and Owens, *The Canonisation of Daniel Defoe*, 1.

[36] *Ibid.*, 9.

[37] *Ibid.*, 148.

[38] P.N. Furbank and W.R. Owens, *Defoe De-Attributions: A Critique of J.R. Moore's Checklist*, London, 1994, xiii.

[39] Arthur Wellesley Secord, *Studies in the Narrative Method of Defoe*, Urbana: IL, 1924. Secord links Defoe's Robinson Crusoe to contemporary English seafaring tales – especially the account of Robert Knox's captivity in Ceylon (published in 1681) and Captain William Dampier's accounts of his voyages (published in 1697). Secord does

by arguing that Defoe was abreast of the science of his day and that Defoe had constructed his story by copying travel narration.

Subsequently, Defoe scholars began to pay attention to his artistic expression of religious and philosophical positions. R.L. Stamm's1938 study judges that Defoe himself had been unable to see and admit his departure from his orthodox religious roots. Stamm traces Defoe's capacity for sophisticated thinking to this conflict, but also sees there the roots of what he calls Defoe's lack of clarity and dishonesty about his own intentions.[40]

Carrying on the line of analysis that sees Defoe as part of the enlightenment, Ian Watt presents Defoe as a pragmatist – one of the architects of modern individualism. He was one of the pioneers of the literary technique of formal realism, a style that, Watt says, accompanies a larger change: the replacement of "the unified world picture of the Middle Ages with ... a developing but unplanned aggregate of particular individuals having particular experiences at particular times and at Particular places".[41] As far as Watt is concerned, Defoe's religious interests are irrelevant to the story. Watt's 1996 study *Myths of Modern Individualism* reaffirms his earlier analysis of Robin's significance:

> The story shows how an ordinary man, quite alone, is able to subdue nature to his own material purposes, and eventually to triumph over his physical environment. In the context of Crusoe's life in the island, rational ecological and economic labor can be seen as the moral premise which underlies his character.[42]

---

not see Defoe's work as having been influenced by other contemporary stories of imaginary islands. The search of contemporary sources continues to occupy scholarly attention. Defoe's connection to the Netherlands though his work with King William and Robert Harley make it likely that he was acquainted with the Dutch tale, *The Mighty Kingdom of Krinke Kesmes*, a book published in 1708 in Amsterdam. David Fausset argues that "a chain of works led from the utopia to the Robinsonade and from the historical romance to the pseudo-authentic travel report (the crime that Defoe was chiefly accused of). *Krinke Kesmes* was a vital link in that chain, a model without which it is doubtful whether *Crusoe* could ever have been written at all" (David Fausset, *The Strange Surprizing Sources of Robinson Crusoe*, Amsterdam, 1994, 13).

[40] Stamm, *Der aufgeklärte puritanismus Daniel Defoes*, 111.

[41] Ian Watt, *The Rise of the Novel*, Berkley: CA, 1962, 31.

[42] Watt, *Myths of Modern Individualism*, 151.

After Watts' philosophic appreciation in 1957, other scholars turned to an examination of Defoe's literary craftsmanship. Both G.A. Starr and J. Paul Hunter studied Defoe's development of English Protestant written genres – conversion narration and spiritual autobiography. In the 1960s, articles such as J. Paul Hunter's "Friday as a Convert"[43] and books such as G.A. Starr's *Defoe and Spiritual Autobiography*[44] and Hunter's *The Reluctant Pilgrim*[45] demonstrated that Defoe was making artistic use of contemporary popular religious writing.

The work of Paula Backscheider consolidates the modern re-evaluation of Defoe's artistic achievement. She sees his work as part of the eighteenth-century redefinition of the nature and concerns of literature. In her 1986 *Daniel Defoe: Ambition and Innovation*, she argues this case:

> What Defoe did was to join Dryden and other writers in extending the idea of literature beyond the narrow confines of the classical conception – to include periodical essays, history, biography, memoirs and travel books, all forms that every era since the Renaissance has found troublesome …. Literature also came to accept the tasks of collecting knowledge and of interpreting events.[46]

Backscheider presents Defoe as a "writer aware of his roots [in literature]" and aware of his own artistry.[47] Her panoramic biography published in 1989, *Daniel Defoe, His Life*, explains how his writing responded to and shaped the growing public forum of eighteenth-century English political and cultural life. She presents a sympathetic study of Defoe as a man whose poetry, narrative, and political essays illuminate each other. Backscheider sees Defoe as a man who had learned the lessons that Robinson Crusoe cites in the Preface to *Serious Reflections*: the necessity for "invincible Patience",

---

[43] J. Paul Hunter, "Friday as a Convert", *Review of English Studies*, New Series, XIV/55 (1963), 243-48.

[44] G.A. Starr, *Defoe and Spiritual Autobiography* (1965), New York, 1971.

[45] J. Paul Hunter, *The Reluctant Pilgrim: Defoe's Emblematic Method and Quest for Form in Robinson Crusoe*, Baltimore: MD, 1966.

[46] Paula Backscheider, *Daniel Defoe: Ambition and Innovation*, Lexington: KY, 1986, 5.

[47] *Ibid.*, 7.

"indefatigable Application", and "undaunted Resolution". Tracing Defoe's survival through bankruptcy, imprisonment, and political struggles, she says that Defoe "had the power to make himself happy, and if Robinson Crusoe shows a transforming imagination, it is because Defoe had a transforming will".[48]

The present critical climate provides a good time to re-examine Daniel Defoe's *Robinson Crusoe* series because we have the historical distance, the critical tools, and the cultural concerns for the task. Our own communications revolutions have made us able to look back on the way modern culture developed in the eighteenth century. Defoe's interests – the importance of solitude (or to use the current term "privacy"), the moral value of trade, and how to interpret events in our own lives – still interest us today.

Defoe's struggle for cultural respectability

Daniel Defoe wrote at a time when both readers and writers felt that a change was taking place in literature. Some readers and writers who looked to Greek and Latin classical texts as the high point of literary value reviled the changes, even as their own work participated in the revolution. Jonathan Swift's *The Battle of the Books* (1704) is an innovative satire in defense of the traditionalists. Even though the classicists despised the new kinds of literature and their authors, Swift and his friends Pope, and Gay live on in their parodies of classical genres, not in the creation of new epics or tragedies. The traditionalists attacked the innovators for their failure to work within established literary genres, and some of the innovators, such as Defoe, struggled to find respectable genre labels for their work. As already noted, the term "novel" was not available to Defoe. Furbank and Owens explain that our idea of Defoe as essentially a novelist originated during the 1770s and was the achievement of a bookseller, and proprietor of a fashionable circulating library, Francis Noble.[49]

The term "romance" was the eighteenth-century category for long, imagined prose narrative, but Defoe has Robin treat this term as a slander in his Preface to *Serious Reflections*:

---

[48] Backscheider, *Daniel Defoe, His Life*, 427.

[49] P.N. Furbank and W. R. Owens, *A Critical Bibliography of Daniel Defoe*, London, 1994, xv.

> I have heard, that the envious and ill-disposed Part of the World have
> rais'd some Objections against the two first Volumes, on Pretence, *for
> want of a better Reason*; That (*as they say*) the Story is feign'd, that
> the Names are borrow'd, and that it is all a Romance.

Defoe's contemporary Aphra Behn makes the same kind of disclaimer
in her *Epistle Dedicatory* for her story *Oroonoko:*

> If there be any thing that seems Romantick, I beseech your Lordship
> to consider, these Countries do, in all things, so far differ from ours,
> that they produce unconceivable Wonders .... What I have mention'd I
> have taken care shou'd be Truth, let the Critical Reader judge as he
> pleases.[50]

These two protests demonstrate some of the emotional force of these
authors' search for a respectable literary genre for their work. Chapter
Four of this study will examine some of the popular genres that sprung
up at the same time as works that were later called novels.

London readers did not have the modern novel as a familiar genre,
but they did have one genre that modern readers lack: the pamphlet
exchange, a genre very familiar to Defoe. This mode of writing shows
some of the interactive characteristics of oral debate. Early eighteenth-
century pamphlets discuss current events; they allude to other
pamphlet texts; they were written and printed quickly in a colloquial
style that imitates other genres and often uses satire, irony, and
invective; they often combine prefaces that address the reader directly
with texts in other genres. Pamphlets were often reprinted with new
introductory comments by the author. In all these features, the three
volumes of the *Robinson Crusoe* series resemble Defoe's pamphlets.

Looking back at the first volume of the *Robinson Crusoe* series, we
can see that Robin is an energetic and sympathetic character, but he is
far from being a heroic figure by any standard – Classical,
Renaissance, or Elizabethan. In fact he is often a fool. He is
interesting not only because he suffers and conquers, but because he
analyzes and reflects on his situation. He dramatizes himself, debates
with himself, changes his mind, and mocks himself. Robin's account

---

[50] Aphra Behn, "Epistle Dedicatory", *Oroonoko* (London, 1688), ed. Joanna Lipking,
New York, 1997, 7.

shows him not only arguing with himself, but also intermittently aware of his own clownish behavior.

The events of the first volume can seem heroic to modern readers for whom the survival of the individual narrator is a favorite theme. Robin constructs a self-sustaining economy on his island. But he does not set up a colony or a center of trade. Robin's survival testifies to his patience and application, but his fortune comes to him as trust income from his partner in Brazil and from the various colonial and religious institutions that had guarded his financial rights under Portuguese colonial law.

Contemporary abridgments and criticism indicate that Defoe's first readers focused on Robin's suffering and survival in the first volume. Close reading of all three volumes shows that the second and third volumes reiterate other themes that the first readers misunderstood or ignored.

Literary genre as a speech act
Twenty-first-century schools of literary criticism build their approaches to literary genre on the studies of speech and literature undertaken by linguists and literary scholars in the previous century. The prime achievement of this earlier work was discovering and exploring the force of conventional rules in language use. Both structural and transformational linguistics focused attention on hidden structures and processes in spoken language. Twentieth-century linguistics also explored the use of conventional rules of language use in speech genre and in literary genre as part of the dialogue between reader and author. The work of linguistic philosophers J.L. Austin and John Searle in Speech Act Theory examined the social and linguistic preconditions for effective speech acts.[51] J. Paul Grice followed this lead by exploring how shared conventions of quality, quantity, relevance, and manner illuminate conversational interchange.[52] Elizabeth Traugott and Mary Louise Pratt showed that the conventions of literary genre in any given culture illuminate the implicit

---

[51] J.L. Austin, *How To Do Things With Words* (1955), eds J.O. Urmson and Mariana Sbisa, 2nd edn, Oxford, 1992; John Searle, *Speech Acts: An Essay in the Philosophy of Language*, London, 1969.
[52] J.P. Grice, *Studies in the Way of Words*, Cambridge: MA, 1989.

communication in the writer's choice of genre.[53] Culler suggests that "Novels [can be] treated … as real instances of a broad class of discourses: narrative display texts".[54] These texts set up a dialogue between reader and writer. Shared discourse conventions of genre and reading methods help a display text work. Shaping these insights into a critical series called "New Historicism: Studies in Cultural Poetics", the Shakespeare scholar Stephen Greenblatt points out how all authors "depend upon collective genres, narrative patterns, and linguistic conventions".[55] This work helps explain how difficult it can be for readers to interpret innovative texts such as Defoe's *The Life and Strange Surprising Adventures of Robinson Crusoe.*

Culler goes one step further in 1988 when he calls on critics to develop a linguistics of writing that would explore the ways a text can imply meanings.[56] To uncover the rules of speech, linguists have to idealize speech. Culler reminds us that writing and reading literature are not like coding and decoding a message: "A linguistics of writing, by contrast [with a linguistics of speech], would be one that gives a central place to those aspects of language set aside by [the transformational-generative] model, whether they are associated with the written character or with features of speech neglected by linguistic idealization."[57]

Twenty-first-century critics study not only at how works are constructed, but also how they are received and interpreted. To readers and critics today, it seems clear that literature fits into a wide array of communication styles. Film, video, music, and text – all shape public culture. Literary scholarship that takes account of cultural dialogue is better able to appreciate Defoe's work than earlier approaches. Once we see literature as an interaction between author and reader, we can

---

[53] Elizabeth Traugott and Mary Louise Pratt, *Linguistics for Students of Literature*, New York, 1980, 241: "Just as there are types and categories of illocutionary acts at the sentence level, so there are types and categories of extended utterances at the discourse level. Some obvious examples are sermons, interviews, prayers, letters, advertisements, oaths, press releases, stories, and speeches. These are referred to as 'speech genres.' Literary genres will also be identified as speech genres."

[54] Jonathan Culler, *Framing the Sign: Criticism and Its Institutions*, Oxford, 1988, 211.

[55] Stephen Greenblatt, *Shakespearean Negotiations*, Berkeley: CA 1988, 5.

[56] Culler, *Framing the Sign: Criticism and Its Institutions*, 217.

[57] *Ibid.*, 222.

look at what readers make of it in terms of communication success and communication failure.

Without abandoning the close attention to textual structure, literary critics at the end of the twentieth-century turned their attention also to the way literary texts participate in their culture. Wolfgang Iser summarizes this progression in his 1989 collection of essays, *Prospecting: From Reader Response to Literary Anthropology*. His brief historical account of this progression in criticism brings us to the current state of affairs:

> The three key concepts of current literary theory – structure, function and communication – have joined together through a sort of historical chain-reaction. The dominance of the structure concept led to the emergence of a function concept, and this has led, in turn, to an ever-increasing interest in communication.[58]

The political valence of literary genre

When Defoe was writing, the rules for public communication were changing in England. Defoe, the businessman-turned-writer, grew up in a new era of mass literacy and virtually uncensored publication, but he came of age in a time of re-imposition of government control. He tripped over the new rules.

American readers of English literature might assume that freedom of speech is an English tradition. Not so. Frederick Siebert shows that since the introduction of the printing press to England the crown had claimed the right to control the press. In the more than two-hundred years of printing in England, the government had limited printing presses to London, Cambridge and Oxford. It had insisted on pre-publication censorship. Writers and rulers had developed conventions that allowed for political commentary behind a screen of literary devices. The development of English Protestantism was accompanied by a widespread increase in literacy, a deluge of uncensored pamphlets, and an appeal to popular assent that broke all the old agreements. During the period of political turmoil in England between 1640 and 1660 – a period that included the Civil Wars 1642-46 and 1648-49 and then the Commonwealth period from 1649 to 1660 – the

---

[58] Wolfgang Iser, *Prospecting: From Reader Response to Literary Anthropology*, Baltimore: MD, 1989, 230.

crown lost its control over the press, but the restored Stuart monarchy reasserted this right. Then in the Bloodless Revolution of 1688, Parliament claimed the right to censor.[59]

In 1695, when Daniel Defoe was thirty-five-years old, pre-publication censorship ended, but it ended by accident. The censorship law lapsed. Parliament failed to renew it. The legal change came because of party infighting, not because Parliament believed in the freedom of speech. Neither the crown nor Parliament gave up their desire to censor printed material, as Defoe was to discover. Nevertheless, the abolition of pre-publication censorship changed the rules of public discourse at a time when Defoe was becoming interested in public affairs.

Pre-publication censorship had driven authors to use allusion, symbol, metaphor, irony, and dramatic voice to avoid direct political argumentation. Annabelle Patterson argues that state censorship made exotic settings and characters self-protective as well as artistic choices. She points out that even before print made written texts available to a wide reading public, Western culture had developed the category of written literature. Patterson reminds her readers: "[the] concept of 'literature,' as a kind of discourse with rules of its own … has for centuries been thought to be capable of protecting writers who have tried to abide by those rules."[60] Such classification created a public space that was removed from direct political involvement, a space which both writers and rulers found useful.

Patterson's analysis emphasizes the political forces that shielded some texts from government repression, but the existing literary conventions allowed no room for the pamphlets, satires, or journal essays that sprang up during the English revolution – a *de facto* censorship holiday. These genres continued to grow in the early eighteenth century. Once the category of realistic novel was developed, this kind of segregation of literature from other kinds of writing again allowed writers to take shelter from government scrutiny, but the genre "realistic novel" did not yet exist for Defoe. When the genre was recognized as literature, it still excluded the large

---

[59] Frederick Seaton Siebert, *Freedom of the Press in England 1476-1766: The Rise and Decline of Government Controls*, Urbana: IL, 1952, 22.

[60] Annabelle Patterson, *Censorship and Interpretation: The Conditions of Writing and Reading in Early Modern England* (1984), Madison: WI, 1990, 4.

bulk of Defoe's writing, covering, essentially, five works written during five years of his thirty-four year career. Discourse Analysis, with its focus on genre conventions, pries open categories to allow the study of Defoe's neglected work. It also provides a tool for examining the contemporary writing that formed its context.

A new critical framework: Relevance Theory

Linguistic analysis and the history of censorship in England help us see that Defoe's first readers were not guided by genre conventions as they read *The Life and Strange Surprising Adventures of Robinson Crusoe*. A critical theory that goes beyond the exploration of shared convention is needed to explain how Defoe's admiring readers missed some of his important themes. Speech Act Theory, which analyzes both speech and literature from the bottom up as rule-based behavior, is of limited use. Dan Sperber and Dierdre Wilson offer a radical development to Speech Act Theory. Their Relevance Theory comes at language study from the top down – as part of the human ability to communicate. They argue that the exploration of speech genres distracted scholars from the primary distinction between "two different modes of communication: the coding-decoding mode and the inferential mode".[61] Claiming that the inferential mode is primary, they say that "languages are indispensable not for communication, but for information processing".[62] Language can be decoded because it is such a highly structured component of human communication. They give credit to J. Paul Grice for "an idea of fundamental importance: that the very act of communicating creates expectations which it then exploits".[63]

Sperber and Wilson's book opens with the broad simple question: "How do human beings communicate with one another?"[64] Most simply, they say, communication involves mutual recognition of a desire to communicate. Even before a listener interprets, the speaker has made interpretive choices:

---

[61] Dan Sperber and Dierdre Wilson, *Relevance: Communication and Cognition*, 2nd edn, Oxford, 1995, 7.
[62] *Ibid.*, 171.
[63] *Ibid.*, 37.
[64] *Ibid.*, 1.

> We see verbal communication as involving a speaker producing an utterance as a public interpretation of one of her thoughts, and the hearer constructing a mental interpretation of this utterance, and hence of the original thought. Let us say that an utterance is an *interpretive expression* or a thought of the speaker's, and that the hearer makes an *interpretive assumption* about the speaker's informative intention.[65]

It is the shared assumptions of speaker and listener that make communication possible. The listener knows that the speaker is trying to communicate something relevant in the situation using shared resources of language, culture, and experience:

> … all the hearer can take for granted is that an utterance is intended as an interpretation of one of the speaker's thoughts …. If the speaker has done her job correctly, all the hearer has to do is start computing, in the order of accessibility, those implications which might be relevant to him [*sic*],[66] and continue to add them to the overall interpretation of the utterance until it is relevant enough to be consistent with the principle of relevance.[67]

Sperber and Wilson use common experience to support their model of communication. They say, "People certainly do not express themselves literally all the time, and when they do not, there is no intuition that a norm has been transgressed".[68]

The complexity of their model challenges the older simple models of speech as the transmission of a message:

> … an utterance used as an interpretation of someone else's thought is always, in the first place, an interpretation of one's understating of that other person's thought. When we talk of utterances used to interpret someone else's thought, it should be clear, then, that we are always talking of second-degree interpretations.[69]

---

[65] *Ibid.*, 230-31 (emphases in the original).

[66] Sperber and Wilson use alternating masculine and feminine third-person singular pronouns in order to be gender inclusive, which has the advantage of avoiding the wordy "his or her" used in the present study.

[67] Sperber and Wilson, *Relevance*, 234.

[68] *Ibid.*, 230.

[69] *Ibid.*, 238.

According to Sperber and Wilson, when people explicate what they hear, they explicate both the literal utterance and the implications. In both kinds of explication the listener must use encyclopedic information to resolve any potential ambiguities. The speaker and listener share a presumption of relevance: the speaker intended an ostensive communication to lead the hearer to the most easily accessible mutually manifest information.[70] The shared context of the utterance is part of the speaker's communication and part of the listener's explication.

Sperber and Wilson's proposal allows for the indeterminacy and failure that can shape the listener's interpretation. If the listener finds a sufficiently relevant meaning he or she may stop explicating before arriving at the meaning that the speaker intended. In this respect, they argue, their proposal matches normal experience more closely than a model whose goal is a single uniform interpretation. Successful communication does not simply depend on the communicative competence of the speaker or writer, according to this theory. Both speaker and listener assume that the speaker will appeal to contextual information or memories possessed by the listener, and the speaker will try to make it as easy as possible for the listener to find the implication. The listener must judge whether the speaker is speaking for him or herself or is echoing someone's position.

Sperber and Wilson's distinction between the speaker's utterance as *description* or *interpretation* (italics theirs)[71] cuts across the traditional boundary between literal and figurative language: "We are arguing that there is a continuum of cases rather than a dividing line between metaphorical and literal utterances on the one hand, between ironical utterances and other echoic utterances on the other hand."[72]

Sperber and Wilson treat irony as a special kind of echoic speech. Often echoic speech indicates agreement, however, in irony, the speaker represents the thoughts of another in order to call the ideas represented into question. An ironic echo is fairly easy to recognize in oral communication. Speakers signal ironic intention by using an intonation pattern that does not match the literal interpretation of an utterance. In written communication irony is easy to recognize when

---

[70] *Ibid.*, 185-95.
[71] *Ibid.*, 232.
[72] *Ibid.*, 242.

we know the writer or when the writer changes voices in the text, speaking non-ironically at some point. Once the reader has caught on to the irony, the reader quickly picks out the contradictions or lies in the speaker's claims.

Compared to other writers of his day, Defoe did not always give his readers clues to his ironic intention by changing voices in the texts that he claimed to be ironic. The convention of anonymous publication prevented readers from inferring his irony from his identity. Fast readers misread him. Again and again, these readers felt tricked by Defoe. Sperber and Wilson's Relevance Theory provides a framework for addressing the confusion between author and narrator that plagued Defoe.

Who decides what's relevant?

Relevance Theory provides a way to analyze communication failure as well as communication success. Defoe is famous for both. In the next two chapters we will examine the situation and structure of two early Defoe works – two paradigmatic examples of publication success and publication failure. Research libraries have preserved the eighteenth-century pamphlets that give us the contemporary responses to Defoe's writing, so we do not have to trust our own guesses about the readers' responses. We can observe the way these texts were interpreted by their readers as well as how they were shaped by Defoe's intentions.

When Defoe wrote *The Life and Strange Surprising Adventures of Robinson Crusoe*, he claimed his story had a clear lesson about listening to the voice of Providence. He found that readers ignored the lesson, missed his mockery of Robin, and affirmed Robin's island survival as an adventure. Faced with readers who idealized his foolish hero and with abridgers who modified his story to fit their desires for a sentimental hero, Defoe tried to reiterate his lesson in sequels. Defoe's effort to educate his readers on what he thought to be the true meaning of solitude, on Providence, and on the moral force of trade failed miserably. Meanwhile his critique of English piety and imperial violence was ignored. His hero, the eternally adolescent narrator Robinson Crusoe, survived amazingly well, however, as an icon of the indomitable individual.

In Chapters Four to Eight we will examine the literary dialogue between Defoe and his readers in the three-volume *Robinson Crusoe* series. Defoe's struggle to establish his interpretation closes with an ambiguous victory. Robin's energy, independence, and spiritual strength make him a hero for modern individuals. Robin's ordeals in the first volume represent the challenge of isolation even to readers who live in modern cities. Defoe had hoped to teach his readers how to listen to the voice of Providence. The attempt to discern God's Providence in everyday life was one Defoe shared with many of his contemporaries[73] Defoe's concern for the spiritual health of his country proved prophetic, but his hope for a world united by trade is still unrealized.

Robin's career, after he left the island at the end of the first volume, developed Defoe's ideas about trade and religion in the new global economy, but *The Farther Adventures* and *Serious Reflections* failed to reassert the author's control of the story. Defoe himself was not defeated – he stopped writing fiction and returned to obviously didactic writing, publishing influential books on the English economy, on trade, and on family structure. Like his Robin, he cut his losses and left his island. Relevance Theory provides a framework for appreciating the paradox that Defoe's classic achievement is also a failed speech act.

---

[73] J.D.D. Clark makes this point in his article entitled "Providence, Predestination, and Progress: Or Did the Enlightenment Fail?", *Albion*, XXXV/4 (Winter 2003), 559-89. Clark argues that "Providential discourse [was] not … swept away at an early date but survived] in large quantity into the nineteenth century and later" (561). He points out that "that reputed spokesman for modernism, Daniel Defoe, conventionally dealt with the issues of human vicissitude in a providential context …. Defoe's fiction had a dominant ethical dimension, but this dimension was a specifically providential one, obscured by later preoccupations that both abbreviated his titles and 'modernized' the themes in his plots" (563).

CHAPTER TWO

PRINT DISCOURSE IN DEFOE'S DAY

Defoe's dissenter convictions kept him from a career in government, university, or church, but they also gave him a passion for connecting philosophy, religion, and practice. In his early philosophical poem *Jure Divino* (likely begun in 1701)[1] and an *Essay upon Projects*,[2] he tried to speak to the educated elite. He failed. But when he turned to pamphlets addressing the public on hot political issues, he found his voice, and he found an audience. He shaped the public debate, and the pamphlet debate shaped him as an author. In *The True-Born Englishman*,[3] one of Defoe's proudest achievements, we can observe the characteristic features of pamphlet writing, features that dominated Defoe's subsequent writing.

Londoners in the late seventeenth century loved political pamphlets. They had grown up on the pamphlet debates of the revolution, and they were eager to follow the latest arguments. In the early eighteenth-century England, religion, business, and politics fostered literacy. Many ordinary people wrote regularly – letters to friends, letters to newspapers, journals, and devotional meditations. This everyday writing became the basis for new genres of print discourse developed by newspaper writers and pamphleteers.[4] The colloquial style and speed of response make these pamphlets like face-to-face debate, and coffee houses provided places for reading and discussion of pamphlets and newspapers.

---

[1] Backscheider, *Daniel Defoe, His Life*, 161.

[2] Daniel Defoe, *An Essay upon Projects*, London, 1697.

[3] Daniel Defoe, *The True-Born Englishman* (1700), in *The Shortest-Way with the Dissenters and Other Pamphlets by Daniel Defoe*, Oxford, 1927.

[4] J. Paul Hunter traces the links between the growth of literacy in England and the development of the novel. He points out that, "the steepest acceleration in literacy occurred early on in the seventeenth century, at least three generations before the novel began in any meaningful sense to emerge" (*Before Novels*, New York, 1990, 67).

University-educated writers despised the new genres, but at the same time they entered into the public debates with their own satires and parodies of everyday popular writing. Despite the relaxation of pre-publication government censorship, pamphlet and news writers kept up the convention of publishing anonymously. The writers used the conventions of a masquerade culture that made the writer's identity an open secret but put all texts on an equal footing.

A charter for a new age: ***The True-Born Englishman***
Defoe jumped into the middle of a political fight with his verse broadside *The True-Born Englishman*. William of Orange, the Protestant husband of James II's daughter Mary, was under attack for being foreign. Since William had not been born in England the charge was obviously true, but the motive for the charge was opposition to William's request that his Dutch Guards should not be disbanded after the Treaty of Ryswick had been signed.[5] As *Stadholder* of the Netherlands he was the leader of a European coalition opposing France. Once he became King of England, he used the English navy and army in the struggle against Louis XIV's European expansion.[6] William was Protestant, but not Anglican, so his leadership did not completely satisfy the leaders of that church. Defoe's pamphlet hit William's critics by attacking as un-English the idea that public office could be awarded on the grounds of one's English ancestry, since the claim to a pure English ancestry was absurd.

This poem – a topical political composition in rhymed couplets of iambic pentameter – was written in a popular pamphlet genre. Defoe's pamphlet elicited a spate of pamphlet responses.[7] His pamphlet rose to the top of the pamphlet pile. It was reprinted in a 1717 two-volume set called *A Collection of the Best English Poetry*.[8] Defoe added a second

---

[5] "Notes to *The True-Born Englishman*", in *The Shortest Way with the Dissenters and Other Pamphlets by Daniel Defoe*, 241.

[6] William took the throne after negotiation with the Convention Parliament, in the bloodless "Glorious Revolution" of 1688 that included the Toleration Act (1689) allowing non-Anglican congregations to meet. See J.G.A. Pocock, "The Fourth English Civil War", in *The Revolution of 1688-1689: Changing Perspectives*, ed. Lois G. Schwoerer, Cambridge, 1992, 55.

[7] Defoe scholars trace twenty-two editions of the poem in Defoe's lifetime and at least eleven pamphlet responses (P.N. Furbank and W.R. Owens, *A Critical Bibliography of Daniel Defoe*, 20).

[8] *Ibid.*, 21.

prose preface, which he called an "Explanatory Preface" for the ninth edition published in 1701, and "this appeared in most of the subsequent editions".[9] The phrase "true-born Englishman" became a catchword.

Defoe's pamphlet is a complicated piece of irony, with sections in several different styles and voices. It begins with a short prose "Preface" and a four-page verse "Introduction" to the forty-eight-page poem. The poet calls on "Satyr" to speak to the nation about its history and its present discord. In Part I Satyr reviews English history to show that "scarce one Family is left alive, / Which does not from some Foreigner derive". In Part II Satyr describes English character, modulating into a justification for the 1688 revolution ("When Kings the Sword of Justice first lay down, / They are no Kings, though they possess the Crown") and an account of William's accession to the English throne. A song in praise of William by "Britannia" precedes the one-page "Conclusion". The final stanza speaks in the self-mocking voice of an Englishman addressing his countrymen on the nature of true English greatness:

> Cou'd but our Ancestors retrieve their Fate,
> And see their off-spring thus degenerate;
> How we contend for Birth and Names unknown,
> And build on their past Actions, not our own;
> They'd cancel Records, and their Tombs deface,
> And openly disown the Vile Degenerate Race:
> For Fame of Families is all a Cheat,
> *'Tis Personal Virtue only makes us Great.*[10]

The pamphlet as an offensive defense

Defoe designed his pamphlet to raise public support for King William by challenging the cultural assumptions behind the attacks on William as a foreigner. Defoe supported William's European vision and his continental Protestantism, but those points were not the topic of his pamphlet. Instead, Defoe reviewed English history in the hope of changing the terms of the public discourse. His subsequent use of this pamphlet as his self-identification shows that he thought he had succeeded in making his political point. In 1703 he used the poem as

---

[9] *Ibid.*, 20.
[10] Defoe, *The True-Born Englishman*, 71.

his signature, referring to himself as "the Author of The True-Born Englishman".[11]

Defoe's pamphlet was one of many printed replies to John Tutchin's attack on King William, *The Foreigner*. Tutchin's work was advertised in the *Flying Post*, 31 July-1 August 1700. Defoe's response in late December 1700 came after two other anonymous verse replies. Defoe changed the terms of the debate. After *The True-Born Englishman* was published, other writers – including Tutchin – responded to Defoe's poem. Most of the responses cited by Furbank and Owens allude to Defoe's title. The list includes the following: *An Answer to a Late Abusive Pamphlet, Intituled, The True-Born Englishman &c. Together with The True Character of a True Englishman*; *A Satyr, On a True Born Dutch-Skipper*; *The True-Born Welshman*; *English Men no Bastards*; and *The True-Born Hugonot: or, Daniel de Foe, a Satyr*.[12]

The style of *The True-Born Englishman* is vigorous and direct, but not elegant. The couplet rhymes are rough, and often the iambic pentameter rhythm is forced. The vocabulary is inventive; under Defoe's pen the nouns "panegyrick" and "bugbear" become verbs. The diction is colloquial, and several phrases allude to the terms of contemporary political discussion: the Devil "needs no standing-Army Government" and "No Nonconforming Sects disturb his Reign."

The speaker claims the poem's lack of polish as a guarantee of his integrity. He asserts that the poem is the direct, open expression of a man who is not trying to protect himself. In the verse "Introduction", the poet advises Satyr "'Tis pointed Truth must manage this Dispute / And down-right English *Englishmen* confute". In the "Explanatory Preface", Defoe added another comment on the style: "The hasty Errors of my Verse I made my Excuse for before; and since the time I have been upon it has been but little, and my Leisure less, I have all along strove rather to make the thoughts Explicite, than the Poem Correct."[13]

The speaker of the poem asks Satyr to put her "native England" in the best possible light, but the poem gives a history of the English population in crude and derogatory terms:

---

[11] Furbank and Owens, *A Critical Bibliography of Daniel Defoe*, 3.
[12] *Ibid.*, 21.
[13] Defoe, "Explanatory Preface", in *The True-Born Englishman*, 27-28.

> We have been *Europe's* Sink, *the Jakes* where she
> Voids all her Offal Out-cast Progeny
> From our Fifth *Henry's* time, the Strolling Bands
>   Of banish'd Fugitives from Neighb'ring Lands,
>   Have here a certain Sanctuary found:
> *The Eternal Refuge of the Vagabond.*[14]

The poet lists the many invading armies who have settled down and formed the English people. He ridicules the idea that Englishness could be a matter of pure bloodlines:

> *A True-Born Englishman*'s a Contradiction
> In Speech an Irony, in Fact a Fiction.[15]

By way of contrast to a supposed inherited merit, the poet praises spiritual and moral qualities of individuals as the basis for national identity. In the "Explanatory Preface", he emphasizes his position:

> Our *English* Nation may Value themselves for their *Wit, Wealth and Courage*, and I believe few Nations will dispute it with them; but for long Originals, and Ancient *True-Born* Families of *English*, I wou'd advise them to wave the Discourse. A *True English* Man is one that deserves a Character, and I have no were [*sic*] lessened him, that I know of; but as for a *True-Born* English *Man*, I confess I do not understand him.[16]

The good qualities the poet claims for true English men are courage and a love of fighting on the behalf of others, although even these compliments are tinged with sarcasm:

> Fierce as the *Britain*; as the *Roman* brave
> And less inclin'd to conquer than to Save;
> Eager to fight and lavish of their Blood
> And equally of *Fear* and *Forecast* void.[17]

Some respondents reacted to Defoe's identification of himself as an Englishman by reviling him as a "Cuckoo" who had "defiled his

---

[14] Defoe, *The True-Born Englishman*, 39.
[15] *Ibid.*, 43.
[16] Defoe, "Explanatory Preface", in *The True-Born Englishman*, 24.
[17] *Ibid.*, 45.

own Nest".[18] This angry reaction seems to have been exactly the response Defoe had hoped to provoke. He wanted his readers to feel defensive anger in the hope that they would then go beyond anger to join him in affirming his vision of Englishmen as impetuous, fierce, brave, and generous.

ᐧIn the poem itself Defoe writes about what he hopes to accomplish by his pamphlet. The poem gives people a chance to confront their delusions about what makes a true Englishman. By their response to his harsh irony, the readers will reveal themselves to be foolish or wise. The phrase "true-born Englishman" is a banter:

> A Banter made to be a Test of Fools,
> Which those that use it justly ridicules. [19]

Defoe uses the term "banter" both to describe his poem and as the label for a kind of discourse. In the original "Preface" he says:

> As to Vices, who can dispute our Intemperance, while an *Honest Drunken Fellow* is a Character in a Mans Praise? All our Reformations are Banters, and will be so, till our Magistrates and Gentry Reform themselves by way of Example.[20]

The term appears again in his "Explanatory Preface," where he explains the motive for his pamphlet:

> But when I see the Town full of Lampoons and Invectives against *Dutchmen, Only because they are Foreigners*, and the King Reproached and Insulted by Insolent Pedants, and Ballad-making Poets, for employing Foreigners, and for being a Foreigner himself, I confess my self moved by it to remind our Nation of their own Original, thereby to let them see what a Banter is put upon our selves in it; since speaking of *English-men ab Origine*, we are really all Foreigners our selves.[21]

By "banter" Defoe seems to mean an inadvertent self-betrayal. It is something a person says which demonstrates that he or she has failed

---

[18] Defoe, *The True-Born Englishman*, "Notes", 241.
[19] Defoe, *The True-Born Englishman*, 43.
[20] Defoe, Preface, in *ibid.*, 29.
[21] Defoe, "Explanatory Preface", in *ibid.*, 25.

to engage in self-criticism. Defoe's verse broadside uncovers the banter of English pride in ancestry. The banter, however, is not only a self-indictment, but also an opportunity for the speaker to hear his or her own words and to reform. The fool who fails to listen will be justly ridiculed by his or her own words. Defoe stresses the term in his long "Introduction" because contemporary pamphlet responses to Tutchin show that some of his readers had not got to the stage of reflection. The pamphlet's popularity, however, and Defoe's repeated self-identification as its author indicates that Defoe thought most of his readers affirmed what he was doing. After reading his poem, most readers could not boast of their ancestry without feeling foolish.

Defoe's abusive and derogatory tone toward the foreign invaders whose descendants populate England echoes all the contemporary anti-William and anti-Dutch invective and applies it to the earlier immigrants. Relevance Theory would predict that the readers would perceive that the poem is an interpretive echo and understand it as an attack on misplaced pride. This reaction seems to be that of most contemporaries. The poet speaks more directly – in Relevance Theory terms, "descriptively" – to his readers in the opening "Preface" and the longer "Explanatory Preface". In the initial "Preface" he says he is targeting "such who enjoy the Peace and Protection of the present Government, and yet abuse and affront the King who procur'd it". The "Explanatory Preface" goes beyond a simple political debate to imagine a kind of sociology of healthy national character: "If I were to write a Reverse to the *Satyr*, I would examine all the Nations of *Europe*, and prove that those Nations which are most mix'd are the best, and have the least of Barbarism and Brutality among them."[22]

Political pamphlets during the Bloodless Revolution

The True-Born Englishman is just one of Defoe's contributions to the major debate of the day. Backscheider calls this debate "one of the most sustained pamphlet wars in history, one that labeled Englishmen 'Jacobites' or 'revolution' men for the rest of their lives".[23] The issue was William's legitimacy as king. The validity of his rule depended on Parliament's having the authory to invite him to be king. The pamphlet writing that accompanied the Bloodless Revolution in 1688 had made the case for Parliament's action on two grounds: the weight

---

[22] *Ibid.*, 23.
[23] Backscheider, *Daniel Defoe, His Life*, 48.

of English tradition and the natural rights of mankind. Both of these arguments appealed to their readers' self-worth. The historical argument traced what was called "the Ancient Constitution" – a long history of English self-government through Anglo-Saxon institutions and their recognition by William I – whom these pamphlet writers called "William the Norman", rather than "William the Conqueror". The natural rights argument rested on the value of natural human reason, shared by all men. While most of the writers based their case on "the Ancient Constitution",[24] some pamphlets explicitly called for a reformulation of the government, and they used terms such as "contract" and "Constitution of the Realm".[25]

Many of Defoe's Dissenter friends supported King William with arguments based on natural law, and so, usually, did Defoe:

> He joined a number of Dissenters, including his classmate Timothy Cruso, in publishing his opinions about the legality of William's accession .... Morton, Cruso, and Defoe all adhered to the theory of contract government, and Defoe consistently defended it throughout his life.[26]

Later that year Defoe would begin a long verse essay, *Jure Divino*, reasoning "from the theory of the nature of man and a deeply Protestant belief in every man's ability to test law and legal authority ... by his own reason".[27]

The pamphlet exchange that included Defoe's *The True-Born Englishman* shows the opportunity for political discussion in this period. The events accompanying his contemporaneous pamphlet *Legion's Memorial* show the risks of political involvement. Defoe escaped trouble, though Backscheider thinks "... the fact that he had not only gotten away with but gained great success ... probably misled Defoe".[28]

---

[24] The nature of the English constitution had been the subject of intense debate in the seventeenth century, as J.G.A. Pocock shows in his study *The Ancient Constitution and the Feudal Law* (1957), Cambridge, 1987, 211-34.

[25] Lois G. Schwoerer, "The Bill of Rights: Epitome of the Revolution of 1688-9", in *Three British Revolutions: 1641, 1688, 1776*, ed. J.G.A. Pocock, Princeton: NJ, 1980, 232-36.

[26] Backscheider, *Daniel Defoe, His Life*, 48-49.

[27] Paula Backscheider, "The Verse Essay, John Locke and Defoe's *Jure Divino*", *English Literary History*, 55 (Spring 1988), 114.

[28] Backscheider, *Daniel Defoe, His Life*, 80-81.

In 1701 the citizen leaders of Kent[29] petitioned Parliament to approve funds to protect against a potential invasion from France. Backscheider points out that this petition was legal. One of the early Restoration laws under Charles II set out conditions for petitions to the King. Nevertheless, such petitions were not welcome or encouraged:

> The British Bill of Rights stated: 'It is the right of subjects to petition the King and all commitments and prosecution for such petitioning are illegal.' Even so, when the citizens of Kent petitioned Parliament to mount a defense against the danger of an invasion from France the petitioners were cautious. They observed the stipulations in the 1661 act against 'tumultuous petitions,' which required any petition bearing more than twenty signatures to be approved by at least three justices of the peace from the county or by a majority of the Grand Jury.[30]

Parliament arrested the men who brought the petition, and called it "Scandalous, Insolent, and Seditious".[31] As Siebert explains, the common understanding of these terms came from the idea that a king's actions should not be judged by ordinary people:

> ... the crime of seditious libel depends on the contemporary view of the relation between the ruler and the subject. In the seventeenth century the ruler retained many of the characteristics of the feudal overlord. He was the fountainhead of justice and law. His acts were beyond popular criticism.[32]

Defoe's abrasive protest to the House of Commons, *Legion's Memorial*, claimed to speak in the name of "all the good People of England". It supported the right of Englishmen to address Parliament, and drew its title from its claim to speak for innumerable protesters. This pamphlet was published anonymously. Furbank and Owens list it as one of Defoe's works. They point out that it "was widely attributed to Defoe by contemporaries".[33] Defoe seems to have accepted public

---

[29] According to Backscheider, these included "the justices of the peace, the grand jury, some Whig gentlemen and freeholders of Kent" (*ibid.*, 78).
[30] *Ibid.*, 79.
[31] Quoted in *ibid.*, 79.
[32] Siebert, *Freedom of the Press in England 1476-1776*, 299.
[33] Furbank and Owens, *A Critical Bibliography of Daniel Defoe*, 27.

congratulations for his work. The Kentish Petition incident ended in a triumph for the petitioners and Defoe:

> The Commons voted the king his supplies and endorsed new alliances to thwart the French. When the five men from Kent were released, Londoners collected £200 and held a banquet at Mercers Chapel for them Defoe 'was placed' 'next the Worthies.'[34]

When he wrote *The True-Born Englishman* in 1700 and *Legion's Memorial* in 1701, Defoe was self-confident in his career as a businessman with a legitimate role in politics. He had followed his father as a London Freeman, and he had been a member of the Butchers' company since 1687. As a Dissenter from the Church of England, he could not, by the Test Act of 1673, attend university or hold any Crown or military office, but he participated in local self-government in London, serving on juries and as a local magistrate.[35] Under King William, who had been enthroned in 1689, Defoe felt empowered to speak on national priorities, as he did in his *An Essay upon Projects* (1697), mentioned earlier. Backscheider describes eleven pamphlets by Defoe between 1693 and 1701 that supported William's policies: "Even when Defoe wrote about speculation and abuse in the new credit economy ... he considered William and national interests." [36] Many of the pamphlets focused on specific practical issues such as William's request to maintain a standing army The sub topic, however, was the legitimacy of William's rule and the role of Parliament in the monarchy. In his history of the period, David Ogg presents Defoe as "the only English man of letters who was honoured with the king's recognition".[37]

The True-Born Englishman was part of a long development of the institutions and practices of public space for political controversy in England The 1695 lapse of pre-publication censorship gave the pamphlet writers new freedom to speak out on political theory, but there was no presumption of free speech on political issues. During the seventeenth century, this national debate over the nature of the monarchy had emerged into pamphlet exchanges whenever political

---

[34] Backscheider, *Daniel Defoe, His Life*, 80.

[35] *Ibid.*, 41.

[36] *Ibid.*, 72.

[37] David Ogg, *England in the Reigns of James II and William III*, Oxford, 1984, 464.

turmoil obstructed the operations of government censorship. Two such periods came during the period of political turmoil in England between 1640 and 1660, and at the time of the Bloodless Revolution in 1688. Each of these periods was followed by a renewal of pre-publication censorship. Pamphlet numbers grew from twenty-two in 1640 to nearly two thousand in 1642, but then to restrain the pamphleteers Parliament issued a Licensing Order in 1642 and again in 1643.[38] Pamphlet numbers rose again at the time of the Bloodless Revolution. Under William and Mary pre-publication censorship was reinstated through the Stationers Company and men who were appointed "deputy licenser" or "inspector of printing presses". The censoring agency, however, was Parliament, not the crown. Siebert reports:

> One searches in vain in the documents of the period for an official statement to this effect, but nevertheless William and the succeeding monarchs made no claims to prerogative rights over printing. From then on Parliament was supreme in the control of the press. [39]

Eighteenth-century pamphlets continued a long tradition of political pamphleteering extending back to Elizabethan times.[40] They also continued and developed the dramatic style of these pamphlets. Nigel Smith's study *Literature and Revolution* argues that pamphlet exchanges took the place of the theatre in society. When the revolution closed the theatres, "the theatrical migrated into pamphlets and newsbooks".[41] Defoe inherited this pamphlet tradition of political discourse:

> A broad and shared faith in the virtue and efficacy of public rhetoric had been replaced, under the pressure of political division, by a large number of different ways of fashioning a (sometimes oblique)

---

[38] Nancy Armstrong and Leonard Tennenhouse, *The Imaginary Puritan: Literature, Intellectual Labor, and the Origins of Personal Life*, Berkeley: CA, 1992, 66.

[39] Siebert, *Freedom of the Press in England 1476-1766*, 300.

[40] See the studies by Sandra Clark, *Elizabethan Pamphleteers: Popular Moralistic Pamphlets 1580-1640*, Rutherford: NJ, 1983, and Herbert Grabes, *Das englische Pamphlet: Politische und religiöse Polemik am Begin Neuzeit*, Tübingen, 1990.

[41] Nigel Smith, *Literature and Revolution in England, 1640-1660*, New Haven: CT, 1994, 11.

political narrative .... Fictionalizing had supplemented or replaced controversializing.[42]

These pamphlets were speech acts in a double sense: they exerted political pressure and they cast their readers as actors in the national drama.

Revolution in literature

Defoe began writing pamphlets at a time of radical changes in literature. The changes are clear and demonstrable. Moreover they were self-conscious, and they proceeded on several different levels of print culture. The perception of being in a revolution was "nearly universal", says J. Paul Hunter: "New readers, new modes of literary production, changing tastes, and a growing belief that traditional forms and conventions were too constricted and rigid to represent modern reality or to reach modern readers collaborated to mean – in the eyes of both proponents and critics – that much modern writing was taking radical new directions."[43]

Readers of Swift and Pope know that these men were engaged in a cultural struggle over the role of classical culture in intellectual life – a quarrel brought to life in Swift's satire *The Battle of the Books*. The quarrel was a media event at the time, as literary historian Joseph Levine reports:

> It began quietly in London in 1690 with an apparently innocuous event .... In a short time the air was filled with books and pamphlets, charges and countercharges, high principle and low invective. It was the beginning of one of the more raucous events in English intellectual history.[44]

While this public quarrel was going on among the educated, another revolution was going on as new genres of popular writing gained a market among a new reading public. The pamphlet exchanges, newspapers, travel tales, wonder books, and family guides changed English literature. New forms expressed new ideas and new

---

[42] *Ibid.*, 53.

[43] Hunter, *Before Novels*, 10.

[44] Joseph M. Levine, *The Battle of the Books, History and Literature in the Augustan Age*, Ithaca: NY, 1991, 1.

English political, social, and economic institutions. Siebert's study of press freedom points out the interconnections:

> The decline of government controls in the eighteenth century parallels the growth of private enterprise capitalism and the increase in democratic processes in the government. It is extremely difficult to assess the priority of one or the other either chronologically or in intensity. All three were inextricably interrelated.[45]

Many of these institutional and social changes were shaped by a religiously based emphasis on the spiritual importance of ordinary life. Such a concern was both radically old and strikingly new. Charles Taylor traces the "affirmation of ordinary life" as the root of "a second major aspect of the modern identity".[46] Taylor sees this affirmation "foreshadowed and initiated, in all its facets, in the spirituality of the [sixteenth-century] Reformers",[47] but he finds "its origin in Judaeo-Christian spirituality".[48] The spiritual theme was old, but its literary expression was new. Hunter's study emphasizes the spiritual force behind the increase in literacy: "A number of other factors – political, social, and economic – in fact supported the argument from piety. But piety was the most acceptable, most persuasive, and perhaps the most fundamental basis for literacy.[49]

Writing as part of an ordinary life
Ordinary life itself changed. In the last part of the seventeenth century ordinary people started writing. Individuals began to incorporate reading and writing into their spiritual discipline. Ordinary people wrote to communicate, to organize their lives, and to help trace the workings of Providence in their experiences. They wrote letters, ledgers, diaries, and spiritual meditations. Hunter points out that the side offect of this this religiously-motivated everyday writing was a change in the type and topic of literature: "readers, publishers and other bit players in traditional literary history played a powerful role in creating a new textual species responsive to human concerns about

---

[45] Siebert, *Freedom of the Press in England 1476-1766*, vi.
[46] Charles Taylor, *Sources of the Self, The Making of the Modern Identity*, Cambridge: MA, 1989, 211.
[47] *Ibid.*, 218
[48] *Ibid.*, 83.
[49] Hunter, *Before Novels*, 83.

the structure of everyday life as well as about the feelings that flow from – and inspire – ordinary actions."[50]

Jürgen Habermas finds the roots of the novel in this conjunction of different kinds of everyday writing. Business and government began to use letter-writing, and personal mobility led to personal correspondence. Soon correspondents separated business writing from personal letters. The conventions of personal letters demanded the appearance of spontaneity and intimacy. The spontaneity was probably a self-conscious and calculated style.[51] Nevertheless, during the seventeenth century personal letters became the place for intimate communication and for self-reflection. Habermas credits letter writing with leading to diary writing. He traces the growth of a public sphere to a change in consciousness rooted in this personal writing:

> In the intimate sphere of the conjugal family privatized individuals viewed themselves as ... persons capable of entering into 'purely human' relations with one another. The literary form of these at the time was the letter. It is no accident that the eighteenth century became the century of the letter: through letter writing the individual unfolded himself in his subjectivity ... the diary became a letter addressed to the sender, and the first-person narrative became a conversation with one's self addressed to another person.[52]

The practice of writing diaries became a spiritual self-discipline, with a form of its own that made use of the detailed observation of everyday life and thought:

> Diaries proliferated in England and Scotland in the early seventeenth century and a little later in America ... they must have been very common, perhaps almost universal among those who were both devout and literate, whatever their religious persuasion .... 'Saints' kept diaries for their own benefit – behavior that would help reveal the state of their souls and to provide a basis for review of life patterns.[53]

---

[50] *Ibid.*, 5.

[51] Ingrid Tieken-Boon van Ostade, "Eighteenth-century Letters and Journals as Evidence: Studying Society through the Individual", in *Literature and the New Interdisciplinarity: Poetics, Linguistics, History*, eds Roger D. Sell and Peter Verdonk, Amsterdam, 1994, 179.

[52] Jürgen Habermas, *The Structural Transformation of the Public Sphere*, trans. Thomas Burger, Cambridge: MA, 1991, 48-49.

[53] Hunter, *Before Novels*, 304.

One of the goals of diary writing was to help the diarist recognize the hand of God's Providence in the events of his or her life. The epistemological foundation for this goal was "the sense that the details of the world can be observed fully enough that the ordering pattern behind them can be discovered and described".[54]

Diaries became spiritual ledgers, kept by middle-class Christians who also kept financial ledgers. Protestant religious culture comfortably works with biblical images of God as a large property-owner and Christians as stewards of God's property, property that includes themselves. David Little's re-working of Weber points out that in the tradition of thought springing from John Calvin economic activity was in no way antithetical to Christianity:

> This sort of pattern [of voluntary action], then, with all its economic overtones, is *specially related to and bound up with* the eschatological purposes of God. What man was created to be – a freely obedient being who responds gratefully to the gifts of God, ardently sharing them with all his brothers and turning them to corporate use – is put by Calvin again and again in the language of economic action.[55]

Similar to diaries, shorter meditations formed another genre of everyday writing. The genre embodied the Puritan assumption that ordinary things nourish spiritual life. This spiritual exercise was given a Greek name ("Meletetics") and explained by the scientist Robert Boyle.[56] Boyle's method, says Hunter, "simply involves an insistence on close observation – a close reading – of even the smallest and most trivial things encountered in daily life".[57] The habit of occasional meditation formed "a new kind of reading public, one with verbal habits and expectations that novelists soon would learn to exploit".[58]

Personal letters, diaries and meditations on ordinary events would provide templates for many of the best-selling books and pamphlets of early eighteenth-century London. These were the kinds of writing

---

[54] *Ibid.*, 309.

[55] David Little, *Religion, Order, and Law: A Study in Pre-Revolutionary England*, New York, 1969, 66.

[56] Hunter, *Before Novels*, 204.

[57] Hunter lists such varied topics as the following: "His Horse stumbling upon a very fair way", "Upon the want of Sleep", and "Upon comparing the Clock and his watch" (*ibid.*, 202).

[58] *Ibid.*, 201.

many people did every day. Many readers had written their own spiritual diaries and had learned how to observe and find significance in the details of the everyday physical world. The popular new print genres of travel narration, providence book, family guidebook, and rational-critical journalism would further expand the interests of these new readers.

New public genres: journalism and travel narrative
The lapse of official censorship in England in 1695 opened the way for the newspapers that supplemented the officially sanctioned parliamentary news publications. In 1600, the Restoration government of Charles II still thought it controlled the press, when it gave Roger L'Estrange the right to publish news in payment for his work as censor.[59] Later, Secretary of State Williamson got that right.[60] These official journals were only a small part of the public press. Habermas cites the familiar list in his history of the growth of the public sphere: "Defoe's *Review*, Tutchin's *Observator*, and Swift's *Examiner* were discussed in clubs and coffee houses, at home and in the streets."[61] These newspapers incorporated material from some of the new kinds of personal writing and new kinds of popular print genres such as travel reports.

One early newspaper Habermas does not mention is one that Defoe imitated: John Dunton's innovative journal, *The Athenian Gazette: Or Casuistical Mercury* (1691-1697). The journal's title evokes a people who delight in hearing new ideas (Acts 17.21). Dunton uses a couplet from a 1683 poem by Robert Wilde as an epigraph: "We are all tainted with the *Athenian* Itch / News, and new Things do the whole World bewitch."[62] Dunton pioneered interactive journalis by asking his readers to submit questions to be answered by the members of the "Athenian Society".[63] He received so many questions that after only a

---

[59] Siebert, *Freedom of the Press in England 1476-1766*, 292 n.

[60] *Ibid.*, 295-96.

[61] Habermas, *The Structural Transformation of the Public Sphere*, 59.

[62] Hunter, *Before Novels*, 377 n. 1.

[63] *Ibid.*, 13. Hunter reports that Dunton gradually introduced the idea of a society behind the journal: "Less than two months into the periodical, Dunton began to hint that a formal group was involved in his project, and a year later he announced that a society of the learned, 'the Athenian society,' was responsible for its contents. Actually, the society consisted of three people."

week he started publishing his journal twice a week and asked readers to hold their questions until he had cleared the backlog.[64]

In 1704, when Defoe started his journal, *The Review*, he copied this kind of interaction with readers. Dunton complained bitterly about Defoe's imitation:

> This man [Defoe] has done me a sensible wrong, by interloping with my 'Question Project.' Losers may have leave to speak; and I here declare, I am [two hundred pounds] the worse for De Foe's clogging my 'Question-Project.'[65]

The lessons from Alexander Selkirk's story

Newspapers and pamphlets were just two elements of a marketplace crowded with texts at the turn of eighteenth century. They re-circulated material from the new print genres such as travel literature. Richard Steele made the story of Alexander Selkirk's rescue from the Island of Juan Fernandez into a London story by interviewing Selkirk for his newspaper, *The Englishman*.[66]

Selkirk's solitary life on the island is surely one of the inspirations for *Robinson Crusoe*. The public interpretation given to that solitary stay is also part of the readers' context for Defoe's story. Woodes Rogers' 1712 account of the rescue makes it a religious lesson. Rogers says that "nothing but the Divine Providence could have supported any Man" in such circumstances. Rogers also provides a practical lesson for his London reader when he suggests Selkirk's "plain and temperate" life on the island was much more healthful than that offered by London. Poor Selkirk "lost much of his Strength and Agility" back in England.[67]

Selkirk had become something of a curiosity in London after his rescue. Steele's interview with Selkirk was printed on 3 December 1713. It gives the tale a psychological interpretation:

---

[64] *Ibid.*, 12.

[65] John Dunton, *The Life and Errors of John Dunton Citizen of London* (1704), London, 1818, 423.

[66] Richard Steele, *The Englishman*, XXVI/3 (December 1713), ed. Rae Blanchard, Oxford, 1955, 106-109.

[67] Woodes Rogers, *A cruising voyage round the world: first to the South-Sea, thence to the East-Indies, and homewards by the Cape of Good Hope, begun in 1708 and finish'd in 1711*, London, 1712, 131.

> Desire of society was as strong a Call upon him [as the Necessities of Hunger and Thirst] …. He grew dejected languid, and melancholy … till by Degrees, by the Force of Reason, and frequent reading of the Scriptures, and turning his Thoughts upon the Study of Navigation, after the Space of eighteen Months, he grew thoroughly reconciled to his Conditions. When he had made this Conquest, the Vigour of his Health, Disengagement from the World, a constant, chearful, serene Sky and a temperate Air, made his Life one continual Feast, and his Being much more joyful than it had before been irksome.[68]

According to Steele, Selkirk became so contented on the island that when his rescuers came, he was not particularly interested in being rescued:

> When the Ship which brought him off the island came in, he received them with the greatest Indifference, with relation to the Prospect of going off with them, but with great Satisfaction in an Opportunity to refresh and help them. The Man frequently bewailed his Return to the World, which could not, he said, with all its Enjoyments, restore him to the Tranquility of his Solitude.[69]

Steele thinks that Selkirk's story proves how hard it is to be Christian in the middle of London society. After the castaway had been in London for some time, Selkirk had become so coarsened by life in the city that he was unrecognizable.

Orators in print
The print culture of the early eighteenth century was open and personally engaging for very many Englishmen. It thrived in cities where participants could meet on the street, but it also formed readers into communities that crossed geographical boundaries. This culture was something new in world history, as Benedict Anderson points out: "print-capitalism … made it possible for rapidly growing numbers of people to think about themselves, and to relate themselves to others, in profoundly new ways."[70] Writers and a mass readership were just inventing the conventions of public mass discourse. The new forms of writing – the travel narratives and the early novels in the form of

---

[68] *Ibid.*, 170.
[69] *Ibid.*, 173.
[70] Benedict Anderson, *Imagined Communities*, 2nd edn, London, 1991, 36.

personal narrative – fostered a new kind of social entity, a reading public. Jürgen Habermas traces its growth in his "Inquiry into a Category of Bourgeois Society". In Habermas' analysis the aristocracy or even the developing civil service did not shape the public sphere. Families and friends reading novels aloud to each other shaped it. Habermas says that this reading public became a force for change in the power structures of society.

What was new about this pressure group was the way its members related to each other: "the standards of 'reason' and the forms of the 'law' to which the public wanted to subject domination and thereby change it in substance reveal their sociological meaning only in the recognition of the fact that it was private people who related to each other in it as a public."[71] Elizabeth Eisenstein reminds us that the changes were not simple. While one form of community was weakened, others developed: "The displacement of pulpit by press ... points to an explanation for the weakening of local community ties ... a reading public was not only more dispersed; it was also more atomistic and individualistic than a hearing one."[72] Nevertheless, "urban populations were not only pulled apart, they were also linked in new ways by the more impersonal channels of communication".[73] This early print culture retained some of the features of oral culture. Eisenstein warns that "we shall need to be cautious about assuming, as did McLuhan and other authorities, that the spread of habits of silent scanning invariably diminished recourse to the spoken word".[74] The pamphlet-reading culture of England combined the public exposure offered by print with features typical of oral culture.

In Defoe's time, pamphlets typically responded to printed versions of spoken discourse such as sermons and proclamations as well as other pamphlets. The interval between a pamphlet and its response could be a matter of days, and the style of the prose typically resembled spoken language. Often pamphlets formed a series of exchanges extending over months. These exchanges raised public interest in their topics, to the profit of the publishers, as Hunter points out:

---

[71] Habermas, *The Structural Transformation of the Public Sphere*, 28.
[72] Elizabeth L. Eisenstein, *The Printing Revolution in Early Modern Europe* (1983), Cambridge, 1992, 94.
[73] *Ibid.*, 9.
[74] *Ibid.*, 92.

A pamphlet taking a particular position or offering a certain interpretation often was followed by answers, replies, rejoinders, defenses, and various shades of attack and sympathetic response, sometimes all written by the same writer or by others within the same stable. A clever promoter could keep a good pseudo-controversy in the public press for days or even weeks.[75]

In the same vein, Siebert notes that one of the pressures leading to the pamphlet wars was the desire of printers who had finished their apprenticeship to set up their own print shops. When Parliament declined to renew the Licensing Act, the printers' interests were important:

The Commons followed Locke's reasoning if not his exact words by emphasizing the commercial restraints contained in the Act. Of the eighteen reasons advanced for refusal to continue the Act, thirteen were directed against the restraints on the printing and allied trades.[76]

The very features which modern analysis cites to distinguish speech from writing are the characteristic features which mark eighteenth-century pamphlet writing, and these are clear in Defoe's *The True-Born Englishman*. These pamphlets were composed quickly and printed without much editing – or they try to give the appearance of having been composed quickly. They were often addressed to acquaintances or familiar antagonists. Summarizing the modern conventions governing public writing, Traugott and Pratt say that written language is deliberate, formal, and carefully edited as opposed to speech.[77] Obviously this characterization does not hold for eighteenth-century pamphlets.

Print reading experiences in our time may obscure the open, interactive, and personal nature of pamphlet dialogue in the early eighteenth century. However, twenty-first-century readers may understand eighteenth-century pamphlet culture by analogy to new social networking web technology and the quick chat of text messaging. Unlike formal written communication of our day, this emerging genre relies on spontaneity, colloquial style, and immediacy of response. E-mail writers disregard and sometimes deliberately

---

[75] Hunter, *Before Novels*, 177.
[76] Siebert, *Freedom of the Press in England 1476-1766*, 261.
[77] Traugott and Pratt, *Linguistics for Students of Literature*, 271.

violate print norms, while text messaging has developed a para-language of its own.

The pamphlet-reading culture in London

Eighteenth-century pamphlets cultivated a group of readers who followed political controversies. The pamphlets' focus on topical issues, colloquial style, and low price appealed to a large public. Pamphlets opened a dialogue with their readers, implicitly encouraging their readers to respond in print or in public discussion. Clubs and coffee houses served as distribution and discussion centers. Jack Lindsay's study of Defoe's London, *The Monster City*, lists several famous clubs including the Kit Cat Club and the Hanover Club. Lindsay says that there were as many as five-hundred coffee houses:

> For a penny at the door, you could take your seat by the fire, smoke a pipe, join in the talk or listen. Foreigners were astonished at the way men aired their ideas.[78]

Habermas estimates that there were three-thousand coffee houses in London in the first decade of the eighteenth century.[79] Backscheider says of Defoe:

> He was probably part of the unusually long-lived literary group composed of Dissenting ministers and laymen that met at Chews' Coffeehouse on Bow Lane. Satires of Defoe occasionally mentioned his presence at 'Sue's' another name for this coffeehouse.[80]

Hunter quotes a Swiss traveler's account of London coffee houses: "Workmen habitually begin the day by going to coffee-rooms in order to read the latest news."[81]

London readers, printers, and writers often knew each other personally. Although London was the largest city in England, its population was still only half a million.[82] Many writers were public

---

[78] Jack Lindsay, *The Monster City: Defoe's London 1688-1730*, New York, 1978, 55-56.
[79] Habermas, *The Structural Transformation of the Public Sphere*, 32.
[80] Backscheider, *Daniel Defoe, His Life*, 48.
[81] Hunter, *Before Novels*, 174.
[82] Lindsay, *The Monster City*, vii.

figures. The title page of Dunton's autobiography, *Life and Errors*, promises comments on his fellow printers and booksellers as well as "More than a Thousand Contemporary Divines, and other Persons of Literary Eminence".[83] Many of the pamphlet writers of London in the early eighteenth century formed open groups of correspondents who interacted over years.

The traditional canon of English literature has included writers such as Dryden, Pope, Swift, Steele, and Addison and it has relegated their opponents to explanatory footnotes. The contemporary debate, however, was less one-sided than the impression created by canonization. Newspapers written by Swift, Steele, and Addison relied on the same public who read the newspapers of their opponents. In tracing Defoe's career as a writer, we see names reappear as men who wrote pamphlets that elicited Defoe's response or writers who responded to him. Two of these men – John Tutchin and John Dunton – have already figured in this chapter. Tutchin wrote about the same political issues that aroused Defoe, and got into the same kind of political trouble.[84] John Dunton and Defoe were fellow Dissenters. Dunton's wife was one of the daughters of Samuel Annesly, the pastor whom Defoe's parents had followed out of the Anglican Church in 1662. Dunton's autobiography, mentioned earlier, criticizes and praises Defoe at several different points. He sums up his opinion with a magisterial flourish:

> De Foe has Piety enough for an Author, and Courage enough for a Martyr. And, in a word, if ever any, Daniel De Foe is 'a True Englishman;' and for that reason, he is more respected by men of honour and sense than he can be affronted by Alderman B--- and Justice S---, and the rest of the Western Blockheads."[85]

An early interaction between John Dunton and Jonathan Swift illuminates the close ties between London writers, whether friends or antagonists. This incident also underscores the difficulty in distinguishing between direct and ironic discourse. Swift wrote an ode for Dunton's *Athenian Gazette.* It seems possible, says Hunter, that Swift was gulled by Dunton into writing for his journal. Hunter cannot

---

[83] Dunton, *Life and Errors*, Title Page.
[84] Siebert, *Freedom of the Press in England 1476-1766*, 278.
[85] Dunton, *Life and Errors*, 425.

decide whether Swift's ode was a genuine tribute or an elaborate hoax. The fact that Dunton published Swift's ode *An Ode to the Athenian Society* on the first of April and the fact that Swift mounted "an elaborate attack on Dunton in *A Tale of a Tub*"[86] seems to weight the decision in favor of a hoax, but it also emphasizes the intimate antagonism between these contemporaries.

Anonymous pamphlets in a masquerade culture

Modern scholars can trace interconnections between writers, but often they cannot determine who wrote which pamphlets because so many different people wrote so often. The fact that so many pamphlets drew published responses indicates that readers understood the publication of a pamphlet as an invitation to respond. The Civil War had produced a "new kind of author" as well as a new kind of reader, as Nigel Smith argues.[87] The difficulty in determining who wrote what and whether they wrote directly or ironically comes from the system of publication, which penalized open political discussion, even after the lapse of pre-publication censorship. When Parliament took over the role of censor, it followed the old royal idea that any public discussion whatsoever of government affairs was impertinent and seditious.

In earlier generations when pre-publication censorship was enforced, the writer's access to public space had been under constant unspoken negotiation. Writers couched their political opinions in allegory or fable. When they criticized government, they published illegally, anonymously. In the new system, after 1695, the government turned to post-publication censorship, but did not change its view of critical writing. It is no wonder that writers of political pamphlets wanted to remain anonymous even after the lapse of the Licensing Act.

When Queen Anne came to the throne in 1702, she tried to get Parliament to pass a new Licensing Act. The attempt failed. Then Queen Anne tried to control the press by royal proclamation. She issued proclamations on 26 March 1702, 24 February 1704, 25 May 1704, 20 December 1705, and 15 March 1714/15.[88] In June 1712, Queen Anne's government tried a new approach by introducing a bill in Parliament to prohibit anonymous publication. Such a prohibition

---

[86] Hunter, *Before Novels*, 13.
[87] Smith, *Literature and Revolution in England*, 32-35.
[88] Siebert, *Freedom of the Press in England 1476-1766*, 270.

would have made it easier for the government to prosecute offending writers. This bill, too, failed. The printers wanted to keep anonymity as an option for writers. As Siebert reports: "opposition to the bill came not from the Whigs alone but from the London printers who, although willing to accept registration of presses and apprentices and to append their printers' marks to each publication, were opposed to the clause requiring the author's name to appear on every piece of printing."[89]

The convention of authorial anonymity caused Defoe trouble, but he used it for most of his writing career. Defoe's metaphoric description of his work as a stage performance reveals his ambivalent desire to be both recognized and hidden. Defoe was irritated when linked to publications he disowned. Nevertheless, he continued to use the convention of anonymous publication for his own pamphlets, his journalism, and for longer works such as his *Family Instructor* and *Robinson Crusoe*. In the Preface to *The Serious Reflections* he says that he published his work anonymously because he was afraid the readers would pre-judge it. He wanted readers to respond to his work, not to his reputation.

Anonymous equality in masquerade
The London masquerades of the day provide an analogy to the shadow-world of anonymous publication at this time. The London masquerades were both commercial and social. These evening parties held in public gardens to which revelers wore masks and costumes or concealing cloaks were a species of audience-participation drama. Terry Castle's 1986 study, *Masquerade and Civilization*, describes the phenomenon and notes its significance:

> Throughout the eighteenth century the masked assembly, that 'promiscuous Gathering,' was at once a highly visible public institution and a highly charged image – a social phenomenon of expansive proportions and a cultural sign of considerable potency. It is easy to forget the pervasiveness and magnitude of these events. During the second and third decades of the century, Count Heidegger's elaborate masquerades at the Haymarket drew up to a thousand antic 'masks' weekly.[90]

---

[89] *Ibid.*, 307.
[90] Terry Castle, *Masquerade and Civilization*, Stanford: CA, 1986, 2.

Some features of these Masquerade assemblies closely resemble the conventions of anonymous pamphlet writing of the day. Just as a costume was a statement demanding interpretation, the style and themes of an anonymous publication invited speculation on the author's identity. Just as a pamphlet could speak in an ironic voice, so a costume could represent a comment on social class. Descriptive analysis of the London Masquerade in this period points out the ways this kind of entertainment allowed people to move in the society without being identified by family or position. People who took part were simultaneously in society and free to criticize its structures. According to Castle's analysis, dress was usually ironic:

> Costume ideally represented an inversion of one's nature. At its most piquant it expressed a violation of cultural categories. If one may speak of the rhetoric of masquerade, a tropology of costume, the controlling figure was the antithesis: one was obliged to impersonate a being opposite, in some essential feature, to oneself. The conventional relationship between costume and wearer was ironic, one that replicated a conceptual scandal.[91]

Defoe speaks disparagingly of masquerades in his *Review*:

> In short, the whole nation is now one great masquerade. – No men seem to act the part they aim at, or aim at the part they act.[92]

Defoe's comments here reveal his attachment to theater, which often appears as an analogy for his work as a writer. Defoe's comments about his journalism and pamphlet writing reveal both his consciousness of putting on a performance and his enjoyment of performing. He created several roles during his career. Defoe's self-presentation as a performer calls for an interpretive theory that acknowledges his delight in satire and irony.

In 1705, near the beginning of his career as a journalist, Defoe adapts the commonplace metaphor of life as a stage when he explains his role. The *Review* is his stage, and his texts are on stage with him. In the Preface to the first bound volume he imagines "twenty or thirty volumes of this work on the stage".[93] By the use of this metaphor he

---

[91] *Ibid.*, 5.
[92] Daniel Defoe, *Review*, IX/83, quoted in Curtis, *The Elusive Daniel Defoe*, 123.
[93] Daniel Defoe, *Review*, I/5, ed, A.W. Secord, New York, 1938, 22.

implies an agreement between writer and reader about the nature of their relationship. He implies that anyone reading his *Review* would understand that they were watching a public dramatic performance. As in all drama, the audience is expected to perceive dramatic irony. Similarly, the complex voice in Defoe's *The True-Born Englishman* depends on the readers' ability to perceive the particular irony of a banter.

Defoe's pamphlets characteristically used dramatic voice to present his case. Parts of his *Family Instructor* and *The Farther Adventures* read like dialogue in a play. Putting an argument in various voices was considered an ethically motivated rhetorical technique, as Backscheider points out:

> Defoe often quotes the lines from St Paul's description of his ministry: 'I am made all things to all men, that I might by all means save some' …. In fact the idea is common in the eighteenth century. Samuel Johnson's *Idler* no. 85 reads, 'Truth like beauty varies its fashion, and is best recommended by different dresses to different minds.' Defoe often uses the line 'all things to all men' as he tries to bring others to his opinion. His pleasure in assumed voices comes from what he believes is the skillful performance of his job: to bring the mistaken to truth.[94]

Role-play may have been a reputable argumentative strategy, but one of Defoe's most convincing roles was that of the plain-speaking businessman who scorns role-playing. In this respect, his role is the kind of ironic parody that a masquerade costume provided. Defoe's written reports to Robert Harley, his patron, show that while he was acting the role of the sympathetic English businessman for the Scots, he was working as a political agent for Harley. His public pamphlets claim "I scorn the employment of an emissary, a spy, or a mercenary", and Curtis says that he acted "honest and open, impartial and calm".[95] Defoe's report to Robert Harley shows a different picture:

> Defoe presents himself to Harley …. 'I am all to Every one that I may Gain some.' Most significantly, he is operating under a variety of disguises, and, far from being calm, Defoe is aroused by the

---

[94] Backscheider, *Daniel Defoe, His Life*, 299.
[95] Curtis, *The Elusive Daniel Defoe*, 118.

> prodigious dexterity required by all these disguises to a pitch of excitement revealed by the exuberant tone of the letter.[96]

Defoe's contemporary opponents accused him of hypocrisy. Some modern scholars think he was carried away by his acting ability. Curtis sees an unresolved conflict between Defoe's two voices in *The Review*. She judges that for Defoe the plain-speaking world has moral superiority, but thinks that the "worldly Mr. Review" would rationalize acting a secret part.[97] Defoe's theatre metaphor may provide an explanation of his stance. Defoe often seems surprised when his readers take him literally. For him, writing is performance, not confession. Defoe's use of irony and dramatic voice in his early pamphlets shows that he expects his readers to recognize his irony and welcome its salutary shock.

London society loved and hated anonymous pamphlets the same way it loved and hated the masquerades. Castle asserts that the masquerades angered their critics because they functioned as a "material devaluation of the unitary notions of the self".[98] Defoe's critics make this same complaint when they charged that he had no unified shape. Backscheider quotes a 1715 pamphlet describing Defoe: he was "An *Animal* who shifts his Shape oftner than *Proteus*, and goes backwards and forwards like a Hunted Hare".[99] The masquerade gatherings were successful precisely because they gave people permission to meet others without the limitations of family or social roles. Anonymous pamphlets, too, gave people the chance to address their fellows in an open forum.

At a masquerade, the everyday social identities of the maskers could be discovered by investigation. Anonymous pamphlets challenged their readers to listen to the voice of a fellow Englishman and judge his arguments without knowing for sure who had written them. The mask of anonymity could be removed by gossip, by government investigation, or by the reader's inferences. Until the author was named, the pamphlet called its readers to exercise their intelligence in a forum where print made all speakers equal.

---

[96] *Ibid.*, 119.
[97] *Ibid.*, 123.
[98] Castle, *Masquerade and Civilization*, 4.
[99] Backscheider, *Daniel Defoe, His Life*, 350.

CHAPTER THREE

A LONG BATTLE OVER *THE SHORTEST-WAY*

Defoe's anonymous pamphlet, *The Shortest-Way with the Dissenters*, became the focus of a political controversy in the turbulent London of December 1702. The sudden death of King William and the accession of Anne upset the tolerant system William had installed. Backscheider reports that:

> William's death unleashed an intimidating amount of anti-Dissenting feeling. A mob celebrating William's death destroyed a meeting-house in Newcastle-under-Lyme.[1]

Anglican Tories looked for ways to punish the Dissenters who had enjoyed King William's protection, and the Dissenters were frightened. Defoe's ironic pamphlet precipitated a legal battle that transformed his life and inaugurated a new kind of government approach to public opinion. Defoe expressed his anger and fear over current political events in ways that aroused its readers' passion and the government's alarm. It evoked an immediate warrant for the author's discovery and arrest. Eventually it led to Defoe's conviction for seditious libel. This trial and judgment changed Defoe from a businessman with political interests to an entrepreneurial writer and political commentator. The pamphlet is Defoe's most famous failure.

The Shortest-Way with the Dissenters was a great success in attracting attention. Important people read it and reacted strongly and quickly. Both the House of Commons and the Crown perceived the pamphlet as threatening. In court, the government prosecutors presented their case as a simple story: Defoe was a lunatic who had written a pamphlet which incited violence against Dissenters, attacked the Scots, and impugned the Queen's concern for her Dissenter

---

[1] Backscheider, *Daniel Defoe, His Life*, 90.

subjects. This dangerous attack had been traced to its source and Defoe should be punished.

The original edition of Defoe's offending twenty-nine page pamphlet *The Shortest-Way with the Dissenters: or Proposals for the Establishment of the Church* has no preface or introduction. The title page does not list an author or printer, but simply says that it is printed in London in 1702. The text begins by quoting a fable from a well-known Tory writer. It ends with an imitation prayer asking that the "Sons of Error" be "rooted out from the Face of the Land forever."[2]

The pamphlet pretends to be a confrontation between the Anglican speaker and his opponents – the Dissenters. At the beginning it sets up a physical confrontation between the speaker's party – the "we" – and their opponents – the "you". As the pamphlet proceeds, however, the imagined speaker erases the opponents from the scene by speaking about them rather than to them. The speaker says, "We have been huff'd and bully'd with your Act of Tolleration"[3] but later, "Now let use examine the Reasons they pretend to give why we shou'd be favourable to them, why we should continue to tolerate them among us".[4] As Nigel Smith points out, this oratorical mode was a common one for the genre: "The sense given in the printed puritan satire of a heavily dramatic function in the *persona* tells us much about attitudes which early modern people had towards controversial writing: it was really an extension of an orally delivered performance."[5]

The introductory fable introduces a violent subtext. It pictures a cock forced to try to survive on a stable floor. Instead of begging for space, the cock admonishes the horses: "Pray Gentlefolks let us stand still, for fear we should tread upon one another." The pamphlet speaker applies this fable to "some People in the World" who "now they are *unpearcht* ... begin with Aesop's Cock to Preach up Peace and Union and the Christian Duties of Moderation".[6]

For nine pages the imagined speaker surveys Anglican church history from the time of James I, focusing on the recent fourteen years of "Oppression". The reference for this period is to the fourteen years

---

[2] Daniel Defoe, *The Shortest-Way with the Dissenters: Or, proposals for the Establishment of the Church* (London, 1702), in *The Shortest Way with the Dissenters and Other Pamphlets by Daniel Defoe*, Oxford, 1927, 29.

[3] *Ibid.*, 3.

[4] *Ibid.*, 12.

[5] Smith, *Literature and Revolution in England*, 297.

[6] Defoe, *The Shortest-Way with the Dissenters*, 1.

since the Toleration Act of 1689 brought in by King William. This law allowed Dissenter congregations to meet. These last years, says the speaker, – "the Days of her Humiliation and Tribulation"[7] – have culminated in the "sufferings of the Episcopal Clergy in Scotland"[8] and the threat of a Scottish Presbyterian take-over of the Church of England Convocation.[9] The speaker feels that the recent accession of Anne to the throne and her promise to protect the established church have toppled the Dissenters off their perch in the national power structure.

The pamphlet raises and answers five possible objections to harsh treatment of Dissenters. These objections range from practical – "they are very Numerous"[10] to public relations – "This will be Cruelty in its Nature, and Barbarous to all the World".[11] Hidden in the middle of the list is the burning issue of the day – the newly-crowned Queen Anne's intention with regard to the Dissenters: "The Queen has promis'd them, to continue them in their tolerated Liberty."[12] At last the speaker proposes a solution – get rid of Dissenters by exile and execution:

> If one severe Law were made, and punctually executed, that who ever was found at a Conventicle, shou'd be Banished the Nation, and the Preacher be Hang'd, we shou'd soon see an end of the Tale, they wou'd all come to Church: and one Age wou'd make us all One again.[13]

The speaker piles up violent images and metaphors. Dissenters are like snakes, blood-sucking vipers, toads, weeds, disease, or festering wounds. The pamphlet concludes with some vaguely biblical-sounding calls to action: "Let us crucifie the Thieves" and "Let all true Sons of so Holy an Oppressed Mother ... harden their Hearts against those who have oppres'd her".[14]

---

[7] *Ibid.*, 2.
[8] *Ibid.*, 10.
[9] *Ibid.*, 11.
[10] *Ibid.*, 12.
[11] *Ibid.*, 18.
[12] *Ibid.*, 16.
[13] *Ibid.*, 21.
[14]*Ibid.*, 29.

Government officials at the highest level saw the pamphlet as a threat to civil order. Robert Harley, Speaker of the House of Commons – the man who would later become Defoe's patron – persuaded the Lord Treasurer, Sidney Godolphin, to instruct Daniel Finch – the Earl of Nottingham and Secretary of State for the Southern Region – to find and arrest the writer of the pamphlet.[15] Nottingham traced the pamphlet through George Croome, the printer, to Edward Bellamy who had taken the manuscript from Defoe.[16] On 24 February 1703, the Crown in the Justice Hall in the Old Bailey indicted Defoe, in his absence. The indictment quoted pages 2, 3, 4, 6, 10, 11, 12, 13, 16, 18, 19, and 21 of the pamphlet.[17] The next day the House of Commons lodged its formal complaint against the pamphlet and ordered it to be burned.

In political context of the time, Defoe's arrest and trial for seditious libel is one early instance of the government's attempt to control public opinion in the absence of pre-publication censorship. His punishment is known today because of its effect on his life and his importance in literary history, but Defoe's arrest did not silence the public discussion. While he was in hiding, others were writing on the same topic and facing the same charges:

> An article appearing in The *Observator* for 8-11 December 1702, entitled 'Some further Remarks on Occasional Conformity', irritated the majority in the Commons. John How, the printer, Benjamin Bragg, the publisher, and John Tutchin, the author, were arrested and later released. A few months later another article on the same subject in the 9-12 February 1703 issue again aroused the House, but this time the three men absconded.[18]

The two charges by the House and by the Crown were different, but "Neither charge treated *The Shortest-Way with the Dissenters* as irony or parody".[19] The House found that the pamphlet incited sedition by what it said or implied about Parliament. The Crown accused Defoe of trying to cause discord between the Queen and her Protestant subjects. Defoe hid while he tried to get friends to negotiate terms with the

---

[15] Backscheider, *Daniel Defoe, His Life*, 100.

[16] *Ibid.*, 101.

[17] Moore, *A Checklist of the Writings of Daniel Defoe*, Item 50.

[18] Siebert, *Freedom of the Press in England 1476-1766*, 278.

[19] Backscheider, *Daniel Defoe, His Life*, 103.

government, but an informer – who anonymously collected fifty pounds – turned him in. On 21 May he was arrested "at the house of a Spittalfields weaver".[20]

Although Defoe was given a public trial in front of a group of justices, these men had very little scope for action. Before the trial a judge had already made the determination that the pamphlet was seditious. That determination was the basis for trial. All that the justices were asked to determine was whether or not the defendant, Daniel Defoe, had written *The Shortest-Way with the Dissenters*. That was an easy task. Not only did the Government have a chain of witnesses, but also Defoe admitted writing the piece. The prosecution did not argue that Defoe had been presumptuous to discuss public affairs, the usual basis for a charge of sedition. The prosecution argued that Defoe's pamphlet would have a harmful effect on public confidence in the Queen and would arouse public fear of Scotland.

Defoe was up before powerful men who had cause to dislike him and his satiric pen. Backscheider details the ways these men would have felt attacked by earlier Defoe pamphlets.[21] Similar analysis is provided by J.R. Moore in his essay, "Defoe in the Pillory". Moore quotes and explains the satires Defoe had written earlier against the men who were now his judges. He comments, "Perhaps the wonder is not so much that he was punished so severely, but that he escaped at all".[22] Defoe pleaded guilty to having written the pamphlet. In response to his appeal for mercy, the Queen's attorney general "responded with an eloquent speech elaborating the defiance and danger in Defoe's pamphlet". Defoe was sentenced to stand in the pillory for an hour at noon three times, to pay a fine worth about £134, and to remain in Newgate until he could find "good sureties to be of good behaviour for the space of seven years". In effect this was an automatic sentence to another three months in jail, since the next court session was not until the following October and the release date 8 November.[23]

The sentence was delayed by Defoe's attempts to negotiate an avoidance of the pillory. These attempts failed. Finally, he stood in the pillory on 29, 30, and 31 July 1703 about a city block away from his

---

[20] *Ibid.*, 104.
[21] *Ibid.*, 109.
[22] J.R. Moore, *"Defoe in the Pillory" and Other Studies*, Bloomington: IN, 1939, 31.
[23] Backscheider, *Daniel Defoe, His Life*, 110, 119, 124.

house in Cornhill, London.[24] In London at this time the pillory was not only physically uncomfortable, legally crippling, and personally humiliating, but also life-threatening. Onlookers were allowed to assault the victim. Nevertheless, Defoe survived his experience defiantly because friends and supporters surrounded him as he stood exposed to public humiliation.

The limits of public dialogue

The story from Defoe's side is just as simple. He insists that he was not starting a quarrel, but was responding to public attack on the Dissenters. He says that his pamphlet simply echoes the kinds of anti-Dissenter rhetoric current in London, bringing out all its violent implications. His defense is that the government is unfairly taking his ironic echo as if it were straightforward call for action.

In December 1702, as soon as he realized that the government considered his pamphlet dangerous, he went into hiding with friends in London. These friends were probably members of the "sect of dissenters call'd Baptists, or Antepaedo Baptists" to whom he refers in his *Tour*[25] and the same Spitalfield weavers whom he championed in a later pamphlet.[26] Spitalfield was just outside the city boundaries of London at that time, but it was close to Defoe's house in Cornhill. It was the area where Huguenot refugees – many of them silk merchants and weavers – had settled after the revocation of the Edict of Nantes in 1685. It is likely that English Dissenters felt the proposal for an act against Occasional Conformity as a parallel threat to their fellowship. Early in January 1703, while hiding from arrest, Defoe published a four-page pamphlet: *A Brief Explanation of a late Pamphlet, entitul'd The Shortest Way with the Dissenters*. He appeals to the readers' sense of justice, insisting that his pamphlet is a response to other published writers, "a fair answer to several books published in this *Liberty of the Press*".[27]

---

[24] *Ibid.*, 117; Furbank and Owens, *Critical Bibliography of Daniel Defoe*, Item 43.

[25] Daniel Defoe, *A Tour Through the Whole Island of Great Britain*, abridged and edited P.N. Furbank, W.R. Owens, A.J. Coulson, New Haven: CN, 1991, 165.

[26] Furbank and Owens, *Critical Bibliography of Daniel Defoe*, Item 203P.

[27] Daniel Defoe, *A Brief Explanation of A late pamphlet, entitul'd The Shortest Way with the Dissenters*, *The Shortest Way with the Dissenters: [Taken from Dr Sach---ll's Sermon] or Proposals for the Establishment of the Church*. By the Author of the True-born English-Man (London, 1703), Library of English Literature Microfiche, 1976, Fiche 40136, 18.

He sent his wife to talk to Secretary of State Nottingham, who refused to negotiate. On 28 February 1703, still hiding, he published a second edition of *The Shortest-Way with the Dissenters*. He reprinted his four-page explanation at the end of the pamphlet, and for this edition he changed the title page to anchor the text in contemporary political discussion. The new version reads as follows: "Taken from Dr. Sach-----ll's Sermon and Others" and "By the author of the True-Born English-Man". These changes identified himself as the outspoken supporter of King William and his opponent as one of the most prominent high church Anglicans. In May 1702 the Reverend Henry Sacheverell had preached and then published a sermon arguing that the English government depended on the Anglican Church and that Dissenters were enemies of the Anglican Church. The last section of the sermon, the application, called on supporters of the Anglican Church to "Hang out the *Bloody Flag*, and *Banner* of Defiance rather than offering Nonconformists oaths and offices".[28] Others had echoed his phrases and ideas during the summer of 1702. The phrase "bloody flag" may have contemporary reference to the buccaneer *jolie rouge* flag. Peter Leeson's study of pirates notes that "buccaneers flew red flags, which communicated to targets they would take 'no quarter' if they were resisted".[29]

Rather than silencing Defoe, his arrest sent him into a frenzy of publication. In mid-July, after his sentencing, but eleven days before the date for his standing in the pillory, he published a bitter commentary on his experience in the introduction to a poem called *More Reformation: A Satyr upon Himself, by the author of the True-Born Englishman*.[30] On 22 July 1703, only a week before standing in the pillory, he published a collection of his essays entitled *A True Collection of the Writings of the Author of the True Born English-man*.[31] This collection is a self-defense on two fronts. Firstly, the collection marshaled his best defense: "he included his best, most popular works and arranged them to show steady support for the

---

[28] Backscheider, *Daniel Defoe, His Life*, 91.

[29] Peter Leeson, *The Invisible Hook: The Hidden Economics of Pirates*, Princeton: NJ, 2009, 91.

[30] Daniel Defoe, *More Reformation. A Satyr upon himself. By the author of the true born English-man*. London, 1703: 18th Century Collections Online (Y.1707) 1325658-1001.

[31] Daniel Defoe, *A True Collection of the Writings of the Author of the True Born English-man*, London, 1703.

Protestant religion, the Protestant succession, and moral reform."[32] But the collection also responds to media profiteering on his trouble. On 17 April, while Defoe was in hiding, the printer John How had gathered some Defoe pamphlets and published them as *A Collection of the Writings of the Author of the True-Born English-Man.*[33] Defoe objected to this collection on several grounds, and the initial *"True"* in Defoe's title alludes to the fact that his collection was at least partly a response to How's. Defoe's true collection, however, incited public scorn for the way it demonstrated Defoe's pretentions to respectability. The volume included a portrait of Defoe in a wig and gown.[34]

On the same day as the *True Collection*, 22 July 1703, Defoe published *The Shortest Way to Peace and Union,* claiming that this was an essay he had written back in 1699 when William was king. He uses it to show that he would have had no desire to upset the government. In the pamphlet Defoe argues that under the Toleration Act of 1689, the Dissenters' "true interest is bound up in the prosperity of the present establishment". If a Dissenter were guilty of wanting to change the system, that Dissenter "should be sent to Bedlam not to Newgate".[35] His return to the dangerous phrase "the shortest way" in this pamphlet is a prominent feature of his self-defense, although the introduction says, "I shall be very wary how I prescribe more Short Ways, without the Direction of my superiors".[36]

The climax of this series of texts is "A Hymn to the Pillory",[37] which was handed out to the crowd while Defoe stood in the pillory. In this poem he attempts to turn his humiliation into an indictment of the government. He gives a roll-call of great men who have stood in the pillory:

> Bastwick, Pryn, Hunt, Hollinsby, and Pye,
> Men of unspotted Honesty;
> Men that had Learning, Wit and Sence,

---

[32] Backscheider, *Daniel Defoe, His Life*, 127.

[33] Moore, *A Checklist of the Writings of Daniel Defoe*, Item 25.

[34] Backscheider, *Daniel Defoe, His Life*, 128.

[35] Daniel Defoe, *The Shortest Way to Peace and Union* (1703), in *The Writings of Daniel Defoe*, ed. J.R. Moore, University Microfilms, number 57, 7.

[36] *Ibid.*, 22.

[37] Daniel Defoe, *A Hymn to the Pillory* (London, 1703), in *The Shortest Way with the Dissenters and Other Pamphlets*, Oxford, 1974.

And more than most Men have had since.

He calls for equal treatment: "Let all that merit equal Punishment, / Stand there with him, and we are all Content." Then he gives a list of people in England who deserve punishment. He starts with Sachaverell, but includes a wide range of targets:

> There would the Fam'd S[achevere]ll stand,
> With Trumpet of Sedition in his Hand
> Sounding the first *Crusado* in the Land.
>> He from a Church of *England* Pulpit first
>> All his Dissenting Brethren Curst;
>> Doom'd them to Satan for a Prey,
>>> And first found out *the shortest way*;

Defoe indicts large groups of people: "all the States-men" who "Armies, Fleet, and Men betray / And Ruine all *the shortest way*". He turns to "*Jobbers*, and *Brokers* of the City Stocks / ... Who make our Banks and Companies obey, / Or sink'em all *the shortest way*". He would like to see "those Justices upon thy Bench, / who vilely break the Laws they should defend". Defoe works the phrase "the shortest way" into many of the indictments. He ends the poem with a flourish:

> Tell them 'twas because he was too bold,
> And told those Truths, which shou'd not ha'been told.
>> Extol the Justice of the Land,
>> Who Punish what they will not understand.
> . . . .
> Tell 'em the M[en] that plac'd him here,
> Are Sc[anda]ls to the Times,
>> Are at a loss to find his Guilt,
>> And can't Commit his Crimes.

Besides flaunting the dangerous phrase "the shortest way", Defoe draws attention to his physical situation in the pillory. He metaphorically characterizes the pillory with twenty-five different images. It is a "Stool of State", a "Throne", a "Pulpit", a "Great Engine", and "Monster of the Law", as well as a person with brows, face, and front. The largest group of metaphors – seven of the twenty-five – compares the pillory to a theater. That comparison is his attempt to define the physical situation. It epitomizes the way he had tried to defend himself. Rather than accepting silence and passivity, Defoe translated his time in the pillory into a dramatic performance.

Defoe's defense failed to engage the government in dialogue, but it succeeded in rallying an effective crowd of supporters at the pillory: "By all accounts, Defoe's pillory was ringed with protectors, and the only things thrown at him were flowers."[38] There seems to be no surviving record naming those who protected him in the pillory. Backscheider surmises that it was the common London citizens who surrounded him. She credits his writing on behalf of the poor and his view that the ordinary citizens should rule Parliament. Defoe's Dissenter friends are more likely protectors than an anonymous crowd of the poor. Even though Defoe complained that the Dissenters had not supported him in his ordeal, there is evidence that Defoe had many close and loyal friends in the Dissenting community. Whoever his supporters were, the remarkable fact is that this non-violent mob scene occurred little more than a year after the anti-Dissenter mob-violence in London following King William's death.[39]

From the perspective of three centuries later, we should see these events as a milestone in the development of a public forum for political discussion. Defoe argued his case in a public space, and he suffered his punishment both in a physical and intellectual public square. The controversy convinced the government that it had to take a hand in shaping public opinion.

Pamphleteers did respond to Defoe's work. Their texts had something of the quick response time of spoken dialogue, and some of the sarcastic flavor of oral debate. Many of the pamphlet responses mocked him by echoing his title. Furbank and Owens list seven of the contemporary responses, including John Dunton's *the Shortest Way with Whores and Rogues* and Mary Astell's *A Fair Way with Dissenters and their Patrons.*

The popular support Defoe received as he stood in the pillory showed that a public opinion existed, but Defoe's damaged reputation and his own emotional reaction show the limits of such support. The fact that he had stood in the pillory remained a taunt his opponents could use against him for the rest of his life. Backscheider assembles a sampling of the scornful allusions made in 1717, 1719, and 1723 to

---

[38] Backscheider, *Daniel Defoe, His Life*, 118.
[39] *Ibid.*, 90.

Defoe's experience.[40] Defoe himself continues to refer back to this pamphlet and his pillory experience for years. Backscheider quotes his comment four years later in the *Review* of 1708.[41] Paul Alkon quotes a comment Defoe made eight years later, in 1712.[42] In his 1715 *Appeal*, Defoe says "during the Heat of the first Fury of High-flying; I fell a Sacrifice for writing against the Rage and Madness of that High Party, and in the Service of the Dissenters".[43]

Anatomy of a failure

The Shortest-Way with the Dissenters was a terrible failure. Rather than shaming his opponent, Sacheverell, Defoe disgraced himself. The pamphlet and its interpretation have become a treasure trove for critics. Backscheider cites several recent studies of *The Shortest-Way with the Dissenters*.[44] These studies, in turn, cite other studies. Paul Alkon, for example, lists fifteen studies by a veritable Who's Who of eighteenth-century scholars.[45] For students of the period, Defoe's failed irony provides a stunning contrast to Swift's successful irony in *A Modest Proposal*.

Most critics agree that Defoe failed, and they think his explanations of what he was trying to do also fail. Many critics think that Defoe's explanations are simply public relations bluster; he could not admit he had lost a fight. A very small number of critics take his pamphlet as a deliberate martyrdom and his explanations as part of the elaborate deception. I argue that even though the original title page did not help the readers perceive irony in the pamphlet, there were textual clues that could have led to a sympathetic reading. The difference in perspective between Defoe, the disenfranchised Dissenter, and most of his first readers explains why they could not see the ironies that were glaringly obvious to him. Relevance Theory explains why Defoe's irony was invisible to many of its first London readers.

Critics who focus on the structural details of the text claim that Defoe did not play by the rules of the game. In orthodox irony the text contains an obvious wink to the reader. Defoe's speaker, however,

---

[40] Backscheider, *Daniel Defoe, His Life*, 436.

[41] *Ibid.*, 119.

[42] Paul Alkon, "Defoe's Argument in *The Shortest Way with the Dissenters*", *Modern Philology*, XXXVII/2 (May 1976), S14.

[43] Defoe, "An Appeal to Honour and Justice", 171.

[44] Backscheider, *Daniel Defoe, His Life*, 555 n.22.

[45] Alkon, "Defoe's Argument", S13.

never hints that he is wearing a mask, so the text fails to provide a "framework or backdrop against which we can judge the central fiction and perceive it as a shocking, shameful, or ludicrous distortion of reality".[46] This deliberate dropping of the ironic mask is clear, for example, in Swift's *A Modest Proposal*. These critics claim that Defoe did not keep track of what he was doing. He failed because he was carried away with his role-playing.[47]

Two critics who think Defoe had a plan, Miriam Leranbaum and Paul Alkon, see Defoe as setting out to trick his audience. They think he sacrificed himself in order to make a point that he thought could not be made any other way. Leranbaum argues that Defoe wanted to imitate the High Church party in order to frighten the rest of the country. Alkon agrees, and examines the techniques Defoe copied from these High Church writers. He argues that Defoe's essay is designed to divide the Anglican party by trapping High Church readers into condoning its virulence. Alkon says:

> It *is* skillful rhetoric … a major achievement of *The Shortest Way* is the effective employment for worthier purposes of arguments most often designed to harden the heart. At great personal cost, Defoe turned such methods around to catch and awaken the silenced Anglican conscience.[48]

Leranbaum, too, thinks that Defoe wrote his pamphlet to trick the Anglican extremists – called colloquially the "high flyers" – into publicly exposing their murderous intentions: "His disappointment lay not in failing to effect this aim … but in failing to gain the support of his secondary audience, those moderates whom he thought of as his allies."[49] She says Defoe intended his pamphlet to expose the high church party to national disgrace and he came up with his strategy in imitation of a pamphlet hoax he had witnessed as a young man when a Jacobite censor was tricked by a Whig writer and lost his job as a result. The incident Leranbaum cites is a censorship scandal that took place in January 1693 when Defoe was thirty-three years old. Siebert

---

[46] Miriam Leranbaum, "'An Irony Not Unusual': Defoe's Shortest Way with the Dissenters", *Huntington Library Quarterly*, LXXIII/3 (September 1974), 228.
[47] *Ibid.*, 227-30.
[48] Alkon, "Defoe's Argument", S23.
[49] Leranbaum, "'An Irony Not Unusual'", 245.

credits this scandal with causing so much inter-party quarreling that it led to the abandonment of the censorship system.[50]

Relevance Theory analysis allows critics to track reasons other than Defoe's incompetence or self-sacrifice for the reception of Defoe's pamphlet. At this distance we can see irony in his text, but we can also suggest three reasons why Defoe's audience failed to see it. In the first place, Defoe failed to calculate how the fear he aroused would distract readers from his argument. In the second place, the clues to the text's ironic purpose appealed to events in English church history that Defoe interpreted differently from many of his readers. The High Church party really did think they had suffered under King William, and they could think that the Pilgrims' exile to New England was generosity from King James I. A third factor in the pamphlet's reception is the puzzle-solving reading patterns that London publications encouraged. Such reading focused readers' curiosity on the author's identity rather than his message.

Defoe was trying to elicit an emotional reaction as well as intellectual consent to logical analysis. In his January 1703 *Brief Explanation*, Defoe says that his goal was to startle all his readers into distancing themselves from the pamphlet: "when the Persecution and Destruction of the *Dissenters, the very Thing they* [high Anglicans] *drive at*, is put into plain *English*, the whole Nation will start at the Notion, and condemn the Author to be hang'd for his Impudence." On the next page he describes again the kind of aversion response he had expected: "when the Thing they mean is put into plain *English*, the whole Nation replies with the *Assyrian* Captain, *Is thy servant a dog that he should do these Things?*"[51] The hypocritical protest of a murderous official in the court of the King of Syria is noted in II Kings 8.13. Defoe uses it several times in his pamphlets, so Furbank and Owens consider it one of his stylistic fingerprints.[52]

Defoe uses another metaphor to explain what kind of reaction he had hoped to evoke. This metaphor appears in the Preface to *A True Collection*, published only a week before Defoe stood in the pillory.

---

[50] Siebert, *Freedom of the Press in England 1476-1766*, 260.
[51] Defoe, *Brief Explanation*, 19.
[52] Furbank and Owens, *Critical Bibliography of Daniel Defoe*, Items 68 and 72P.

There he says he had tried to construct an "Argument" and "draw a Picture which shew'd a Face".[53]

The two different kinds of pattern recognition – through logical analysis or through a global reaction – ring true to common experience. When Defoe talks about drawing a picture, he is talking about eliciting the kind of experience people can have when they catch an unflattering sight of themselves in a mirror. He was not trying to divide the Anglican parties but unite them. What happened, though, is that he frightened everyone except the High Church fanatics. Defoe had mistaken the High Church party. He had expected them to be shamed by the echo of their arguments. The Dissenters saw a murderous attack, but some High Church party members publicly admired the pamphlet.

Rather than uniting the country against threats of violence, Defoe had united the country against himself. The readers' horror or glee kept them from close analysis of the pamphlet's arguments. Then in self-defense, they all put the monster face on Daniel Defoe.

Defoe used common anti-Dissenter invective that dated back fifteen years to King William's 1688 Edict of Toleration: "'crucified between thieves' (the 'thieves' were the Dissenters and the Catholics, both enemies of the Church of England) and 'vipers in the bosom' (The Dissenters who had been given too many rights and had enriched themselves hypocritically)."[54] Even more threatening than the vocabulary of the High Church party, however, was the use of rhetoric that circumvented normal moral evaluation. These techniques include the creation of an impersonal speaker, the inversion of moral vocabulary, and the use of indeterminate and depersonalizing metaphors. Paul Alkon's study of the pamphlet explains "how such models of intolerance were made appealing, especially to those who were later appalled".[55] Alkon's analysis helps us sympathize with the readers who missed the irony.

Alkon points out that Defoe's creation of an impersonal speaker in *The Shortest-Way with the Dissenters* deprives his readers of one of the most important means of ethical evaluation – a speaker whose

---

[53] Daniel Defoe, *A True Collection of the Writings of the Author of the True Born English-man*, 4-5.
[54] Backscheider, *Daniel Defoe, His Life*, 96.
[55] Alkon, "Defoe's Argument", S12.

character we can judge.[56] Another technique, which Alkon says Defoe copied from Sacheverell, is the "inversion of moral vocabulary". Defoe accomplishes this inversion, for example, when he calls the exile of the Puritans to New England, "too much lenity of King James the First".[57]

Yet another technique Alkon points out is the use of metaphors that "increase confusion about what both Defoe and his speaker intend".[58] These metaphors imply that political repression will be similar to good farming practices or sound financial management: "We can never enjoy a settled uninterrupted Union and Tranquility in this Nation, till the spirit of Whiggism, faction and Schism is melted down like the Old-Money."[59] Here the Whigs – or their spirits – are compared to inanimate objects – old coins – whose destruction had been a positive economic measure for the nation in the recoinage of 1696. This kind of metaphor will ring differently in the ears of those being compared to coins than it does in the ears of those being compared to the coiners.

Defoe's banter, a successful hoax or a failed test?

While most critics think Defoe failed because he did not know what he was doing, both Alkon and Leranbaum think accurate imitation of Tory polemic was a necessary part of Defoe's larger plan to trick his readers. Leranbaum says, "Defoe's banter strove for authenticity and sought to trap his primary audience into self-betrayal".[60] She implies that Defoe admitted playing a trick on his opponents when he called his pamphlet a "banter".

Leranbaum's argument hangs on her interpretation of the noun "banter". She insists that for Defoe the word means a "hoax". The word was so new that John Locke pointed it out as a newly coined word in 1690, and uses it as an example of how words are created in his *Essay on Human Understanding*.[61] The *Oxford English Dictionary* cites Jonathan Swift's ridicule of this term in both the *Apology* to *Tale*

---

[56] *Ibid.*, S14.

[57] Defoe, *The Shortest-Way with the Dissenters*, 8.

[58] Alkon, "Defoe's Argument", S18.

[59] Defoe, *The Shortest-Way with the Dissenters*, 23.

[60] Leranbaum, "'An Irony Not Unusual'", 231.

[61] John Locke, *An Essay Concerning Human Understanding* (1689), Amherst: MA, 1995, 387.

of a Tub (1710*)* and in *The Tatler*, Number 230, as well as Locke's discussion. The *OED* lists three noun meanings contemporary with Defoe: "1. Wanton nonsense talked in ridicule of a subject or person, 2. An instance of such ridicule, a merry jest, 3. A matter of ridicule or jest." As a verb, the *OED* lists three meanings in this time period: "1. to make fun of (a person), to hold up to ridicule, 2. to ridicule, make a jest of a thing, 3. to impose upon (a person) originally in jest, to delude, cheat, trick." These meanings support Leranbaum, but they do not allow the possibility that Defoe had a slightly different meaning when he used the word.

Leranbaum argues that Defoe used the word banter "in the sense of 'joke,' 'hoax,' 'deception,' and as a verb, 'to play a joke upon,' 'to hoax,' or 'to deceive'".[62] Her analysis presents Defoe's pamphlet as the product of a conscious, deliberate self-sacrifice in a particular political situation. She points out that Defoe was very much aware of the pamphlet's legal status, and thus of the risk he was running. She thinks he wanted to seduce the High Flyers into agreeing with his pamphlet. He would then embarrass them by coming forward as its author.

Leranbaum's hypothesis that Defoe was playing a trick does not plausibly explain his original intention, however. He did not have a political power base that he could trust to rescue him from the anger of the tricked. If Defoe had been deliberately trying to divide the public into two groups – the one tricked by the pamphlet and the other seeing its irony – he would have known that those who were tricked would be in the recently elected Parliament, which was almost entirely Tory. In that case, having been shamed, they could not be expected to be conciliatory to Dissenter interests.

Leranbaum's argument that Defoe had consciously set himself up as a sacrificial lamb certainly does not explain his subsequent behavior. Later on, he complains that the Dissenters were not grateful for his efforts, but he cannot have expected political support from them. Their lack of political power was part of what drove him to irony. Nevertheless, Leranbaum's focus on the word "banter" as important to Defoe is perceptive, as is her attention to the close relationship between the words "banter" and "irony" for Defoe.

---

[62] Leranbaum, "'An Irony Not Unusual'", 245.

Defoe called the pamphlet irony before he claimed it was banter. Leranbaum notes that the *Brief Explanation* uses the word irony. The phrase "Banter upon the high-flying Church-Men" replaces that word in the reprinted *Shortest-Way* in January 1703.[63] The term "irony" is a very old one in rhetoric, but Sperber and Wilson argue that the conventional explanation of irony – reversal of literal meaning – never did explain a wide range of ironic language: "there are many examples of irony which fall outside the scope of the classical definition of irony as saying one thing and meaning the opposite."[64] Sperber and Wilson's approach sees the traditional examples of irony as just one type of a broader pattern of echoic speech: "[a] speaker can use an echoic utterance to convey a whole range of attitudes and emotions, ranging from outright acceptance and endorsement to outright rejection and dissociation."[65]

The crucial step in identifying irony is the reader's recognition that the pamphlet is interpretative language – that it is echoic speech. In speaking, the contrast between the words and a situation often gives the signal – as for example, when one is thanked for spilling a cup of coffee. In writing, a contrast between labels and reality provide the dissonance. The title page often gives initiated readers the clues they need, as naïve readers have discovered after having taken seriously an article in the American satiric journal *The Onion*. Defoe defended his original pamphlet as being within the bounds of conventional irony, even though he had not given his readers any orientation to his purpose. The new title page of his second edition gave his readers crucial new information to point them toward an ironic interpretation. The partially spelled-out name of another writer was a common clue to the author's intention. It indicates that the subsequent essay will attack the named opponent by giving an ironic echo of that person's writing. It establishes the pamphlet as an attack on Sacheverell's sermon. The new title page also identifies the author in terms of his support for King William. As we have seen, Defoe's *True-Born Englishman* had caused enough of a stir in January of 1701 so that Defoe could expect the public to remember that pamphlet's support of King William and his toleration policies.

---

[63] *Ibid.*, 244.
[64] Sperber and Wilson, *Relevance*, 241.
[65] *Ibid.*, 240.

These two contextual clues did not change the body of the pamphlet. They simply brought out the implications of material already there. Defoe must have thought that his exaggerated echo of High Church rhetoric – his opening references to the Church of England's "suffering" and "humiliation" under King William – would have signaled his ironic intention. In fact, the terms seemed sarcastic to Dissenters, but accurate description to the High Church readers.

Defoe was playing with rage and fear when he echoed the High Church rhetoric, yet he seemed surprised to be the target of the strong public emotional reaction his pamphlet precipitated. Backscheider says, "Defoe had imitated the code of the High Church too well, and for a brief period, they quoted his anonymous pamphlet as they had Sacheverell, and the Dissenters were truly alarmed".[66] Furbank and Owens take this line of analysis as well: "His hoax was so amazingly successful that those whom he had tricked, both churchmen and Dissenters, could never forgive him, and in their furious retaliation it is impossible to disentangle the stupidity from the malice."[67] The public anger was so intense because it fed off the reaction of fear Defoe noted.

Defoe certainly had an astonishing ability to pick up Tory catch phrases and to mimic the particular rhetorical patterns they employed in their anti-Dissenter polemic. Looking at the text with the knowledge that Defoe wrote it, however, we can spot signals of ironic intention in *The Shortest-Way with the Dissenters*. One such signal is the pamphlet's form of discourse. It looks like a sermon, but is not one. All sermons, whether they were the high-church Anglican sermons of Sacheverell, the latitudinarian Anglican sermons noted by John Evelyn, or the Dissenter sermons Defoe listened to, began with a careful examination of a Bible text.[68] To substitute a Fable for the Bible makes it a parody of a sermon. Another notable signal is the closing injunction to "crucify the Thieves". This deliberate echo of a Biblical mob scene must have seemed to Defoe a warning to readers that the pamphlet was ironic.

A theatrical signal of Defoe's irony is the deterioration of the speaker's mental state as he speaks. The speaker moves from self-

---

[66] Backscheider, *Daniel Defoe, His Life*, 100.

[67] Furbank and Owens, *Critical Bibliography of Daniel Defoe*, 148.

[68] Leranbaum cites Evelyn's notes on the sermons he heard, "'An Irony Not Unusual'", 231n.

confidence to paranoid frenzy. He speaks first as part of the "purest and most flourishing Church in the World".[69] Then he becomes righteously indignant, claiming to be presenting "the Church of England's just Resentments".[70] Eventually, he works himself into a frenzy and says it would be more rational to "summon our own [children] to a general Massacre" than tolerate the Dissenters.[71] His conclusion claims that the alternative to exterminating the Dissenters is for the Anglicans to kill their own children. The speaker has clearly left any reasonable argument behind. Defoe might well have expected readers to notice.

As outrageous as the sermon parody is the rewriting of English history. The speaker says that the exile of Puritans in the time of James I was generosity. Defoe's friends and teachers had emigrated to America partly because they were not allowed into Oxford or Cambridge. Defoe himself was well aware of the stressful re-negotiation of the Massachusetts Bay Charter in 1698 as well as the ravages of King Philip's War in 1675. To Defoe, the claim that James had given the Puritans "great Privileges, Grants, and suitable Powers, [kept] them under Protection and defend[ed] them against all Invaders"[72] must have seemed transparently false. Since Cotton Mather's *Magnalia Christi Americana*,[73] with its record of Puritan suffering and achievement, had been published in London and Boston in 1702, Defoe expected his readers to be aware of the Puritan settlers' experience in America.

Defoe fills his pamphlet with this series of complicated distortions. When Defoe later drew attention to "Contents, the Nature of the Thing, and the Manner of the Stile",[74] it seems likely that it is this kind of violation of reasonable public discourse he meant. He claims that his audience should have understood that his words were ironic.

No matter how clearly specific elements of the pamphlet signal its ironic intention to later readers, we are left with fact that they failed. Previous literary analysis has presented the pamphlet as a personal

---

[69] Defoe, *The Shortest-Way with the Dissenters*, 2.

[70] *Ibid.*,16.

[71] *Ibid.*, 20.

[72] *Ibid.*, 5.

[73] Cotton Mather, *Magnalia Christie Americana: or the ecclesiastical history of New England from its first planting in the year 1620. unto the year of our Lord 1698*, London, 1702.

[74] Defoe, "Brief Explanation", 17.

failure or a self-sacrificial hoax. Relevance Theory analysis, however, better explains the failure as the breakdown of an overloaded communication system.

The political context

Sperber and Wilson explain that interpretation is as much a matter of emotion as logic. Listeners look for an argument's relevance to themselves rather than looking for relevance to a topic. If a text arouses strong emotions, the reader may not hear the logic of the text.

When we look at the political situation we find the causes for Defoe's anger as well as for the division and fear in his readers. From his perspective, a quarrel within the Dissenter community turned into a legal battle that threatened his civic and economic life. His own desperation led him to mimic the rage of some readers and articulate the nightmares of others.

The change in government with King William's death brought to the surface the struggle between the old power of the aristocracy based on agricultural wealth and the new power of the merchants and traders based on cash and credit. During King William's lifetime, the struggle had expressed itself as conflict over the support for a standing army. The new issue was participation in communion. The new Tory Parliament was installed in July 1702, and High Church Anglicans introduced a bill to cut Dissenters off from participation in local government or from trade with any level of government, by forbidding the practice called "occasional conformity" – a practice Dissenters had developed to comply with the Act of Uniformity's requirement that public office be held only by communicants in the Church of England.

The Bill against Occasional Conformity followed months of rising tension for Dissenters. Queen Anne's actions and speeches seemed to encourage Anglican aggression. Her quick replacement of moderate Whig statesmen, her appointment of six Tory colonels to replace six Whig colonels in the City Commission of Lieutenancy, and her May 1702 speech expressing an inclination "to countenance those who have the truest Zeal to support [the Church of England]" had inflamed anti-Dissent feeling.[75] It seemed that Queen Anne threatened to reverse King William's toleration of Protestant Dissent.

---

[75] *Ibid.*, 90.

Under William, the Dissenters had become self-confident in their civic participation and assured of England's Protestant future. Just before his death William III had successfully negotiated the 1701 Act of Settlement, which had stipulated that the throne would pass to the Electress Sophia, the Protestant granddaughter of James I. The Act of Settlement put restrictions on the foreign interests of a foreign-born king, but it showed that the country was broadly united. The Act of Settlement reaffirmed the exclusion of Roman Catholics from the throne, a stipulation of the 1689 Bill of Rights. As David Ogg says, "this measure develops and completes the Bill of Rights ... once more, it asserts the uncompromising Protestantism of seventeenth-century England".[76]

The parliamentary action against the economic and political participation of Dissenters in national life took advantage of a long-simmering argument within the Dissenter community and between High Church Anglicans and strong Dissenters. It threatened to make communion in the Anglican rite more exclusive than it had been, and re-visited the exclusionary oaths that had marked the previous half-century of revolution. The whole nation was suffering from a kind of oath whiplash. During the Civil War everyone had taken several loyalty oaths of various types. As new oaths were demanded, various groups refused them. Refusal of the oaths in the 1662 Act of Uniformity had stripped some eighteen-hundred Dissenting preachers of their churches, and had made these preachers' congregations into second-class citizens.[77] Refusal of the 1689 oath of fidelity to William and Mary created a new group of outcasts. These Anglican clergymen were called the "non-jurors". David Ogg reports that in 1698:

> ... the nation lost a body of men, usually estimated at about 400 in number, many of them distinguished by character and learning .... The new oaths, in spite of the fact that the old phrase 'rightful and lawful' had been deleted, were abhorrent to all consistent believers in the doctrine of Non-Resistance, for whom the Lord's Anointed was still James.[78]

---

[76] Ogg, *England in the Reigns of James II and William III*, 469.
[77] Backscheider, *Daniel Defoe, His Life*, 7.
[78] Ogg, *England in the Reigns of James II and William III*, 233.

Backscheider lists the oaths and summarizes the emotional and intellectual consequences:

> Many men of James Foe's generation had been bound by oath to support Charles I, Parliament, the Solemn Oath and Covenant, Cromwell, and then Charles II and the Non-Resistance Act. Such demands made a generation that believed all oaths were binding under God reconsider the idea that church and state, religious and legal codes were inseparable.[79]

The intellectual and emotional struggle over the status of oaths cut across institutional ties. Christian communities became engaged with the question of sincerity in Church affiliation. Some Anglican Church leaders and some Dissenters, such as Defoe, made a public stir about the practice of "occasional conformity". This term referred to the practice of members of non-Anglican churches attending Anglican worship and participating in the communion service. The practice had grown up among Dissenters as a way to live within the letter of the 1673 Test Act for civil, military, or crown office. Under this Act, every office holder had to take "an Oath of Allegiance and communion in the Church of England within three months of taking office".[80] Since Presbyterians and other Dissenters agreed with 33 of the 39 Anglican articles, many were able to consider taking part occasionally in an Anglican church service as an expression of Christian unity. Others, both Anglican and Dissenter, looked on such a use of the Lord's Supper as hypocrisy – and as sin.[81] In 1698, Defoe took it on himself to admonish Sir Humphrey Edwin, the Mayor of London, who visited both a Presbyterian and Anglican church on a Sunday. He republished this pamphlet in 1700 with a preface asking John Howe, the prominent Dissenter minister, to take a public stand on the issue.

Suddenly in 1702 this simmering quarrel became a volcano whose eruption threatened to engulf the Dissenters. The proposed Bill against Occasional Conformity virtually declared Dissenters to be traitors. They would not be allowed participation in any level of government, or any commercial contact with any level of government. For Defoe,

---

[79] Backscheider, *Daniel Defoe, His Life*, 18-19.
[80] *Ibid.*, 84.
[81] *Ibid.*, 85.

such distrust was painful, insulting, and unconstitutional. Defoe did not reverse himself and support the practice he had earlier criticized. Instead he tried the same kind of abusive hyperbolic banter he had used in *The True-Born Englishman*. The Occasional Conformity bill implicitly denied the idea that British subjects were the heirs of a long constitutional history that gave them certain civic rights.

Not only did the proposed bill against Occasional Conformity forbid Dissenter participation in political or economic life, but it also set up a cynical mechanism for stripping Dissenters of their property. Dissenters could be deliberately voted into office so that they could be fined for attending non-Anglican church services. The anti-Dissenter mood of the public made such action plausible. Such fines were levied and collected, as Backscheider reports:

> Critics would later say that the Mansion House had been built with the fines imposed on Dissenters deliberately elected to City offices. If the Dissenter were forced to serve, he could not go to conventicle or he risked loss of office and a 150 [pound] fine the first time he went.[82]

Backscheider summarizes the emotional atmosphere of the period:

> The amount and nature of the abuse from pulpits and the press angered and intimidated even the sturdiest Dissenter. Pamphleteers traced a version of the history of Dissent in order to link Nonconformity with the Puritans who had beheaded Charles I and to preserve the idea that they were 'turbulent and factious spirits,' malcontents, and potential rebels. They were frequently compared to vermin, reptiles, cancer, and disease.[83]

Defoe's test changes the system

Defoe's explanation of *The Shortest-Way with the Dissenters* classifies his text as a banter, and his personal definition of the term focuses on the way he thinks irony works on the speaker who hears his discourse being echoed. In this respect, his definition differs from that of Locke or Swift. His definition of this term supports arguments that the pamphlet was a test or challenge to its readers. As we have seen, Defoe had defined his concept of a banter already in 1701, in his

---

[82] *Ibid.*, 92.
[83] *Ibid.*, 93-94.

polemic *True-Born Englishman*. He had presented it as a special kind of verbal action, a self-test that gives the speaker a chance to hear himself, an echo designed to make those who say it, listen to it. The experience of facing one's self in a verbal mirror is a "Test of Fools", akin to "showing a face". Not all fools pass the test. A hopeless fool fails to realize he is being tested and takes an echo to be agreement. This kind of irony asks readers to do self-analysis rather than condemn others, an unusual demand for polemic.

Defoe's banter test was a different game from the one his readers played regularly. Those readers were used to playing a masquerade game with writers. Anonymous publication trained the readers to respond to new pamphlets with a public guessing game as to the identity of the author. Such a guessing game is quite different from the moral self-examination Defoe was trying to induce with his banter. People were looking for clues, but not for a moral challenge. Immediately after *The Shortest-Way with the Dissenters* appeared, people were speculating about who had written it. Backscheider reports: "Charles Leslie, a journalistic enemy, wrote that he knew of no one who thought a Whig wrote *The Shortest-Way* and told how various High churchmen were rumored to be the author."[84]

A remarkably similar scenario would follow the publication of *Robinson Crusoe*. In 1719 Defoe again tried to explain to his readers that they had missed the irony in his work. The later circumstances, however, were much happier for Defoe. He was not arrested and disgraced for publishing *Robinson Crusoe*. On the contrary, he received fame and admiration that still survives. However, as we shall see, the readers' approval was no guarantee that they heard what Defoe thought he was saying.

Defoe came out of Newgate Prison a changed man. Imprisonment had ruined his entrepreneurial schemes, and public humiliation in the pillory had tainted his reputation. Nevertheless, the controversy had changed the political mood enough so that the English government was having to modify its methods of public control. The stormy public response to the Queen's speech showed the government that England itself was changing from an autocratic system to one more dependant on winning the consent of the governed. The government could not control public opinion, and it could not govern without the support of

---

[84] *Ibid.*, 99.

public opinion. After his time in Newgate, and as part of the condition of his release, Defoe became a pioneer of a new attempt by the government to shape public opinion. This new government plan involved both prevention and attack. They hired people to write for them and they arrested writers whose work went against the current government line. Facing prosecution for libel became a relatively common experience for a journalist. Nine years later, in 1713, Defoe would be arrested for libel once more, but this arrest was not a scandal. By then, arrest for libel had become part of the cost of doing journalism. The very different circumstances of his second arrest for libel, in 1713, demonstrate that the public debate had become an increasingly self-conscious performance.

After the *Shortest-Way with the Dissenters* controversy Defoe could no longer function as a London businessman with an interest in government. His roof-tile factory had failed. Men who had been pilloried lost their right to vote and were not able to serve on juries.[85] He became a government man with a passion for promoting trade. He constructed two new public roles, one as a journalist and another as an investigator of public opinion. He became a full-time political writer, and he organized a public-opinion investigation service for Robert Harley, the Secretary of State for the North, the man who as Speaker of the House had instigated charges against him and later arranged his discharge from Newgate.

Defoe's second arrest for libel – In April 1713 – threatened to collapse the distinction between his role as a journalist and his role as government propagandist, but the arrest did not threaten him the way the 1703 arrest had done. Many of the political issues and players were the same then as in 1703, but the country had changed. Such an arrest was now part of the drama of politics, and Defoe himself had become one of the authors of that drama. The charges against him were laid in retaliation for government charges he had suggested against an opponent. The opponent, out on bail, fled to France, with Defoe jeering in print.[86]

When he was charged with seditious libel and arrested on 13 April 1713, Defoe took it as an annoyance. He wrote to his mentor, Harley:

---

[85] *Ibid.*, 116.
[86] Daniel Defoe, *The Letters of Daniel Defoe*, ed. George Harris Healey, Oxford, 1955, 406n.

> I Believe the greatest Injury they can do me is the Expence and the
> surprise. *The first* the wound which your Ldpp knows I had So lately
> makes me ill able to bear. *The last* I hope will wear off.[87]

This kind of treason charge had become no more than a political card
to play in the game of shaping opinion. The publication of anti-
government pamphlets was common in this period, and was still
prosecuted as seditious libel. Backscheider's summary points out that
the government method of prosecution as a way to control the press
was not working:

> The government lost control completely; perhaps one of the best signs
> is that almost every journalist in London would be arrested at least
> once in the next two years. London was inundated with partisan
> periodicals.[88]

Official charges of sedition had become self-defeating. The charge
of seditious libel had led to the downfall of the previous Whig
government several years earlier. Defoe's old opponent Sacheverell
had survived a conviction for libel and had become a popular hero in a
scenario reminiscent of Defoe's own triumph at the pillory. The Whig
government charged Sacheverell with seditious libel, and succeeded in
impeaching him. He was supported, however, by the Lords and by the
public, so his exile to a new pulpit in Wales became a triumphal
procession.[89]

Defoe's arrest in 1713 was part of an effort by Ridpath and other
Scots journalists to humiliate the Tory government that employed
Defoe. Defoe's arrest was staged for the press coverage. Ridpath
described the scene in his journal *The Flying Post*. Defoe countered
Ridpath's story with the charge that Ridpath had arranged a dramatic
arrest scene just so he could write it up in the papers. Defoe, too, was
part of the publicity machine, and his response was public in *The
Review* of 16 and 18 April 1713.[90] The readers were the audience for
the performance. These men struggled over who would write the
dominant script, not over treason to their nation.

---

[87] *Ibid.*, 407 (emphasis in the original).
[88] Backscheider, *Daniel Defoe, His Life*, 273.
[89] *Ibid.*, 264-69.
[90] Daniel Defoe, *Review*, ed. A.W. Secord, New York, 1938, IX,167-70.

Defoe walks off stage

Defoe's public analysis of his 1713 arrest comes in his *Appeal to Honour and Justice* published by J. Baker in 1715 with Defoe's name on the title page.[91] This public statement appeared after Defoe suffered the loss of his political role as government writer when his patron, Harley, lost his position. Defoe himself was vilified for his political writing, and he went through a career crisis at this time of government change: "Defoe's reputation had never been worse. He looked like a thoroughly discredited hack, and his character had been destroyed by reports [of scandal]."[92]

Defoe was no longer a political agent. Political changes had pushed him aside, but these same changes had quieted his political anxieties. George I had taken the throne, and the attempt by James II's son to arouse a revolution in Scotland had failed. Since Defoe no longer had to worry about the Protestant succession, he turned from partisan political writing to broader themes. First, however, he published *An Appeal to Honour and Justice*, a book that appeared under his name and referred back to all his earlier writing. In effect, Defoe was declaring that the day of anonymous political publication was over. Defoe surveyed his whole career in public life, asserting that he had acted with "honesty" – a term he would develop later at great length in *Serious Reflections during the Life and Surprising Adventures of Robinson Crusoe.*

To his contemporaries, and perhaps to Defoe himself at the age of fifty-five, this *Appeal to Honour and Justice* must have seemed a farewell to power. No one predicted that his most influential work was still to come or that it would come out of his dramatic writing on his two favorite subjects: international trade and social morality. Four years after his *Appeal to Honour and Justice*, Defoe published *The Life and Strange Surprising Adventures of Robinson Crusoe*, a political story that would change the public forum his pamphlets had helped create.

---

[91] Daniel Defoe, *An Appeal to Honour and Justice*, London, 1715, title page.
[92] Backscheider, *Daniel Defoe, His Life*, 349.

CHAPTER FOUR

PIRATING *ROBINSON CRUSOE*

Why was Defoe's story both widely read and repeatedly abridged? It was exciting and relevant to its readers. It was topical, touching on the Orinoco coast, survival, plantations, and piracy. It fit popular genres: autobiography, spiritual self-analysis, and shipwreck stories. Defoe attempted to engage his contemporaries by this ironic imitation of popular genres. When readers looked at the text, however, they read it as an affirmation of both contemporary genres and imperialistic adventure. The abridged versions focused this popular interpretation of the text and eventually prevailed in the market.

The sequence of texts and abridgements as a dialogue
The history of Daniel Defoe's *The Life and Strange Surprising Adventures of Robinson Crusoe*[1] is nearly as strange and surprising as the adventures of its main character. No sooner was it published than it was kidnapped by other London publishers, who brought out their own abridged versions. When Defoe tried to reclaim the book through threats of legal action and through the publication of a second and third volume, he failed. He and his publisher soon gave up the fight over the text. There is even some evidence that suggests that when the

---

[1] The |LIFE| And | Strange Surprizing | ADVENTURES | Of | Robinson Crusoe, | of York, Mariner: | Who lived Eight and Twenty Years, | all alone in an un-inhabited Island on the | Coast of America, near the Mouth of | the Great River of Oroonoque; | Having been cast on Shore by Shipwreck, where-| in all the Man perished but himself. | WITH| an Account how he was at last as strangely deli-| ver'd by PYRATES. | [Rule] | *Written by Himself."* This description of the first edition title is given by Henry Clinton Hutchings in his *Robinson Crusoe and Its Printing 1719-1731*, New York, 1925, 52. Early eighteenth century capitalization and spelling often does not match modern usage. When I refer to the first volume of Defoe's series, I will use shortened title with modern spelling and capitalization. I will also give page references from Norton Critical Edition, 2nd edn.

book was serialized in 1720, the year after its first publication, Defoe
himself helped in that abridgement.

Defoe claimed that the changes made to *The Life and Strange
Surprising Adventures of Robinson Crusoe* by its pirate abridgers
radically altered the book. We will examine that claim and show that
the amazing success of Defoe's classic story is at least partly a re-
writing of his text by its readers. The sequence of texts and
abridgements amounts to a dialogue between Defoe and the abridgers.

The spadework for this study is Erhard Dahl's survey of all the
English editions of *The Life and Strange Surprising Adventures of
Robinson Crusoe* for the hundred years after its first publication. In his
1977 study Dahl reports: "They range all the way from the complete
364-page volume to a drastically shortened 8-page penny pamphlet."[2]

This re-writing took place so quickly, and the abridgements were
so popular, that the original text was overshadowed by the abridged
versions. All the abridgements focused on the first volume of the
series, and the chapbooks cut the first volume itself down to the island
adventure. These alterations made the book available to a broad
public. Dahl judges that the abridgements made the book into a much
greater cultural force than it might have been:

> Such changes in the text, price, and form probably resulted in Defoe's
> novel having an influence in England beyond its original public. That
> public, though socially in the middle class, was very limited in
> numbers.[3]

We know that Defoe was a writer with a political agenda and we
know that he had been a propaganda writer for Robert Harley's
government. He is less well known for his volumes of advice on
marriage and raising children, though he published books of advice
just before writing the *Robinson Crusoe* series. Thinking of Defoe as
an ethical advisor may strain our categories, but Defoe tries to present
his castaway narrative as a kind of parable, with Robinson Crusoe as a
spiritual exemplar. In "Robinson Crusoe's Preface" to *Serious*

---

[2] Erhard Dahl, *Die Kürtzungen des "Robinson Crusoe" in England zwischen 1719
und 1819 vor dem Hintergrund des zeitgenössichen Druckgewerbes, Verlagswesens
und Lespublikums*, Frankfurt am Main, 1977, 7 (my translation here and hereafter).
[3] *Ibid.*, 8.

Reflections, when Robin is defending the truth of his account, he says, "here is the just and only good end of all parable or allegoric history brought to pass, *viz.,* for moral and religious improvement".[4]

Defoe's earlier works show his skill at putting political argument into first-person narration. This personalized argumentation was a pattern Defoe pioneered. The method elicits identification and empathy, and it also appealed to contemporary cognitive theory. Locke's *Essay on Human Understanding*, with its emphasis on the importance of personal experience in knowledge was going through editions and revisions in the early eighteenth century, and it was a popular book. Certainly Defoe himself studied Locke. The sale catalogue of Defoe's library lists two copies of Locke's *Essay on Human Understanding* – a 1695 edition and a 1705 edition, the 1705 *Thoughts on Education*, two pamphlets on finance, a 1690 edition of *Two Treatises on Civil Government,* and a 1714 edition of the *Works.*[5]

We should not bc surprised to find that the *Robinson Crusoe* texts explore more than the emotional sufferings of a castaway. Defoe's Dissenter religious tradition saw trade and commerce as Christian vocations. His tradition also stressed the importance of community in a Christian life. A careful reading of the *Robinson Crusoe* series reveals that international trade is an important theme of these texts. Careful reading also reveals that Defoe's religious concerns are at the heart of the *Robinson Crusoe* series.

The first volume
The Life and Strange Surprising Adventures of Robinson Crusoe, Mariner; who lived eight and twenty years all alone, on an uninhabited Island on the coast of America, near the mouth of the great river of Oroonoque; having been cast on shore by shipwreck, wherein all the men perished but himself. With an Account how he was at last strangely delivered by Pyrates. Written by Himself was published on 25 April 1719. The title itself shows how this text appealed to the contemporary interests in travel, trade, piracy, exotic cultures, investment in the Caribbean, and autobiography.

---

[4] Defoe, *Serious Reflections*, xii.
[5] Olive Payne, *The Libraries of Daniel Defoe and Phillips Farewall*, (1731), ed. Helmut Heidenreich, Berlin, 1970, Items 164, 193, 987, 1029, 1075, 1162, and OM23.

Defoe's text was published anonymously, without the kind of dedication to a political or commercial leader that accompanied authentic travel stories of the period. William Dampier, whose 1697 narrative, *A New Voyage Round the World*, started a revival of interest in travel narration, dedicated his immensely popular account to the head of the Royal Society.[6] Edward Cooke offered his *Voyage to the South Sea and round the world perform'd in the years 1708, 1709, and* 1710 to the Lord High Treasurer of Britain.[7] Woodes Rogers dedicated his account, *A Cruising Voyage Round the World ... Begun in 1708 and Finish'd in 1711*, to its commercial backers, the merchants of Bristol.[8] All of these accounts assume public knowledge and acceptance of the buccaneer/privateer/pirate culture that had grown up in the Caribbean. Dampier's first volume tells how he switched from his original money making plans – cutting logwood to be used for dye – to joining a privateering attack on Porto Bello the Spanish settlement at Panama.[9]

Defoe wrote a preface addressing readers in the voice of an anonymous editor. At first glance this editor's praise for the text appears to authenticate it as factual, but on closer examination this testimony is only an opinion. The editor says he "believes the Thing to be a just History of Fact; neither is there any appearance of Fiction in it".[10] The volume sold for five shillings.

The engaging voice of Robinson Crusoe opens the story with the air of simple candor. But there are clues that the hero of this story is an emblematic figure. If we look carefully at this introductory section of the book we can see that Defoe has created a particular type of Englishman. The youngest son of a German immigrant to York, he longs to go to sea. Our narrator is something of a fool, an everyman whose bumbling explorations will be edifying. Both halves of his name turn out to be clues to this role. The family name "Crusoe" has many different echoes besides its immediate political import as an

---

[6] William Dampier, *A New Voyage Round the World, Seventh Ed.*, (1729), ed. N.M. Penzer, London, 1927, Dedication.

[7] Captain Edward Cooke, *A Voyage to the South Seas and round the world, perform'd in the year 1708, 1709, 1710, and 1711* London,1712, Dedication.

[8] Rogers, *A Cruising Voyage Round the World*, Dedication.

[9] Philip Edwards, *The Story of the Voyage: Sea-narratives in Eighteenth-Century England*, Cambridge, 1994, 19.

[10] Defoe, *The Life and Strange Surprisng Adventures of Robinson Crusoe*, 3.

Anglicized version of Kreuznaer, his father's German surname. "Crusoe" could be an allusion to the work of Defoe's classmate at Morton's Academy. Timothy Cruso wrote a popular spiritual guide.[11] It could be an allusion to Rogers' volume *A Cruising Voyage Round the World*. It could be an allusion to Defoe's own *Hymn to the Pillory* "S...ll... sounding the first Crusado in the Land".[12] The simplest interpretation – the assimilation of an immigrant – may be the most interesting. In 1719 the Hanoverian George I was the English King. By making Robin the son of an immigrant trader Defoe reminds the critical reader of the position that he had taken some thirty years previously while supporting the immigrant King William III in his poem *The True-Born Englishman*. Defoe had praised the English people as a nation of immigrants, characterized by virtue and a spirit of freedom. Robin's bold action in *Robinson Crusoe* shows him to be a true son of the German immigrant and a true Englishman.

The name Robinson was a common English name, but its use is not at all simple. The narrator refers to himself as Robinson in the first volume only in his formal literary mode on the title page and at the beginning of his journal.[13] He seems oddly unattached to that name. When he is a young man he is Bob to his friends, as we see in the early incident when he tries out the sea-faring life with a friend. Much later readers may be surprised to hear one of the English pirates at the end of the story addressed as Robinson, without Robin himself taking notice. He is Robin when he bemoans to himself his loneliness on the island, as we learn from what his parrot hears and imitates.[14] The name Robin was a common one, but it was also a tag. In one contemporary travel account, Robin was a name an English sailor gave to a Mosquito Indian who wanted an English name.[15] The name is so common and inglorious that Defoe used the name Robin for a character in Moll Flanders, as Laura Curtis points out: "A third fool is Robin, younger brother of her first lover."[16] Even in modern America

---

[11] Hunter, *Before Novels,* 261.

[12] Michael Shinagel summarizes these theories about the source of the name Crusoe in a footnote in the Norton Critical Edition of *Robinson Crusoe*, 248.

[13] Defoe, *The Life and Strange Surprising Adventures of Robinson Crusoe*, 52.

[14] *Ibid.*, 104.

[15] Michael Shinagel, "Contexts", in Norton Critical Edition of *Robinson Crusoe*, 246.

[16] Curtis, *The Elusive Daniel Defoe*, 149-50.

there is enough familiarity with English folklore to call up Robin
Hood and Robin Goodfellow.

Robin often seems to take his nationality as a personal name. The
Portuguese sea captain who rescues the young Robin after he has
escaped slavery calls him "Senor Inglese" and "Mr. Englishman".[17] At
the end of his stay on his Island, he rescues an English ship captain
who has been marooned by his crew. When they first meet, the captain
asks Robin if he is an angel. Robin replies, "I am a Man, an
Englishman ...".[18] This is what both Defoe and his readers thought
Robin represented. Defoe's quintessential Englishman is inventive,
persistent, energetic, and theatrical. Just as he is able to be a farmer,
herder, butcher, carpenter, potter, and baker, he is able to fill many
social roles. He loves to dramatize himself as a person with social
power. As critics have pointed out, most of the roles he reproduces
come from his observation of English society. He constructs fantasies
in which he is the owner of the island, with a "Castle"[19] and a
"Country Seat".[20] At the end of his island stay he stages a charade in
which he plays "Generalissimo" – with Friday as his "Lieutenant-
General"[21] and "Governor"[22] in order to restore the marooned English
sea captain to the command of his vessel.

Defoe allows Robin the chance to improve on England. His island
is a kind of constitutional monarchy, since all the inhabitants have to
sign a loyalty oath. After he rescues Friday, Friday's father, and a
Spanish soldier, he amuses himself with the idea of his being a king
who allows religious freedom in his domain: "My Man Friday was a
Protestant, his Father was a Pagan and a Cannibal, and the Spaniard
was a Papist: However I allow'd Liberty of Conscience throughout my
Dominions."[23]

The text of the first volume feels like a screen play. The plot takes
shape in a series of dramatic scenes separated by summaries. Some of
the physical scenes are re-played in Robin's mind as he remembers

---

[17] Defoe, *The Life and Strange Surprising Adventures of Robinson Crusoe*, 26.
[18] *Ibid.*, 183.
[19] *Ibid.,* 112.
[20] *Ibid.*, 113.
[21] *Ibid.*, 192.
[22] *Ibid.*, 193.
[23] *Ibid.*, 174.

and reconsiders his life. Robin's life on the island fills about 80 percent of the book, with the remaining 20 percent divided between his life before and after the island adventure. The opening passages of the story establish him as a restless adventurer – he runs away to sea, becomes a sailor, a slave, a trader, and a colonist – always defined primarily by his desire to move on.

There are no chapter divisions, but the volume falls into six sections that cover Robin's life until he returns to London. The story is told in chronological sequence. The longest stretch of the text (124 pages) presents his fifteen years of life alone on the island – roughly half devoted to his ten-month spiritual struggle and half to his fourteen-year physical adventure. The next long section (51 pages) describes his nine years of terror after seeing a footprint on the beach and discovering the cannibal barbecue site. Another long section (48 pages) describes the three years he spent on the island with Friday. In his final year on the island (40 pages), he rescues Spanish castaways and thwarts English pirates. In the 34-page return to civilization, Robin collects his Brazilian fortune in Portugal, distributes cash to his friends, and returns to London, bringing Friday along as a companion.

Editions and piracies of the first volume published in the summer of 1719

Taylor's print shop was surprised and overwhelmed by the public demand for *The Life and Strange Surprising Adventures of Robinson Crusoe*. The first edition (April 1719) sold out, so the publisher rushed out a second edition. Without exact dates the early editions are hard to track, but from an examination of typefaces in the early editions, Lucius Hubbard judges that Taylor kept two compositors busy so that he could put out more copies quickly.[24] Another analysis of the book's printing history, based on a close examination of the type, dates the second edition on May 8, the third edition on June 6, and the fourth edition on August 6.[25] Taylor was a cautious man, and he did not trust

---

[24] Lucius L. Hubbard, "Text Changes in the Taylor Editions of Robinson Crusoe with Remarks on the Cox Edition", *Papers of the Bibliographical Society of America*, XX/1-2 (1926), 32-35.

[25] Keith I. Maslen "The Printers of Robinson Crusoe", *The Library*, VII/1 (June 1952), 126.

the book to keep selling. All of these editions were probably the normal 1,500-copy print runs.[26]

Other printers were not so cautious. Already in August 1719 Edward Cox, a printer and bookseller whose accommodation address was at the Amsterdam Coffee House, published an abridged edition which he sold for only two shillings. Cox had the effrontery to present his piracy as a public service: "To further so good a Design, and make it Circulate thro' all Hands, we have Abridg'd it, and not only made the Book more portable, but lower'd its Price to the Circumstances of most People."[27] At the same time someone else published a pirated edition without giving a name or place of business, with the main character's name spelled "Cruso".[28] This is referred to as the "O" edition. These first two abridgements of Defoe's "octavo" 364-page original cut the original by more than a hundred pages – and at least one of them used a smaller page size. Still they were much longer than the later chapbook abridgements; the Cox version of 1719 had 255 pages.[29]

The first of these pirated abridgements – the Cox version, usually called the "Amsterdam Coffee House" version – was the one that aroused Defoe's public anger. In the Preface to his second volume, *The Farther Adventures of Robinson Crusoe*, Defoe protested the abridgement of his text. Defoe's publisher, William Taylor, threatened Cox with a lawsuit. Taylor reviled Cox and his abridgement in an advertisement in *The St James Post* on 7 August 1719.[30] The adapter had made substantial cuts to the book. There were fewer pages, and each page was smaller. As Hutchins points out: "How much of Taylor's edition has been eliminated can be easily judged when one compares the volumes – Taylor's an octavo, of 364 pages, 37 lines to the page, and Cox's a duodecimo, of 255 pages, 32 lines to the page."[31] The abridgement cut the book in half, as Hubbard's word-count reveals. There are approximately 125,000 words in the original

---

[26] Hubbard, "Text Changes", 22; Keith I. Maslen, "Edition Quantities for *Robinson Crusoe*, 1719", *The Library* XXIV (1969).

[27] Hutchins, *Robinson Crusoe and Its Printing*, 152.

[28] *Ibid.*, 179.

[29] *Ibid.*, 154.

[30] *Ibid.*, 142.

[31] *Ibid.*, 153.

text, but only about 64,000 words in the Amsterdam Coffee House abridgement.[32]

Hutchins's analysis shows that the substantial omissions come in the pre-island and post-island sections of the book. The Amsterdam Coffee House abridgement cuts pages 2-5 in the original down to a page. It omits pages 6-15 of Defoe's text, and reduces six pages in the final section of Defoe's text to two.[33] In the reduced pages 2-5 Robin fails to persuade his father to let him go to sea. In the deleted pages 6-15 Robin is scared into a short-lived repentance by his experience of a storm at sea. The omissions at the end cover Robin's thanks to the guardians of his Brazilian estate – the source of his wealth. Besides cutting these large sections of text, The Amsterdam Coffee House abridgement also reduced Robin's account of his first months on the island.

By contrast with the Amsterdam Coffee House abridgement, the "O" abridgement receives scorn from Defoe scholars. Both Dahl and Hutchins find this abridgement poorly done. Hutchins calls it a "scrubby little volume, badly printed in every way".[34] There are not many copies of it left, and Hutchins speculates that Defoe and Taylor did not object to it because they may never have seen it. The idea that a pirate edition could exist without Defoe's being aware of it tells us something about the publishing conditions of the time as well as indicating the story's instant popularity.

Farther Adventures and further abridgements
Besides protesting against Cox's modification of the text, Defoe quickly wrote a second volume, which he called *The Farther Adventures of Robinson Crusoe*.[35] Taylor published it on 17 August 1719 – less than four months after the first volume. This second volume carries on the story of Robin's island, but Robin is a rover not the father of a colony. The story becomes a picaresque exposé of international trade, with Robin as a naïve observer. He denounces

---

[32] Hubbard, "Text Changes", 48.

[33] Hutchins, *Robinson Crusoe and Its Printing*, 153.

[34] *Ibid.*, 180.

[35] Daniel Defoe, *The Farther Adventures of Robinson Crusoe; Being the Second and Last Part of His Life, and of the Strange Surprising Accounts of His Travels Round Three Parts of the Globe. Written by himself*, London, 1719.

British violence, buys a pirated ship to find himself accused of piracy. He escapes vigilante justice by way of China. In Mongolia he leads an iconoclastic raid on a tribal idol. He finally returns to England, smuggling a Russian prisoner in his entourage. There is a lot of action, but Robin is not at all heroic. His suffering is more ridiculous than pathetic. For readers looking for some of the emotional intensity of Robin's island adventure, this volume continues to disappoint.

Already when he was writing *The Life and Strange Surprising Adventures of Robinson Crusoe,* Defoe realized that he would want to continue Robin's story. The last section of the first volume foreshadows the initial events of the second. By the time Defoe had the second volume ready to print, Cox had abridged the first. In the preface to *The Farther Adventures* Defoe responds directly to the Preface in the Amsterdam Coffee House abridgement. He writes in the voice of "the Editor": "… the abridging this Work as scandalous, as it is knavish and ridiculous, seeing while to shorten the Book, that they may seem to reduce the Value, they strip it of all those Reflections, as well religious as moral, which are not only the greatest Beauty of the Work, but are calculated for the infinite Advantage of the Reader."[36] Meanwhile the first unabridged version of *The Life and Strange Surprising Adventures of Robinson Crusoe* continued to sell briskly.

Not all the piracies were abridgements, and it is possible that not all abridgements were piracies. In 1719 a consortium of publishers in Dublin, where English copyright laws did not apply, printed the first two volumes carefully and sold them bound into one book. Hutchins says "The Dublin Piracy, printed in Dublin 1719, is the only one [piracy] which at all attempts an accurate reprint of Taylor's publication".[37] Shortly after the appearance of *The Farther Adventures of Robinson Crusoe*, a serialized abridgement began running in *Heathcot's Intelligence.* The series ran from 7 October 1719 to 20 October 1720.[38] Hutchins thinks there is good evidence that "the publishing of *Robinson Crusoe* in this tri-weekly newspaper was the result of some arrangement between William Taylor and Heathcot".[39] There is none of the antagonism between Defoe's publisher, Taylor,

---

[36] Defoe, *Farther Adventures*, Preface.
[37] Hutchins, *Robinson Crusoe and Its Printing*, 141.
[38] *Ibid.*, 159.
[39] *Ibid.*, 161.

and Heathcot that appeared between Taylor and Cox in the Defoe preface to *The Farther Adventures*. In fact, at the end of the serial version of the first volume, Heathcot refers the reader to Taylor's publishing house: "Both which volumes (very fit for the Closet or Library of Persons of Fashion) are sold by Mr. TAYLOR, a Bookseller, at the Ship on Pater-noster Row, near St. Paul's Churchyard." Heathcot put another advertisement for both narrative volumes and for the third volume in the 19 October 1720 issue, which carried the last installment of *The Farther Adventures*:

> [A] Third Volume, which containing excellent Meditations, and other divine Subjects, we thing (*sic*) not proper to be inserted in a Publick Paper, but recommend it as a Book highly useful in all Christian Families, especially those who have the other Volumes, and is to be had of Mr. TAYLOR, Bookseller at the SHIP in PATER-NOSTER ROW.[40]

This close connection between the serial version and Defoe's publisher might argue a close connection with Defoe himself. Hutchins notes two unusual features about the serial abridgement. The abridger went to the trouble of re-paragraphing the text, and the abridger took out action sequences rather than moral reflection:

> From the first hundred pages of Taylor's first edition 584 lines are deleted in Heathcot, and from the remaining 264 pages only 41 lines have been deleted in Heathcot. Curiously enough these omitted passages are not the moralizings omitted in 'O', but in many cases are parts of the narrative.[41]

Defoe's political opponents and journalistic rivals were no less busy than the abridgers. Defoe's rival Charles Gildon published a long pamphlet in response to the first and second volumes. He began his response quoting from the fourth edition of *The Life and Strange Surprising Adventures of Robinson Crusoe,* printed on 8 August 1719. While he was composing his critique Defoe published his second volume, so Gildon added a second long section attacking *The Farther Adventures*.[42]

---

[40] *Ibid.*, 162.

[41] *Ibid.*, 163.

[42] Gildon, *The Life Adventures of Mr D_____De F__ of London*, 109.

Taylor dropped his lawsuit against Cox over the Amsterdam Coffee House abridgement after a confusing exchange of charges and counter charges. Cox published an open letter to Taylor in the 29 October *Flying Post*. He flatly denied having made the abridgement, but he hinted that an agent for Defoe had offered him the text:

> When the said book was published, I was on my journey to Scotland. Neither had I, directly or indirectly, any concern in the said book, nor knew anything more of it than this: that a certain person, a few days before I left London, came to me with a part of a sheet, as a specimen of the paper and print, and desired me to buy some of them; and at the same time told me that there had been a wrangling between Mr Taylor and the author about copy-money for the second volume: upon which, I immediately concluded that the author had done it himself in revenge to Mr Taylor, because he could not bring him to his own terms.

Cox goes on to refer to Defoe as "one of the most prostituted pens in the whole world" and to the "author of Crusoe's Don Quixotism". As Hutchins suggests, the letter throws light on "the undercurrents of the London book-trade of 1719".[43]

Serious Reflections

Initial public confusion over whether or not there was such a man as Robinson Crusoe who had actually experienced the events he described soon gave way to common recognition of Defoe as the author of *The Life and Strange Surprising Adventures of Robinson Crusoe*. Cox's letter shows that he knew this before the second volume was published. On 3 August 1720, a year after the publication of *The Farther Adventures*, Defoe came out with a volume called *Serious Reflections during the Life and Surprising Adventures of Robinson Crusoe, With his vision of the Angelick World*. This book was a collection of essays, not a story. As we noted earlier, both Defoe and his publisher treated the three volumes as a series. Taylor wrote a "Publisher's Introduction" to this third volume in order to answer Cox's public letter.

---

[43] Quoted in Hutchins, *Robinson Crusoe and Its Printing*, 143-44.

> Those whose Avarice prevailing over their Honesty, had invaded the Property of this Book by a corrupt Abridgment, have both fail'd in their Hope, and been ashamed of the Fact; shifting off the Guilt as well as they could, tho' weakly, from one to another. The principal Pyrate is gone to his Place and we say no more of him *De mortuis nil nisi bonum*; 'tis Satisfaction enough, that the Attempt has prov'd abortive, as the Baseness of the Design might give them Reason to expect it would.[44]

In the *Serious Reflections*, Robin goes back over his earlier adventures on the island and his trading voyages. There is no new action in this volume aside from a thought-provoking encounter between Robin and an "Old Gentlewoman" in a London salon. Remarkably, however, "Robinson Crusoe's Preface" claims that this third volume has primacy over the other two:

> As the Design of every Thing is said to be first in the Intention and last in the Execution; so I come now to acknowledge to my reader, That the present Work is not merely the Product of the two first Volumes, but the two first Volumes may rather be called the Product of this: The Fable is always made for the Moral, not the Moral for the Fable.[45]

Defoe's claim does not match the reception the first volume of *Robinson Crusoe* had from admiring abridgers in its own time nor does it fit the appreciation the first volume earned from later readers like Rousseau.

By the time Defoe wrote the Preface to the third volume, he had dropped the pose of a detached editor. Now he argues that the story is a kind of parable and that it casts Robin as a wise fool. Speaking in the voice of the character Robinson Crusoe, the Preface responds to Cox's open letter to Taylor, picking up as a complement Cox's sneering allusion to Don Quixote:

---

[44] Defoe, "Publisher's Introduction", in *Serious Reflections*, Unpaginated introductory material.

[45] Defoe, "Robinson Cruesoe's Preface", *Serious Reflections During the Life and Surprising Adventures of Robinson Crusoe*, A2.

> The famous History of *Don Quixot*, a Work which thousands read
> with Pleasure, to one that knows the Meaning of it, was an emblematic
> History of and a just Satyr upon the Duke *de Medina Sidonia*; a
> Person very remarkable at that time in *Spain*: To those who knew the
> original, the figures were lively and easily discovered themselves, as
> they are also here and the Images were just; and there fore when a
> malicious, but foolish Writer, in the abundance of his Gall spoke of
> *the Quixotism of R. Crusoe*, as he called it, he shewed evidently, that
> he knew nothing of what he said; and perhaps will be a little startled,
> when I shall tell him, that what he meant for a Satyr, was the greatest
> of Panegyricks.[46]

Besides this response to Cox, Defoe responds to Gildon, other critics,
and abridgers both in the Preface and in the text of *Serious
Reflections*.

From abridgement to chapbook

Defoe's story became public property very quickly. In 1722, just three
years after the original volume, the London publisher Edward
Midwinter brought out a popular and influential abridgement. This
abridgement in turn went through several editions. Dahl lists a second
edition in 1724, a third in 1726, a fourth in 1733, a fifth in 1735, a
sixth in 1761, and a ninth in 1765.[47] The Midwinter version claims to
represent the whole series of *Robinson Crusoe* texts: "The whole three
volumes faithfully abridged, and set forth with cuts proper to the
subject."[48] What Dahl calls "the first Midwinter" abridgement does
contain elements of all three volumes, but the radically shortened first
volume dominates the text. The abridgement squeezes the first volume
from 364 pages into 192 pages, the second volume from 373 pages
into 141 pages and the 354-page third volume into 39 pages.[49]

Scholars have traced this work to Thomas Gent, a printer from
York who wrote the abridgement when he was an apprentice under the
London printer Edward Midwinter. So far from taking credit for his
achievement, he mentions having abridged *Robinson Crusoe* only as

---

[46] *Ibid.*, A3.

[47] Dahl, *Die Kürzungen*, 174-79, items 4, 5, 7, 9, 11, 21, and 26 in Dahl's list of
abridged versions.

[48] *Ibid.*, 174.

[49] Hutchins, *Robinson Crusoe and Its Printing*, 131-32.

an incidental comment in a completely different controversy. Hutchins quotes the account printed in *The Life of Mr Thomas Gent, Printer, of York: written by Himself*. Gent was accused of having written about the imprisoned Bishop of Rochester. Gent denies having written about the bishop. He expostulates with his former employer: "Me, who am but your servant, and, you know, has wrote nothing for you this long time, except an abridgment of three volumes of 'Crusoe' into one."[50] This particular speech comes from a scene between Gent and Midwinter, both in jail for allegedly having written about the bishop who was in political trouble.

The 1722 Midwinter abridgement makes changes in the first volume similar to those made in the Amsterdam Coffee House and "O" versions. Pre- and post-island events are condensed, and Robin's inner struggles are minimized. Dahl points out:

> Once again the affected passages are Defoe's detailed accounts of Crusoe's actions, his thoughts, and feelings. In order to shape his own volume Gent completely left out Defoe's ending of Volume I.[51]

The success of his first abridgement encouraged Midwinter to sponsor another. The resulting 1730 text is only 82 pages long, including 23 half-page woodcuts.[52] The text claims to be "faithfully epitomized" from the three volumes rather than being "faithfully abridged".[53] Dahl sums up the changes:

> The book offers its readers a text which, in comparison with its original, has been degraded. The well-balanced proportionality between the 'process of improving his lot' and 'process of his spiritual rehabilitation' is destroyed. Robinson's big adventure is no longer spiritual but only material. [54]

This drastic abridgement virtually eliminates *The Farther Adventures of Robinson Crusoe* and *Serious Reflections*. Such deletion was typical of abridgements after 1730. According to Dahl: "The

---

[50] *Ibid.*, 135-36.
[51] Dahl, *Die Kürzungen*, 112.
[52] *Ibid.*, 117.
[53] *Ibid.*, 175.
[54] *Ibid.*, 114.

adventures that Defoe gave Crusoe in China and Russia are rarely
found in altered versions published after 1730."[55] Even Defoe's *The
Life and Strange Surprising Adventures of Robinson Crusoe* was
sharply cut down. Dahl points out that this abridged version resembles
the chapbooks that would further simplify, condense, and popularize
the Robinson myth:

> What makes this similar to a chapbook version is its concentration on
> the prologue and the island stay, the neglect of Crusoe's adventure in
> Europe at the end of Volume I, and the limitation of the text to facts.
> The island experience ends on the seventy-ninth page of the eighty-
> two page second Midwinter abridgement.[56]

All the abridgers rewrote Defoe's text by cutting out material and
by changing his words. Most of them agreed on which material from
the original text to delete and which aspects of his story to rewrite. Pat
Rogers' essay on the chapbooks and abridgements of Robinson
Crusoe aptly summarizes the process: "The shipwreck and its
aftermath in the days, weeks, and months immediately following
clearly constitute the major point of interest for most compilers."[57]
Rogers notes, "early readers were captivated by Crusoe's initial
trauma, possibly because they were familiar with stories of disaster
and delivery in popular theological manuals".[58] The first abridgers all
cast Robin as a repentant rebel forced to atone for his disobedience to
his father's commands.

Rousseau's game version
In 1762, forty-three years after the publication of *The Life and Strange
Surprising Adventures of Robinson Crusoe*, Rousseau picked the book
as one of the textbooks for his imagined student Emile. His rationale
epitomizes the narrative focus all the abridgers put on Robin's
survival on the island. Even so, Rousseau changes the ideological
slant of the abridgements. Whether or not Rousseau actually read all

---

[55] *Ibid.*, 11.
[56] *Ibid.*, 116-17.
[57] Pat Rogers, "Classics and Chapbooks", in *Books and Their Readers in Eighteenth-
Century England*, ed. Isabel Rivers, New York, 1982, 39.
[58] *Ibid.*, 35.

three volumes, they were available in French. A translation of all three volumes done by Saint Hyacinthe and Van Effen was published in Amsterdam in 1720 and 1721, but Rousseau directs readers to *The Life and Strange Surprising Adventures* as if there were only one volume.[59] Rousseau has eyes only for the story of Robin's physical conquest of the island, and he presents the story as "the most satisfactory treatise on natural education".[60]

Emile is to read this book just before adolescence, in what Rousseau calls the third stage of childhood.[61] Rousseau acknowledges that his reading changes Defoe's text, but, he asserts, his reading brings out the true nature of the text:

> Rid of all its lumber, this novel, beginning with the shipwreck of Robinson near his island and concluding with the arrival of the ship that is to take him away, will furnish Emile with both amusement and instruction during the period of life under consideration. I want his head to be turned by it, and to have him busy himself unceasingly with his castle, his goats and his plantations.

When Rousseau recommends Robin's story as a textbook for Emile, he emphasizes the book's egocentric theatricality not its moral example. He calls this section of his educational program the "Game of Robinson Crusoe". Rousseau says: "Robinson Crusoe alone on his island, without the help of his fellows and the tools of the various arts, yet managing to procure food and safety, and even a measure of well-being; here is something of interest for every age, capable of being made attractive to children in a thousand ways."[62]

The *Robinson Crusoe* Rousseau describes is a wonderful game. It is a game whose rules are clear and whose emotional rewards are great. Rousseau obviously rewrites Defoe's story to suit his own requirements for a happy, self-sufficient hero. Rousseau's Robin provides a satisfactory pattern for imitation. The way this narrative

---

[59] Joseph Texte, *Jean Jacques Rousseau and the Cosmopolitan Spirit in Literature: A Study of the Literary Relations Between France and England in the Eighteenth Century*, trans. J.W. Matthews, London, 1899, 24.

[60] Jean Jacques Rousseau, *Emile* (1762), trans and ed. William Boyd, New York, 1956, 84.

[61] *Ibid.*, 70.

[62] *Ibid.*, 84.

had already become the pattern of a genre throughout the world shows that other writers also recognized the formulaic potential of the plot and its ability to satisfy readers.

Reading for relevance

Defoe expressed his political philosophy by means of story. Defoe's first readers, in turn, interpreted *Robinson Crusoe* in line with their own political assumptions, as Relevance Theory predicts. Readers look for textual coherence based on their assumptions of relevance. No self-conscious conspiracy was needed to shape the text into a colonial fantasy. The allusions to sea stories, castaway experiences, the Orinoco River, and pirates made a colonial interpretation plausible and compelling. The great majority of Defoe's readers were simply blind to elements in his texts that call into question the developing British imperial ideology.

An examination of Defoe's three *Robinson Crusoe* volumes shows that some aspects of the texts sharply contradict the earliest interpretations made by both abridgers and critics. The close study of early abridgements, in turn, illuminates both the power of the written text to shape culture and the power of a culture to shape the texts it reads.

Sperber and Wilson's model of reading provides a theoretical framework for the analysis of abridgement as interpretation. For Sperber and Wilson, neither speech nor writing is the simple transmission of ideas. They say that in order to understand a verbal communication, the reader or listener assigns an interpretation based on anticipation of what the writer or speaker will say. The anticipation is a hypothesis based on the verbal clues as well as the listener or reader's interests and the shared cultural context. Their model allows for the possibility of misinterpretation as well as the possibility of creative amplification: "the experimental literature on disambiguation suggests that disambiguation and reference assignment are also to some extent 'top-down' processes: that the hearer makes anticipatory hypotheses about the overall logical structure of the utterance and resolves potential ambiguities and ambivalences on the basis of these." [63]

---

[63] Sperber and Wilson, *Relevance*, 205.

According to Sperber and Wilson, an utterance – or a text – is a cooperative construction whose speaker should provide the listener with clues for interpreting the text. "If the speaker has done her job properly, the end of the utterance should confirm all the provisional choices of content and context that have been made along the route."[64] This analysis goes a long way to explain why abridgers, who thought they understood the story, found some of Defoe's text redundant. It also explains how deletions or modifications of the kind that were done to *The Life and Strange Surprising Adventures of Robinson Crusoe* could shape the reading of the story. The abridgers read Defoe's text as one element in a public market crowded with new genres of texts. Naturally, they tried to make it fit.

---

[64] *Ibid.*, 208.

CHAPTER FIVE

ROBINSON CRUSOE'S TEXTUAL NEIGHBORS

Defoe's volumes shared intellectual space with large number of texts in a wide range of genres as we can see in a survey of publications and cultural activities of 1717, 1718, and 1719 in London. The literary revolution noted above in Chapter Two had produced colonial propaganda, guides for family life, biographies of pirates, and tales of privateering travels – with the associated genre of castaway stories – as well as a wide range of popular newspapers and pamphlets. Many of these new texts echoed themes from seventeenth-century anthologies of English trade, exploration, privateering, and colonization. London booksellers offered texts in all of these new genres, and the older works were still available. Defoe's original long title indicates that he wanted his book to attract readers of these texts. Conversely, popular texts provided the patterns readers and abridgers used to read Defoe's text.

Tales of the Caribbean
Books, pamphlets, and plays about privateers and colonies focused popular attention on the Caribbean during this period. In 1717 Londoners could buy a sixth edition of Dampier's popular text *A New Voyage Round the World.*[1] Dampier had begun his voyage as a trader harvesting wood used for dye. He joined a privateer expedition, and wrote it up when he reached London.

In 1719 at least two pamphlets on Sir Walter Raleigh marked the centennial of his death in 1618 by execution. The pamphlets drew readers' attention to Raleigh's long-abandoned proposal for a British trading colony on the Orinoco River in South America. Defoe was on record as having urged King William to support Raleigh's unfulfilled dream of a colony. The pseudonymous *Memoirs of Sir Walter Raleigh*

---

[1] Bonner, *Captain William Dampier*, 58.

which appeared in 1719 led to another anonymous publication: *An Historical Account of the ... Voyages of Raleigh*. Defoe was one of those who revered the memory of Sir Walter Raleigh as explorer and writer, and some Defoe scholars think Defoe was the author of this second pamphlet. Furbank and Owns reject this pamphlet from the Defoe canon in their 1988 *Canonisation*,[2] but in their 1998 *Critical Bibliography* they change their position, classifying the work as one of their "unresolved problems in attribution".[3]

On the London stage, Thomas Southerne's drama *Oroonoko: A Tragedy*, written in 1695, was "one of the most commonly produced of all the post-Shakespearean tragedies", according to the modern editors of Southerne's work.[4] The novel *Oroonoco* by Aphra Behn had been written seven years earlier in 1688. The novel was still in circulation at the time, and a new illustrated edition came out in 1722.[5] This story of a royal African couple who were betrayed by their own people and by English slave traders, and who heroically resisted enslavement has very little in common with Defoe's *Robinson Crusoe* series except for its location. Nevertheless, its continued popularity drew attention to trade in the Caribbean – this new market for English enterprise.

Guide books and tales of crime and punishment
Spiritual guides were like the Medieval morality play *Everyman* – intimate, predictable, and fascinating. The common practice of writing spiritual journals, discussed earlier, created a market for spiritual guides[6] as well as individual life stories. These genres gave all readers the opportunity to explore their own lives. Defoe himself had helped create the genre of guides with his popular guide, *The Family Instructor*, in 1715.[7] In 1718 he brought out the second volume of this

---

[2] Furbank and Owens, *The Canonisation of Daniel Defoe*, 167.

[3] Furbank and Owens, *Critical Bibliography*, 275.

[4] Robert Jordan and Harold Love, quoted in Preface, to Aphra Behn, *Oroonoko*, ed. Joanna Lipking, Norton Critical Edition, New York, 1997, 125.

[5] Picture caption, in Behn, *Oroonoko*, 120.

[6] J. Paul Hunter describes the guide: "By far the most popular of the identifiable 'kinds' in all the didactic para-literature of the time – and the closest in spirit to the novel" (*Before Novels*, 252).

[7] Daniel Defoe, *The Family instructor, in three parts; I. Relating to fathers and children. II. To masters and servants, III. To husbands and wives. The 8th edition, corrected by the author*, London, 1720.

series. In the first *Family Instructor* Defoe dramatizes the efforts of spiritually lax parents to regain leadership over the lives of their children. The topics in this second set of scenes focus on "a portrait of the ideal master".[8] In these guides, Defoe pioneered the technique of writing his lessons as short dramatic scenes of interpersonal conflict followed by commentary.

London readers enjoyed the moral criticism of contemporary behavior offered by the guide, as J. Paul Hunter's analysis of this tradition indicates: "This large body of 'popular' material, written from various religious political, and social perspectives, critically examines contemporary life in much the same spirit as do belletristic works."[9] Most of these texts relied on the pilgrimage metaphor that Hunter says "lay behind nearly every work of practical divinity" earlier in the century.[10] Like mystery plays, the guide texts themselves seemed to fall outside normal categories of artistic production that gave the author rights to the material. According to Hunter: "Popular didactic materials seemed to most readers and booksellers to belong in the public domain in an ethical sense, whatever legal restrictions might technically apply, and some of the most popular guides appeared anonymously or under some disguise."[11]

A different kind of popular text was the cautionary tale of theft and murder in the form of cheap anonymous biographies of criminals. These often included a section purporting to be the criminal's speech from the gallows warning against a life of crime. Hunter's analysis links the criminal biography and spiritual autobiography: "The widespread belief that truth will out in the final moments before death may help account for the widespread circulation of 'last words' and 'dying speeches' – a small but important subgenre of the late seventeenth and early eighteenth century that often merged with, or became embedded in, criminal biographies and funeral sermons."[12]

English sailors inside and outside the law
In 1719, when Defoe published *The Life and Strange Surprising Adventures of Robinson Crusoe*, the "golden age of piracy" was

---

[8] Backscheider, *Daniel Defoe, His Life*, 424.
[9] Hunter, *Before Novels*, 252.
[10] *Ibid.*, 259.
[11] *Ibid.*, 257.
[12] *Ibid.*, 182.

coming to an end.[13] The age of pirate literature, however, was just beginning. In fact, that age continues into the twenty-first century with the 2009 publication of fiction and analysis – Michael Crichton's *Pirate Latitudes*[14] and Peter Leeson's *The Invisible Hook: The Hidden Economics of Pirates*.[15]

The title of Defoe's first volume had advertised "an account how he was at last as strangely delivere'd by Pyrates". In the story, however, the pirates might be more accurately described as mutineers, who intended to go into piracy but were foiled by Robin's intervention. The suggestion that pirates might rescue shipwrecked sailors illustrates how the facts of maritime life in the early eighteenth century made absolute moral categories hard to maintain. Pirates were tried and hanged. Their stories fit into the crime and punishment genre, but the lines between legal privateering and illegal piracy were not always clear.

English readers in the early 1700s read pirate tales that offered sensational accounts of murder, theft, and punishment. Most pirates died horribly, so their lives were framed as cautionary tales. John Richetti thinks that these tales had the effect of supporting established social hierarchies. "[They were] a social microcosm" illustrating the truth that "brutal democracy and brutal dictatorship are the only possibilities ... when the traditional moral and legal systems of society are abandoned".[16]

Pirates were often cruel and recklessly dissolute, yet some legends from this period picture pirate society as being democratic and free from the arbitrary tyranny of social class and inherited position. The pirate ships operated by a well-known system of rules that gave each member of the crew a vote. To govern their relations with each other, pirate ships, apparently without exception, operated under articles that spelled out the rights and duties of all aboard, from captain to apprentice. These articles were remarkably uniform in both style and substance. Peter Leeson reports: "each crew devised its own constitution, but pirate articles displayed strong similarities across

---

[13] Donald G. Burgess, *The Pirates' Pact: The Secret Alliances Between History's Most Notorious Buccaneers and Colonial America*, New York, 2009, 7.

[14] Michael Crichton, *Pirate Latitudes*, New York, 2009.

[15] Leeson, *The Invisible Hook: The Hidden Economics of Pirates*.

[16] John J. Richetti, *Popular Fiction Before Richardson: Narrative Patterns: 1700-1739* (1969), Oxford, 1992, 80.

crews.">[17] Essentially they expressed the 'laws' of a 'rogue commonwealth'.[18] Leeson thinks that experiments in self-government of the pirate culture influenced Anglo-American political and social systems far beyond the Caribbean. Before examining that claim, we will track the beginnings of this pirate culture.

Buccaneers

The pirates of the early eighteenth century were the heirs of a long history of rebellion and anarchy in the Caribbean, much of it enabled and used by the English government. The political turmoil of civil war, regicide, restoration, and non-violent revolution had kept English adventurers from interfering with the Spanish exploitation of the Americas or the Far East. At the same time, intermittent war with Spain – under Cromwell during the Commonwealth and under William after the Glorious Revolution – had made Spanish treasure ships from the Americas legitimate prey for English adventurers. The Spanish system of colonization entailed regular shipments of treasure from the colonies to Spain. These treasure ships – the Manila-Acapulco ship from the Philippines and treasure ships from Portobello on the Isthmus of Panama – were rich targets for buccaneers, privateers, and pirates.

Under the Commonwealth government England succeeded in building a merchant fleet through the Ship Law of 1651 that required trade with England to ride in English ships. The Commonwealth had failed, however, in its attempt to challenge Spanish control of the Caribbean. The Commonwealth 1655 attack on Hispaniola was a rout, and the conquest of Jamaica a face-saving follow-up. There was no English military or naval force to protect the island from recapture. N.A.M. Rodgers describes the situation in his history of the British Navy:

> For some time it was doubtful if the English would be able to hold on to their new possession in the face of disease, starvation, and Spanish attack. In the late 1650's however, the infant colony discovered a means of livelihood and defense: buccaneering.

The English encouraged the first group of buccaneers – a free-

---

[17] Leeson, *The Invisible Hook*, 60.
[18] Frank Sherry, *Raiders and Rebels*, New York, 1986, 94.

lance group of largely European, non-Spanish outlaw sailors – to settle in Jamaica. Since the Spanish refused to allow any other nation to trade in the Caribbean, since there were English, French, and Spanish settlements, and since these settlements were not well served by Spanish trading ships, the area was ripe for adventurous exploitation: "the situation generated a mixture of trade, smuggling, and low-level hostilities, and gave ample opportunities to pirates and others who hoped to make their fortunes without the necessity of hard work."[19]

English attempts at colonial expansion inadvertently provided more buccaneers. Labor for the colonies on Jamaica and Barbados came from transported English and Irish people, enslaved natives, and imported enslaved Africans. These laborers ran away whenever they could and formed outlaw groups on sea and on land. Cromwell's conquest of Ireland in 1649 provided large numbers of Irish to supplement the poor Englishmen who furnished the initial labor for sugar plantations as the Atlantic slave trade was just beginning: "By 1660 there were at least twelve thousand Irish workers in the West Indies, and nine years later, eight thousand in Barbados alone."[20] Escapes from plantation slavery led to the formation of multi-racial bands of pirates in the Caribbean. These bands eventually caused so much disruption the British government was forced to act against them: "At the request of sugar planters and merchants ... Sir Robert Holmes commissioned a squadron of ships in 1688 to dispatch the buccaneers who had once been based in Jamaica."[21]

This buccaneer society in the Caribbean produced the storyteller Alexander Exquemelin, whose book, the *Buccaneers of America*, gives us a record of the buccaneer culture. Exquemelin himself was a French indentured servant who became a buccaneer.[22] His book "was written in Dutch and first published in Amsterdam in 1678 .... The first English translation was published in London in 1684 and within

---

[19] N.A.M. Rogers, *The Command of the Ocean: A Naval History of Britain 1649-1815*, New York, 2005, 24.

[20] Peter Linebaugh and Marcus Rediker, *The Many-Headed Hydra: Sailors, Slaves, Commoners, and the Hidden History of the Revolutionary Atlantic*, Boston, 2000, 123.

[21] *Ibid.*, 148.

[22] *Ibid.*, 158.

three months a second followed."[23] The story of this book shows how imprecise was the distinction between privateer and pirate. When Exquemelin's book came out, one of the featured characters, Henry Morgan, successfully sued the publisher for defamation of character. Morgan was the privateer who had led a successful attack on the Spanish treasure port Portobello in 1668 and had become Sir Henry Morgan. The Exquemelin volume went on to a corrected second edition in 1704 and a completely revised third edition also in 1704.

Often the pirates or buccaneers got their first ships by mutiny. Typically, part of the crew on a ship would band together and seize the ship, sending its legitimate captain back to shore or putting the captain and any loyalist crew ashore on a deserted island. This kind of mutiny-piracy frequently appears in the authentic travel literature as it does in the first and second volumes of the *Robinson Crusoe* series. It was not far from the privateer travel narrative. The difference between a pirate and a privateer was the authorization by a government to attack its enemies. Sometimes the authorization came after the attack had succeeded. Privateer culture grew in the Caribbean whenever England was at war with Spain or France – as it was during the War of the Spanish Succession (1701-1714). The privateers who attacked Spanish and French ships in the Caribbean performed a useful service for England.

Privateer narratives and the privateer tradition of English exploration

In 1697, with Dampier's *A New Voyage round the World*, privateer travel writing emerged from this Caribbean buccaneer culture as a new genre for a new group of readers – thrill-seekers, philosophers, and investors. Besides trade accounts and sea rescues, this kind of travel narrative brought pictures of exotic foreign cultures home to an English audience. Dampier gave accounts of the Mosquito Indians, and Cooke described cannibal feasts he had heard about. These kinds of accounts were important to philosophers such as Locke, who based his argument against innate ideas on travelers' accounts of hitherto unknown peoples.

By the eighteenth century, England had built up its navy. England had a large merchant marine and had won domination of shipping

---

[23] David Cordingly, *Under the Black Flag: The Romance and the Reality of Life Among the Pirates*, New York, 1995, 40.

routes from the Dutch in wars under Cromwell and the Restoration governments. England was ready to try to dominate the seas. Privateer narratives, maps, tales of sea voyages, and translations of French accounts of travel in China built enthusiasm for sea adventure. The printers were able and willing to fill the public's appetite for first-person accounts of voyages. Bonner reports: "In the fourteen years following Dampier's *New Voyage* [1697] no less than eight completely new collections appeared in London, whereas In the seventy years before Dampier there were but three collections of voyages in English worthy of notice."[24]

These stories were fresh, but they were not completely new. The early eighteenth-century popular texts such as privateer narrative and pirate stories belong to genres that had their roots in the Renaissance development of world exploration and trade, and England's role in that development.

The English story of the age of exploration was different from the French, Portuguese and Spanish tales. Those European nations had staked out colonial empires. The English did not have the army and navy to challenge Spain. The Elizabethan English did their colonial conquest and expansion close to home – in Ireland. They sent out a few voyages of exploration such as Drake's circumnavigation of the globe, or Frobisher's search for a northwest passage. When Drake came back with treasure, it was because he took it from the Spanish who had earlier taken it from the natives of the Americas.

English voyages were exploration attempts by consortia of the landed aristocracy or trading ships sent out by limited stock trading companies. These voyages did not report on the conquest of new worlds but on the discovery of coasts and tides, or on profit and loss of trading expeditions. Accounts of these exploration narratives and trading accounts had been compiled into volumes and published by Richard Hakluyt and Samuel Purchas in the Elizabethan age. Writers of the early eighteenth century, such as Defoe, were aware of the tradition. The sale catalogue of Defoe's library shows two editions of Hakluyt and two editions of Purchas.[25] Defoe self-consciously carried on some of these forms and challenged others.

The eighteenth-century privateer narrative revived a dormant type

---

[24] Bonner, *Captain William Dampier*, 53.
[25] Payne, *The Libraries of Daniel Defoe and Phillips Farewell*, Items 133, 196, 142 and 1018.

of popular text, but it also modified the textual conventions and supplied material for other kinds of collections. This new genre combined features of both the trade account and the exploration report. The new privateer narrative, however, provided a mix of legalized piracy adventure and travel almanac rather than the discovery of new worlds. But Defoe explicitly rejects the stylistic conventions of the privateer narrative. In the introduction to *Farther Adventures*, the "editor" warns readers that he does not intend to waste space on winds and harbors the way other stories of voyages do. He gives no weather reports nor does he celebrate sacking Spanish or native villages. In this second volume, Defoe's character Robin criticizes English privateering raids in search of plunder.

Privateer accounts were focused on setting, not plot or character. The writers normally traced specific voyages from their beginning in England and back to England. Into this matrix of a circular voyage the writer inserted details of harbors and coasts, encyclopedic information on exotic peoples, incidents from the voyage, and details of the contracts setting out the distribution of plunder between the voyagers and backers. J. Paul Hunter's study of the first volume of the Robinson Crusoe series, *The Reluctant Pilgrim*, epitomizes these conventions to argue that *The Life and Strange Surprising Adventures of Robinson Crusoe* follows the conventions of spiritual autobiography rather than those of travel narrative. Hunter's summary of eighteenth-century travel narrative conventions proves his point:

> Basically, the formula may be described as chronological in movement from place to place, topical in describing the particulars of each place. Much geographical detail is given about the places and about the natives and their customs, but there is relatively little emphasis on event .... 'objectivity' of tone and style characterizes the tradition as a whole. An important aspect of this objectivity is the absence of any informing idea of theme.[26]

Unlike many of the Elizabethan documents written as private reports, the privateer narratives were written for publication and edited by their authors. Sailors wrote privateer narratives for income, and their accounts served as a kind of self-advertisement. Successful privateers could get more work leading future privateering expeditions

---

[26] Hunter, *The Reluctant Pilgrim*, 15-16.

– whether financed by the government or by investors. Dampier, who made his first voyage around the world in 1679 as a member of a privateer crew, was later asked to lead a privateering voyage because of his success as a writer. Indeed, the writing of a travel narrative came to be a common response to going on such a voyage. A single expedition might yield several different accounts. One privateering expedition in 1708 furnished material for four narratives; Edward Cooke, Woodes Rogers, Basil Ringrose, and William Funnel all wrote about this voyage.[27] These travel writers claimed to be giving information that could assist trade, but the accounts themselves seem to reckon success in terms of plunder seized in the voyage.

Distinctions between merchants, privateers, and pirates were hard to maintain, with individual captains slipping between categories as circumstances dictated. The line between pirates and privateers was particularly hard to draw, so this line was one that the privateer-writers worked to build into their own works. In the final published text of the most famous of these accounts, the 1697 volume *A New Voyage Round the World*, Dampier distances himself from mutiny and other pirate acts carried out during the voyage. But Dampier was not so far from piracy in his original account. As he edited his manuscript he downplayed the mutiny in which he took part. Dampier and the rest of crew had abandoned Sawkins, their privateer captain, in the Philippines. The literary distancing in the final text developed through several stages of editing the original manuscript, as Philip Edwards' study shows.[28]

Another example of a privateer's attempt to distance himself from piracy comes in the work of William Funnell, who participated in Dampier's 1703 privateering voyage. Funnell tries to emphasize the military and official nature of the original expedition in his account: "We were each of us supplied with all War-like Stores, and very well victualled for nine Months and had Commissions from his Royal Highness the Lord High-Admiral, to proceed in a War-like manner against the French and Spaniards."[29] In the narrative, Funnell tries to

---

[27] Secord, *Studies in the Narrative Method of Defoe*, 105-106.

[28] Edwards, *The Story of the Voyage*, 26-28.

[29] William Funnell, *A Voyage Round the World: containing an Account of Capt. Dampier's Expedition into the South-Seas in the Ship St. George. With his Various Adventures and Engagements &c. Together with a Voyage from the West Coast of Mexico to East India*, London, 1729, Preface.

convey the impression that he and his band of men attacked only Spanish towns but forged alliances with native tribes.

The 1712 volumes by Woodes Rogers and Edward Cooke, which told of the privateering voyage from Bristol, likewise reveal anxiety about the kind of activity that went on in the expedition. Rogers and Cooke carefully explain the power structure of their expedition. In their introductions they explain that they are exploring the opportunities for English trade in the South Seas. Their careful accounts of the meetings of ships councils and their meticulous bookkeeping of the plunder they accumulate have the unintended effect of highlighting their similarity to pirates, who were known to organize themselves as democracies, electing their captains and dividing their plunder.

Quite naturally the privateer narratives mentioned rescues at sea: the increasing number of dangerous sea voyages furnished many such stories. So important was this kind of story to the religious and philosophical debates of the age, however, that publishers developed a whole new genre of "providence" books and "wonder" books for stories of dramatic rescues. In *The Reluctant Pilgrim*, Hunter points out that there was an extensive literature detailing amazing providential rescues from danger on land and at sea: "Many other 'miraculous preservations' were recorded during the late seventeenth and early eighteenth centuries, and Defoe probably knew as much about some of them as he did about Selkirk."[30]

Most Defoe scholars have made his reliance on the Selkirk story an important part of their analysis of *The Life and Strange Surprising Adventures of Robinson Crusoe*. They rightly note that the story was well known in Defoe's London. Woodes Rogers' narrative contained the story of Andrew Selkirk's rescue from the island of Juan Fernandez as well as references to other sailors left on that island in the Pacific. Certainly Defoe knew the Selkirk story from Rogers, Dampier, and from Steele. Steele's emphasis in 1713 on Selkirk's decay back in London and the tranquilizing effects of solitude may have triggered Defoe's contrarian impulses, but Defoe did not need to base his book on the story of Alexander Selkirk.

Hunter returns to a discussion of this genre in *Before Novels*, pointing out the way rescue stories fit into the religious and

---

[30] Hunter, *Reluctant Pilgrim*, 3.

philosophical discussions of the day. The genre offered proof of God's care for particular individuals in the face of a Newtonian clockwork universe: "the global strategy of Providence books ... was to illustrate God's continuing influence in human history."[31] Defoe's essay "On Providence" in *The Serious Reflections* fits into this genre.

The Elizabethan travel epic

The eighteenth-century privateer narratives were the mass-market development of the Elizabethan collections of travel writing. Richard Hakluyt's three-volume *Principall Navigations, Voyages, and Discoveries of the English Nation* was a collection of other peoples' writing, not a history written by Hakluyt. Hakluyt was a cleric and scholar, not an explorer. He "began collecting geographical literature, both printed books and narratives which he solicited from Englishmen who had been somewhere interesting". Serving as chaplain to the English ambassador to France, Hakluyt heard the French speak scornfully about England's lack of "discoveries and notable enterprises by sea".[32] He became a supporter of the study of navigation and an advocate for English colonies.

What began as a small collection expanded as Hakluyt and his successors gathered more material. Hakluyt's collections grew from the 825 pages of the 1589 *Principall Navigations* to the 2000 pages of the second edition in 1600. Samuel Purchas took up Hakluyt's work. *Purchas his Pilgrimage* grew from 752 pages in 1612 to a posthumous edition of 4,262 pages in 1625.[33] These collections juxtaposed various documents into an enormous multi-volume patchwork text, and that text came to exert nation-formative power. It changed the way England thought of itself, and, according to Richard Helgerson's analysis, distinguished England from other European nations:

> Hakluyt's task – the collective task of the various intersecting communities for which his name and his book stand as convenient markers – was thus not merely to record what the English had done and what the world was like, though these are the goals he explicitly set himself. He had also to reinvent both England and the world to

---

[31] Hunter, *Before Novels*, 218.

[32] Mary C. Fuller, *Voyages in Print: English Travel to America 1576-1624*, Cambridge: MA, 1995, 145.

[33] *Ibid.*, 146-49.

make them fit for one another.[34]

Trade records formed the bulk of the early travel collections partly because they were readily available. Hakluyt had collected everything he could find that had to do with Englishmen traveling, in his effort to portray England as a world power. He included the reports of aristocratic explorers like Sir Walter Raleigh, the colonial propaganda for the Virginia colony by Richard Harriot, the trade records of the East India or Muscovy merchants, and even a translation of Bartolome de las Casas' indictment of the Spanish in America. Within Hakluyt's collection, however, the regular, unemotional, list-filled trader accounts came to dominate the text.

These trade records were generated by the kind of instructions that the Muscovy Company gave its travelers for making the required reports. Hakluyt included even the instructions in his collection. The company gave each ship a record book and asked for a record of council decisions, reckoning of the ship's position and progress, the wind and sail settings, as well as detailed notes on the land they saw.[35] The trade records do not have dramatic plots or lively characters. They are interesting only because they are based on trade experiences, as Fuller rightly notes.[36] Nevertheless, the Hakluyt collection became a celebration of trade. It filled the role of a national epic for the modern English nation in that it defined the nation to itself.

The Hakluyt collection was physically impressive – a "handsome black-letter folio" says Helgerson.[37] The sheer weight of the trade documents made traders important national heroes. Helgerson credits the Hakluyt collection with a transformation in national values. By the mid 1620s a contemporary could write praising merchants in terms of merchant virtue rather than an aristocratic search for glory. Helgerson says Hakluyt's work changed the way people were valued: "men of trade are preferred to nobles, and they are preferred not for their magnanimity and valor, but for qualities intrinsic to their commercial activity, for diligence, thrift, and worldly knowledge."[38]

---

[34] Richard Helgerson, *Forms of Nationhood: The Elizabethan Writing of England*, Chicago, 1992, 153.

[35] Fuller, *Voyages in Print*, 3-6.

[36] *Ibid.*, 2.

[37] Helgerson, *Forms of Nationhood*, 175.

[38] *Ibid.*, 188.

The myth of mild English government

Along with the introduction of anthropological curiosities, the travel narratives informed Elizabethan Englishmen about what other European nations were doing. For more than a hundred years European thinkers had been aware that European treatment of native peoples in the New World could be seen as a test of their own moral standing. All of Europe knew about the Spanish conquest of Mexico. The European opinion of the Spanish conquest came to be called the "black legend". William Maltby documents this sixteenth-century judgment.[39] Information on the extermination of the natives in the Caribbean had come through translations of Bartolome de las Casas' *Devastation of the Indies*. The Spanish text was published in 1551.[40] By 1583, "when the growing enmity between Spain and England could no longer be disguised ... the first English language edition of the work appeared in the stalls of London booksellers".[41] The charges Las Casas made against his own people, the Spanish, were also available to English readers through Hakluyt's quotation of his translated *Relacion de la Destrucion de las Indias*:

> 'The Spanish,' he says, 'have not done in those quarters these forty years ... past, neither yet at this present, ought else than tear [the Indians] in pieces, kill them, martyr them, afflict them, torment them, and destroy them by strange sorts of cruelties, never either seen or read or heard of the like ... so far forth as of above three millions of souls that were in the Isle of Hispaniola ... there are not now two hundred natives of the country.[42]

The sale catalogue of Defoe's library shows that the collection contained two copies of Hakluyt's works and a French translation of Las Casas.[43] Robin refers to this legend as common knowledge when he wrestles with his reaction to the cannibals in the first volume of the series.

---

[39] William Maltby, *The Black Legend in England: The Development of Anti-Spanish Sentiment, 1558-1660*, Durham: NC, 1971.

[40] Bill M. Donovan, Introduction, to Bartolome de las Casas, *The Devastation of the Indies* (1551), trans. Herman Briffaul, Baltimore: MD, 1992, 2.

[41] Maltby, *The Black Legend in England*, 15.

[42] Richard Hakluyt, *The Original Writings and Correspondence of the Two Richard Hakluyts*, quoted in Helgerson, *Forms of Nationhood*, 183.

[43] Payne, *Libraries*, Items 133, 196, and 1321.

England had been slow to join the race for the Americas, so Elizabethan English explorers had little exploitation to live down. They tried to turn their outsider position into one of strength. These explorers introduced themselves to the South American tribes as opponents of the Spanish, and tried to make the natives into allies. Privateers such as Raleigh and Drake presented themselves as establishing trade relations with the South American natives in contrast to the Spanish slavery and exploitation. Sir Walter Raleigh's colony in Virginia was supposed to be a "rallying point for the oppressed natives of New Spain", and its establishment was supposed to coincide with Drake's attacks on Spanish settlements in the Caribbean. The English attempted to use cooperative natives and runaway slaves against the Spanish in South America in establishing colonies that would absorb English settlers and purchase English goods, according to Edmund Morgan. Nevertheless, these English colonists had English domination in mind:

> What Hakluyt and Raleigh were affirming was not quite a right of self-determination for the nations held in Spanish bondage. They were clearly bent on substituting English rule for Spanish.[44]

Raleigh's expeditions to Guiana in search of El Dorado serve as the paradigm of that English pattern. Charles Nicholl's 1995 re-telling of Raleigh's ill-fated South American adventure corroborates Edmund Morgan's account: "The narrative recreation of Raleigh's expedition sketches a picture of relations with the Indians that underlines its cordial relations with the natives."[45]

The English approach to colonies envisioned a network of trading settlements. This dream was well publicized by Raleigh's associates such as Richard Hakluyt and Thomas Harriot. Raleigh himself was aware of the importance of public opinion, and tried to argue his case in his published works. Helgerson judges that the English tack might have worked:

> The famous Elizabethan collection of travel narratives by Richard

---

[44] Edmund S. Morgan, *American Slavery American Freedom: The Ordeal of Colonial Virginia*, New York, 1975, 29-30.

[45] Charles Nicholl, *The Creature in the Map: A Journey to El Dorado*, New York, 1995, 37.

Hakluyt presented two models of conquest: the Spanish model of
universal domination and the other model of world trade without the
desire for universal domination. Drake's bold depredations in the
Caribbean and the Pacific mocked this overweening ambition, and the
various English schemes for western planting, Hakluyt's among them,
were meant to bridle it still more effectually. But both depended for
their particular rhetorical force on being seen as parts of a movement
that was essentially different, one that had no such universalist
ambition.[46]

Early eighteenth-century English travel literature shows traces of
the English tradition of seeing themselves as friends of the natives.
This policy informs Aphra Behn's explanation of the way colonists in
Surinam in the 1680s treated the native people. Her narrator says, "we
live with [the natives] in perfect Amity, without daring to command
'em; but on the contrary, caress 'em with all the brotherly and friendly
Affection in the World".[47] Woodes Rogers argued the same case in the
introductory letter to his 1711 narrative: "Besides, the Natives of
Chile, who are a brave People, have such an aversion to the Spaniards
that when they find the Mildness of an English Government they will
readily join us."[48]

The end of the golden age of piracy
By the time Defoe published *The Life and Strange Surprising
Adventures* in 1719, English colonization was mostly a matter of
investment, not exploration. Even in 1659, when Defoe sets his tale, it
would have been extremely unlikely to find an uninhabited fertile
island off the South American coast. Raleigh's 1616 expedition had
been carefully tracked and vigorously opposed by the Spanish. It
would also have been unlikely that any native would never have heard
a gunshot – as Robin claimed for Friday. The story's anachronism is
part of its emblematic style. Peter Hulme's study of the European
encounter with the Caribbean makes such a claim: "By looking back
beyond the great merchant companies to the age of Raleigh, Defoe
could endow Robinson Crusoe with something of the heroism of the

---

[46] Helgerson, *Forms of Nationhood*, 183.
[47] Behn, *Oroonoko*, 8.
[48] Rogers, *A Cruising Voyage Round the World*, xi.

adventurer who risked life and limb as well as capital."[49]

By 1719 the golden age of piracy was over. The future profits from the Caribbean were going to be profits on trade. Defoe's patron Harley thought he had discovered a way to tap the wealth of the new world when he was negotiating the Peace Treaty of Utrecht in 1713. The English obtained the *Assiento*, the contract to bring slaves from Africa to Spanish America. In 1718 the South Sea Company, which had been formed in 1711, began to look like a good investment. George I became a patron of the company, and the company took over the national debt. Soon people started speculating in its stock.

Once the War of the Spanish Succession had ended in the 1713 Treaty of Utrecht, there was no more scope for privateering against Spain or France. With legitimate targets of prey removed, most of the privateers turned pirate – first in the Indian Ocean and then in the Caribbean. They started attacking any and all ships. In the Indian Ocean attacks on the rich Muslim ships carrying pilgrims to Mecca elicited Mogul trade retaliation on the East India Company. The Company arranged for Royal Navy patrols of the sea off of India. The privateers-turned-pirate relocated to the Caribbean. Peter Leeson, in his analysis of the economics of piracy puts the situation in perspective:

> In any one year between 1716 and 1722 roughly 1,000 to 2,000 sea bandits prowled the pirate-infested waters of the Caribbean, Atlantic Ocean, and Indian Ocean. This may not seem especially impressive. But when you put the pirate population in historical perspective it is. … In a good year, then, the pirate population was more than 15 percent of the navy's.[50]

Privateers and pirates converged in life and in popular literature at the time of *The Life and Strange Surprising Adventures*. With peace in Europe in 1713, the English government turned from commissioning privateers to hunting pirates. Charles Johnson's introduction to his 1724 *A General History of the Robberies and Murders of the Most Notorious Pirates* quotes a 1716 British government list of navy ships

---

[49] Peter Hulme, *Colonial Encounters: Europe and the Native Caribbean 1492-1797*, 1986, New York, 1992, 184.
[50] Leeson, *The Invisible Hook*, 9.

to be used for "annoying the Pyrates and the Security of the Trade".[51] The preamble for the list describes the grounds for naval action: "the Pyrates are grown so numerous, that they infest not only the Seas near Jamaica, but even those of the North Continent of America; and ... unless some effectual Means be used, the whole Trade from Great Britain to those Parts, will not be only obstructed, but in imminent Danger of being lost." [52]

The King sent Woodes Rogers to fortify the Island of Providence in the Bahamas, which had been plundered by the Spanish and French in 1700 and taken over by pirates. Johnson identifies Rogers by his privateering success: "late commander of the two Bristol ships, called the Duke and Dutchess [*sic*], that took the rich Acapulco ship, and made a tour round the globe."[53]

English colonies and English pirates
English colonies added another layer of complication to the politics of piracy after the 1719 crackdown on pirates in the Bahamas. The British governors of the East Coast colonies in North America began licensing privateers. Restrictive British laws regulating trade made imported goods prohibitively expensive in North America, so American governors authorized privateers to attack French and Spanish shipping and allowed the privateers to sell their plunder in the colonies. Pirates clustered in the Caribbean since they could sell the goods they captured to the Americans. Frank Sherry reports: "In colonial cities all along the Atlantic coast, privateer loot was imported in defiance of the Navigation Acts and resold openly .... The same merchants and officials who furnished the illegal market for privateer plunder also outfitted expeditions in exchange for guaranteed shares in a ship's loot."[54]

Two twenty-first-century studies of pirates suggest that the link between the pirates of the Caribbean and the United States brought significant political benefits to the United States through the unintended consequences of this privateering commerce. Peter Leeson's study of the economics of piracy points out that the pirates

---

[51] Captain Charles Johnson, *A General History of the Robberies and Murders of the Most Notorious Pirates* (1724), ed. David Cordingly, New York, 1998, 13.
[52] *Ibid.*, 12.
[53] *Ibid.*, 13.
[54] Sherry, *Raiders and Rebels*, 24.

practiced democracy and separation of powers in order to prevent tyranny by the captain. They elected their captain, but put discipline and finances under another officer:

> Captains retained absolute authority in times of battle, enabling pirates to realize the benefits of autocratic control required for success in conflict. However, pirate crews transferred power to allocate provisions, select and distribute loot ... adjudicate crewmember conflicts, and administer discipline to the quartermaster, whom they democratically elected.[55]

Since the features of pirate law were universal and well known, Leeson suggests that pirate government provided a useful model for the kind of separation of powers set up in the United States Constitution.

Another unintended consequence of the link between colonial America and the pirates of the Caribbean, says Donald Burgess was the independence of colonial governors from London:

> Piracy ... was indeed a radical challenge to the English state. Yet that challenge came not from the pirates themselves. It was their patrons, the earnest colonial governors, who through quiet accord and longstanding practice signaled the limits of crown law and the germination of a distinct Atlantic community.
>
> A community that would one day be known as the United States of America. [56]

Utopian pirates

Utopian and revolutionary legends had grown up around the pirates who sailed in the Indian Ocean to prey on ships engaged in the rich trade with the East. The structural political effects on the development of the United States are the surprising fruit of twenty-first-century analysis. The more direct and obvious impact of these legends was both cautionary and escapist – much as the *Pirates of the Caribbean* film series is for twenty-first-century viewers.

Most of the legends involve a kingdom of pirates on the Indian Ocean island of Madagascar. One of these legends has the effect of

---

[55] Leeson, *The Invisible Hook*, 35.
[56] Burgess, *The Pirates' Pact*, 265.

affirming the English state, as noted by Richetti.[57] The English pirate Captain Avery – also known as Every, who captured a Mogul treasure ship in 1694, was the basis of this legend. This story makes him its pirate king. In this story Avery had 700 of his own men. The legend said that Avery married one of the Great Mogul's beautiful daughters. Then he settled in Madagascar with other exotic beauties, lived in state and luxury, and offered to pay off the English national debt for a pardon.[58] As the rumor had it, all the pirates wanted to come home to England, and there were so many pirates willing to pay the British Government for a general pardon that such pardon would have meant "six millions sterling to the Government".[59] Bonner reports as fact that Avery and his crew tried to buy pardons from British governors in the Caribbean. When they failed, they split up and some returned to England by way of Ireland in 1696. The men were soon caught and hanged, but Avery escaped. Charles Johnson's *General History*, in a debunking of the myth, says that Avery returned to England but could not cash in his diamonds, and died a beggar.[60]

Another story is more revolutionary, and its political commentary goes farther than eliminating the English national debt. The story "began to circulate in Europe about a pirate captain named Mission who had founded a socialist republic in Madagascar":

> According to the tale, the amazing Mission came from an old French family and had gone to sea as a boy, rising to become a keen ship's officer .... Although the tale says that Mission and his men took a number of prizes, it insists they never mistreated their captives, and in fact, took great delight in freeing the slaves aboard slave ships. The story tells how Mission and his liberty-loving crew arrived in Madagascar, where Captain Mission married the sister of a local queen. Eventually they were supposed to have set up an ideal pirate society on Madagascar, which they named fittingly enough, Libertalia and which was run on socialistic principles with all property held in common under a democratic government. But Libertalia came to an end when Mission's ship foundered in a

---

[57] Richetti, *Popular Fiction*, 80.
[58] Bonner, *Captain William Dampier*, 80.
[59] *Ibid.*,21-23.
[60] Johnson, *A General History of the Robberies and Murders of the Most Notorious Pirates*, 33.

> hurricane and he was drowned .... [There is] absolutely no evidence
> that a pirate named Mission ever existed.[61]

These legends were based on the long history of European sailors, beginning with the Portuguese in 1500, using Madagascar as a ship-repair and supply base for trade with the Far East. Although the French (1642), the Dutch, and the English (1645) had all tried to set up colonies on Madagascar, the only European groups on the island were pirates who persisted in small groups. By 1690 there were about half a dozen such settlements, but they were not thriving.[62]

One American entrepreneur, a former pirate named Adam Baldridge, did establish a trading post with an easily defended anchorage on St Mary's island off the north coast of Madagascar in 1691. His clients were legitimate traders heading for the Far East as well as the pirates preying on the Red Sea shipping who would return to North American ports to dispose of their loot. He became a kind of king of the pirates, says Sherry: "He had court in his big house on the hill overlooking St. Mary's harbor, dispensing law for both the white and native population. Warring tribes on the main island sought him as an ally, and he often participated in local wars, almost invariably deciding their outcome with his powerful arsenal of European weapons."[63]

Defoe's textual revolution

Defoe takes advantage of the curiosity about piracy, but he does not glorify piracy. After the Robinson Crusoe series he would imagine a pirate, Jack Singleton, who eventually quits robbery and retires incognito to England. In *The Life and Strange Surprising Adventures of Robinson Crusoe* Defoe shows his understanding of the mechanism by which merchant ships became pirates. Robin is rescued from his island by an English ship's captain. But Robin first meets the captain on shore where his crew that has turned pirate has marooned him. Robin restores that captain to the command of his ship. Defoe's analysis puts the blame for the ship's takeover on several leaders and, by implication, on the weak captain. His punishment for the rebel sailors is a kind of boot camp in communal life with the refugee

---

[61] Sherry, *Raiders and Rebels*, 99.
[62] *Ibid.*, 90.
[63] *Ibid.*, 93.

Spanish soldiers who will be coming to the island. In *The Farther Adventures of Robinson Crusoe* he imagines the results of his experiment in socialization.

Rather than tales of capturing Spanish treasure and fighting among pirate crews Defoe will use cannibals and Spanish soldiers to civilize the unruly English seamen. In this first volume of the series Defoe certainly does not affirm the predatory pirates or explorers, but neither does he find the individuals irredeemable.

Defoe's Robin breaks all the conventions of the early eighteenth-century genres – buccaneer, privateer, or pirate. At the same time his tale picks up some of the important elements of the English national epic. As we shall see, he celebrates hard work and patient effort – like the Elizabethan merchant-explorers. He is ready to work with all men and women to establish networks of trust and mutual aid. Like the English explorers who looked for trading partners as well as gold when they came to the Americas, Defoe's hero Robin stumbles into a voyage of self-discovery and political innovation. Rather than plundering Spanish or African towns, Robin discovers how to live in a new climate and rediscovers the crafts of an earlier age. Both his Christianity and his carpentry are do-it-yourself versions. They are not sophisticated, consistent, or even very successful, but they are often comic. By over-identifying Robin with Defoe, critics lose much of the humor in Robin's tale. Restoration of the ironic distance between Defoe and his Robin, reveals Defoe's series as a commentary on English imperial designs, not necessarily an affirmation of these efforts.

CHAPTER SIX

WHAT DEFOE LOST TO THE PIRATES

What did the first readers of Defoe's story see in the book, and what did they miss? We know the book was a best seller, and we know that most of the readers loved it. Even the abridgers loved it. They claimed that their shortened versions did a better job of conveying the story than the original. By looking at the changes made – the reduction of the frame story and the simplification of Robin's character – we can understand their perspective. At the same time we can understand Defoe's claim that the Amsterdam Coffee House abridged text was significantly different from his original, and we can see why he tried to take defensive action against the intellectual property pirates. Defoe thought the frame story provided relevant background information and character development, and he objected to the simplifications of the abridgements.

The reduced frame
All the shortened versions of *The Life and Strange Surprising Adventures of Robinson Crusoe*, starting with the Amsterdam Coffee House abridgement in 1719, cut down the pre-island and post-island sections of the first volume. These cuts affect the way readers think of Robin's father, and so they affect the interpretation of the moral of the story. The nature of fatherly love is a recurring theme in the story. The frame story introduces this theme and brings it in at the end by showing Robin's development from a rebel to a good father. Robin's own father is not a model, and Defoe's story is clearly not a prodigal son story. Before the island adventure Robin rebels against his incompetent father. He learns trade and navigation from other men who take a fatherly interest in his welfare. After he comes back from the island, where he has become something like a father to Friday, Robin repays his debts to his foster fathers. He becomes a foster father to his nephews and he fathers children of his own.

Critics disagree on how to interpret Robin's relationship to his father. For many readers of *Robinson Crusoe* it seems clear that Robin's exile on a deserted island is punishment for disobedience. For early abridgers and for some modern interpreters, Father Crusoe represents God, and Robin's disobedience to his earthly father indicates his rebellion against God's Providence. In one version of this position, Robin is haunted by his father's curse only until he himself realizes that he has been disobedient to both his earthly and his heavenly Father. In another version, adapters simply take Robin's disobedience to his father as a social crime. Both of these interpretations assume that Robin has a wise father who is giving his son good advice. This interpretation also assumes that Defoe pictures God as a domineering autocrat whose commandments amount to the injunction to be content where you are.

Robin does talk about his exile as the result of his disobedience to his father. He thinks of his disobedience as sin intermittently during his stay on his island. These thoughts add to his distress when he has been on the island for twenty-four years, but before he has rescued Friday. He is moved to reflection by a shipwreck on his island:

> I have been in all my Circumstances a *Memento* to those who are touched with the general Plague of Mankind, whence, for ought I know, one half of their Miseries flow: I mean, that of not being satisfy'd with the Station wherein God and Nature has plac'd them; for not to look back upon my primitive Condition and the excellent Advice of my Father, the Opposition to which was, *as I may call it,* my ORIGINAL SIN; my subsequent Mistakes of the same Kind had been the Means of my coming into this miserable Condition.[1] (emphasis in the original)

This is quite a dramatic lament, especially the capitalized phrase "ORIGINAL SIN", but we should notice that his use of the phrase is a pun. The theological term "original sin" refers to the doctrine that since the fall in the Garden of Eden human beings cannot do anything truly good. Here Robin uses the phrase to mean "my first big mistake". What he regrets in this speech is leaving England as the chief of the "subsequent Mistakes of the same Kind" that he lists. Naturally, had he not left England he would never have had a

---

[1] Defoe, *The Life and Strange Surprising Adventures of Robinson Crusoe*, 141.

plantation in Brazil, so the apparent lament about not being satisfied with his condition is not serious. Readers who have followed Robin's career know that he is subject to extravagant mood swings. We are carried along by these emotional fluctuations, but we also learn to step back and wait for the next swing of the pendulum. Defoe teaches readers to question Robin's analysis by holding all the characters at a distance. Such distance is reduced by the abridgements' reduction of the frame story.

Defoe gives no explicit guidance on the interpretation of Robin's father. Nevertheless, he certainly does not say that the story is designed to persuade young men to stay at home. In the Preface to the first volume, the "Editor" suggests the book's purpose: "a religious Application of Events to the Uses to which wise Men always apply them (*viz.*) *to* the Instruction of others by this Example, and to justify and honour the Wisdom of Providence in all the Variety of our Circumstances, let them happen how they will."[2] The Amsterdam Coffee House abridger changes the emphasis of Defoe's statement when he presents his abridged *Robinson Crusoe* as a story for those "who are inclin'd to learn the Art of Patience in submission to the Divine Will". The abridger does not seem to notice the difference between his formulation and the original. He congratulates himself: "Not that we have omitted any material Circumstance worthy of notice; but have observ'd a closer Connection of the author's Sense, and fallen immediately upon Matters of Fact."[3] The abridger had no qualms about changing the details of the story to match its sense, because he knew the story was a fiction – Defoe's imitation of a castaway tale. By the time the Amsterdam Coffee-House text was published, London readers knew that there was no Robinson Crusoe, mariner of York.

The definition of Providence and the role of Providence in the first volume has become a debating point between different approaches to *Robinson Crusoe*. One school, following Ian Watt's 1957 *Rise of the Novel*, finds that the question of a guiding spiritual force of Providence is not relevant to Robin's life. The story "expresses some

---

[2] *Ibid.*, 3.

[3] Amsterdam Coffee House abridgement, *The Life and Strange Surprizing Adventures of Robinson Crusoe. . . deliver'd by Pyrates. Written Originally by Himself, and Now Faithfully Abridg'd in Which Not One Remarkable Circumstance is Omitted*, London, 1719, Preface. I will refer to this abridgement as *Amsterdam Coffee House*.

of the most important tendencies of the life of his time ... profit is Crusoe's only vocation, and the whole world is his territory". Watt sees the "primacy of individual economic advantage"[4] as the main theme of the book. Another school, whose position is summarized by Peter Hulme, celebrates the story's spiritual values as revealed in the "cycles of sin and regeneration that underlie the surface realism". Hulme analyzes the difference between these schools as "constructing two different Defoes". Against Watt's modern Defoe – Defoe/Richardson/Fielding – Hulme sets a seventeenth-century Defoe – Milton/Bunyan/Defoe.[5] The seventeenth-century view of Providence that Hulme sees in Defoe is an inner voice monitoring the sinner's repentance.

The present study argues that Defoe was indeed taking part in the eighteenth-century exploration of Providence – with his concept being neither an interior spiritual awareness nor an external dominating force to which one must submit. The Amsterdam Coffee House abridger affirmed what he perceived to be Robin's submission to Providence. That abridger did not understood Defoe's concept of a dialogue with Providence. Robin is called to action, but he learns to submit – or offer – the events of his life to the interpretation of Providence. The modern division between material and spiritual life misses the Protestant linkage of the two in the Puritan-Dissenter tradition from which Defoe comes.

The Amsterdam Coffee-House abridgement sharply restricts the frame story. Dahl, the scholar who tracked all the early abridgements, thinks this abridgement is well done because the abridger cuts out what he – and Dahl, and Hutchins – perceive as extraneous material. One such block of material comes in the early section where Robin tries to get his parents' permission to go to sea. This negotiation is reduced to thirty per cent of the original, as Dahl explains:

> The abridger dealt with the dialogue in the same way as he did with the representation of Robin's business and his reflections. As with his deletions in reflective passages, his aim is obviously not to alter the dialogue, but simply to remove repetition and apparently superfluous material. For example, the Amsterdam Coffee House abridger gave only 300 words to the dialogue between father and son at the

---

[4] Watt, *Rise of the Novel*, 67.
[5] Hulme, *Colonial Encounters*, 177.

beginning of the novel, on which Defoe used a thousand words.

Dahl thinks that this abridgement, which preserved Father Crusoe's curse in its shortened introduction, maintained the story's moral complexity. In the Amsterdam Coffee House abridgement, as in the original text, Robin is haunted by his father's curse, but at the time of his conversion he realizes that his real rebellion has been his failure to recognize God's deliverance. For Dahl, Robin's discernment is proof of his spiritual growth. Nevertheless, Dahl sees Robin's exile as punishment for Robin's refusal to be content in Yorkshire.

Most of the Amsterdam Coffee-House reductions, according to Dahl, come in the negotiations Robin makes to pick up his life after leaving the island. Dahl does not think that *Robinson Crusoe* is about trade, so he accepts the deletions at the end of the book as unimportant. Dahl agrees with the abridger in seeing little substantive difference between the original and the first abridgement:

> It is possible that Crusoe's inner struggle would have made less impression on the readers of the Amsterdam Coffee-House version than on the readers of the original; the book may not have appeared to them so obviously a religious-allegorical work. However, Crusoe's conflicts of faith would have been clear enough, whether they were the result of his earlier unreligious life or of his disobedience to his parents. Likewise the readers were bound to notice Crusoe's insight into his guilt, his turning to faith, and his conviction of the power of faith. They would have come away with more than simply the outward adventures of Robinson Crusoe.[6]

For Dahl, Robin's conversion is enough evidence of his maturity. Dahl does not even consider the possibility that Defoe may have designed Father Crusoe's long-winded sermons against rebellion to reveal the inadequacies of both the lazy father who delivers them and the son who remembers them with remorse.

The "O" abridgement, also published in the summer of 1719, seems to find the moral of the story only in Robin's punishment for disobedience. Such a reading allows this abridger to simplify Defoe's text more radically than the Amsterdam Coffee House version. In the "O" abridgement, Robin was wrong not to submit to his father's will,

---

[6] Dahl, *Die Kürtzungen*, 109.

and his punishment from God was a twenty-eight year sentence on a desert island. Defoe's antagonist, Charles Gildon, follows that line because he wants to despise Defoe. Gildon says that Defoe seems to have written a story that advised young men to stay at home rather than go out and engage in international trade.[7] Gildon was right to find such advice absurd. He was wrong in taking that to be the point of Defoe's story.

Even some modern interpreters who see the story as one of spiritual growth have been satisfied to assume a crime-and-punishment pattern in the story. In some ways, the organization of Robin's life on the island does follow the pattern of contemporary Protestant spiritual autobiography, as G.A. Starr argues. Such books followed a highly conventional pattern, which outlined the author's inner life up to and including a conversion experience and subsequent episodes of backsliding.[8] The match between the popular contemporary genre and *Robinson Crusoe* is striking, and Starr argues convincingly that Robin's subsequent behavior including his successful farming and pottery work on the island prove that his conversion had been effective.

One weakness in Starr's approach, however, is that it still defines Robin's initial departure from England as sinful. Starr cites several examples of Defoe's praise of "the middle station of life" outside *The Life and Strange Surprising Adventures of Robinson Crusoe*. He says:

> By a single act, Crusoe … defies the joint authority of family, society, and Providence …. [This] is merely the first overt expression of a more fundamental source of trouble: the natural waywardness of every unregenerate man.[9]

It is clear that Robin does identify his disobedience to his father as disobedience to God in his moments of despair on the island, but it is not at all clear that Defoe did.

The trade frame
Reducing *Life and Strange Surprising Adventures of Robinson Crusoe* to an island adventure is easy, but it changes the reader's perspective

---

[7] Gildon, *Life of D___de_F*, 4.
[8] Starr, *Spiritual Autobiography*, 39-40.
[9] *Ibid.*, 79.

on the main character. Instead of an ambitious young man who wants to join the national adventure of trade, Robin becomes a disobedient child. Even before the chapbook abridgements deleted the frame narrative, the early abridgers shortened it by cutting out the realistic details.

The way Defoe made Robin's island life convincing was by focusing readers' attention on the details of everyday life. These details make the island adventure believable even as they obscure the implausibility of the scenario. Peter Hulme points out:

> The Amerindians would certainly not have ignored Crusoe's remarkably fertile island unless they had been driven off by the European competition for Caribbean land, which was in full swing by 1659 .... The realistic *detail* of the text obscures elements of the narrative that ... would have to be called mythic.[10]

The reduction of the pre- and post-island trade story cuts away at the kinds of details that attempt to give the same kind of verisimilitude to trade as the details of life on the island give to the survival story. In Defoe's text, Robin is a restless adventurer. He wants to make his way in the world. While searching for a career as a trader, he falls prey to slavery, shipwreck, and danger from cannibals, but he always returns to his goal of becoming a trader.

The people who help Robin along in his chosen career take over the work that Robin's own father has refused to do. After running away from home, Robin meets people who help him find the kind of work he enjoys. In the early section of the unabridged text Robin meets several adults who set him up in business. They are friends in the new sense of the word that Lawrence Stone points out in his social history of the period: "Not a person to whom one had some emotional attachment, but someone who could help one on in life, with whom one could safely do business or upon whom one was in some way dependent."[11]

A network of trustworthy commercial relationships is the setting for Robin's island adventure. The strength of these relationships

---

[10] Hulme, *Colonial Encounters*, 186.

[11] Lawrence Stone, "The Results of the English revolutions of the Seventeenth Century", in *Three British Revolutions: 1641, 1688, 1776*, ed. J.G.A. Pocock, Princeton, 1980, 79.

demonstrates the flaws in the ideal of a solitary individualistic life on an island. Furthermore, the disinterested support Robin receives from these friends makes Robin into the kind of attractive character who has the reader's sympathy. The integrity of these associates along with the stability of the system of written contracts Robin had put in place before leaving Brazil make Robin rich. After his initial trading voyage, he entrusts his profits to his captain's wife, who remits half of it to him when he sets up his plantation in Brazil.[12] When he returns to London after his long island sojourn, this woman becomes "My principal guide and Privy Councellor" in his financial affairs.[13] In Lisbon, Robin finds out that his Brazilian plantation has been kept going for twenty-eight years, and the agents are ready to hand over accounts. This network is something new: a system of international business operating on the mutual honesty and good will of the participants. All of these participants have family ties, and their family relationships enter into their business affairs, but in this commercial network they operate as individuals in a public network of trust. Many of their business arrangements are made by written contract registered with government offices. Hulme sees their actions as fantasy: "obviously romance wish-fulfillment operating in the economic realm …. But, conterminously, beneficence functions as the agent of narrative coherence, as in a word, the plot."[14]

Defoe gives specific details about Robin's travel home to England and specific details about his financial arrangements. The Amsterdam Coffee House abridgement severely reduces these details. This reduction modifies the effect of Defoe's work by making the frame story less persuasive. The early abridgers reduced the story to an island adventure. Later abridgements cut the frame narrative altogether.

Even before Defoe saw that the abridgers had cut his material on government and international trade from his first volume, he planned a second volume for the story of Robin's trading adventures after his return to the Island. Although Defoe must have written his second volume before seeing the Amsterdam Coffee House abridgement, his Preface to *The Farther Adventures* responds directly to the Preface of the Amsterdam Coffee House abridgement.

---

[12] Defoe, *The Life and Strange Surprising Adventures of Robinson Crusoe*, 28.
[13] *Ibid.*, 218.
[14] Hulme, *Colonial Encounters*, 218.

The last two pages of Defoe's first volume sketch the outlines of the second. Robin tells about the help he gave his nephews in setting up their careers. One of the nephews becomes a sea captain. He offers Robin a chance to revisit his island on the first leg of a trading voyage. Robin takes his nephew up on the proposal. Robin spends his ten-day visit to the island listening to the story of the residents' seven-year experiment in social development, and setting up his own experimental form of colonial government. He then turns to his long-delayed career as an international trader.

Robin's negligent father

Robin's desire to become an international trader was not the only casualty of the abridgements. Another component of the frame story is the reader's perception of Robin's adventurous spirit – what Defoe would later affirm as Robin's "Don Quixotism". The frame story sets up a gap between Defoe the author and Robin the narrator. This gap is crucial for our understanding of Robin's moral stature. The Robin we meet is not the happy child of Rousseau's fantasy. Neither is he a completely trustworthy adult narrator. One of the ways Defoe provides the reader with distance from his protagonist is through Robin's relationship to his father. Robin seems to find no fault with his father, but Defoe gives the readers clues that the old man is not a wise father.

Father Crusoe does not do much in the story. He only appears in the first eight pages of the volume, though his curse haunts Robin periodically during his stay on the island. Father Crusoe has been guilty of neglecting Robin. He seems to think that his son owes him obedience, but he has failed to do his duty by Robin. He has not helped his son find a suitable career. Father Crusoe tells his son to stay at home. He argues that young Robin can live the life of "the middle station", the best kind of life. Robin will be able to "go silently and smoothly through the world and comfortably out of it ... sliding gently through the world".[15] Robin later remembers his father's warning: "if I did take this foolish step, God would not bless me; and I would have leisure hereafter, to reflect upon having neglected his counsel, when there might be none to assist in my recovery."[16] This old man's curse

---

[15] Defoe, *The Life and Strange Surprising Adventures of Robinson Crusoe*, 5.
[16] *Ibid.*, 6.

reverberates in Robin's mind during his first few months on the island. He seems to think that his father was right.

The readers know from the book's title that Robin will disobey his father's commands. Robin's disobedience is in the reader's interest. If he had obeyed his father, there would be no story. Defoe also gives the reader several clues that Robin is justified in his disobedience because Father Crusoe is an example of improvident fatherhood. Defoe is careful to give his readers enough information about father Crusoe so that we can see Father Crusoe's hypocrisy. In his youth, he had been an adventuring trader who had immigrated to England from Germany – information removed from the Amsterdam Coffee-House abridgement. Now he has no sympathy for Robin's desire for adventure. His harsh tone and threatening attitude to Robin suggest why Robin's two older brothers have left home. By drawing this unattractive character Defoe brings up the topic of fatherhood, but he also casts doubt on Robin's discernment.

The biblical examples which Robin's father throws at him – the prophet Baalam sent to predict doom to the enemy, the prodigal son who wasted his inheritance, and Jonah who refused to preach to Nineveh – all misapply biblical texts. Robin has no divine mission to stay at home and slip through life. He is not refusing God's call, and far from wasting his inheritance, he goes off without a penny in his pocket. In Defoe's text, after leaving home Robin does get some money to use as capital on his first voyage from "the Assistance of some of my Relations whom I corresponded with, and who, I believe got my Father, or at least my Mother, to contribute ... to my first Adventure".[17] This grudging provision of capital for his trading career hardly justifies the accusation that he is a wastrel who runs though his inheritance. He embodies the spirit of adventure and trade that was driving England to compete as a trading nation. Robin's disobedience is right, and his later identification of that disobedience as sin is wrong. It is foolish to suggest that Defoe or his readers would have found a nation of stay-at-home sons any kind of happy ending. This realization gives the reader an important angle of vision on the rest of the volume. Robin feels guilty for disobeying his father, but the reader is able to see Father Crusoe's folly. Robin's father is dead when Robin returns to England, a fact that does not distress Robin at all because he

---

[17] *Ibid.*, 14.

is not a prodigal son returning to be forgiven. On the contrary, Robin comes home to England as a rich man able to help out his friends and relatives.

The Amsterdam Coffee House abridger seems to have noticed this problem and tried to improve Father Crusoe's character by adding material that improves Father Crusoe's provision for Robin's career. In Defoe's text Robin is at loose ends. He says his father has given him "a competent Share of Learning, as far as House-Education, and a Country Free-School generally goes, and design'd me for the Law". Robin's father, however, has not taken the necessary steps to start his son's legal career, nor has he consulted his son's inclinations when deciding his career. Robin complains to his mother that at eighteen it "was too late to go Apprentice to a Trade, or Clerk to an Attorney", and that what he really wanted to do was go to sea.[18] In the first abridged version Robin's complaint is deleted, and Robin says, "As for Education, my Father bestowed as much learning upon me as he thought would qualify me for the Law".[19] The Amsterdam Coffee House abridger also adds words to Robin's description of his father: Defoe says: "my Father, who was very ancient" and "a wise and grave Man".[20] The Amsterdam Coffee House text says, "Nay my Father who had Gravity and a Penetrating wit and one whose excellent counsels made him Valuable among his neighbors, could not prevail upon me to forsake my Inclinations".[21]

English fathers and God

The changes to *Robinson Crusoe* made by the alteration in the frame story are not simply matters of Robin's personal guilt or innocence. They alter the political implications of the story.

The conflict over the interpretation of Father Crusoe mirrors the contemporary English conflict over social and family structure. This conflict was not between individualism and community, but between different views of how community should be structured. Ian Watt's insistence that Crusoe's life and wanderings demonstrate both "individualism" and "the dynamic tendency of capitalism itself" has dominated discussion of *Robinson Crusoe* since the original

---

[18] *Ibid.*, 6.
[19] Amsterdam Coffee House, 2.
[20] Defoe, *The Life and Strange Surprising Adventures of Robinson Crusoe*, 1.
[21] Amsterdam Coffee House, 2.

publication of Watt's study.[22] A slightly different formulation sees the intellectual struggle not between individualism and social cooperation, but between two different kinds of social patterns. David Little points out that in the Christian community of Defoe's period the theoretical conflict was between a Renaissance Humanist tradition that emphasized obedience to natural law and a Calvinistic concept of voluntary obedience:

> The impulses within legal thought toward a spirit of free and autonomous economic activity, untrammeled by the traditional legal and political restraints, manifest a 'rich congruence' with some of the conclusions that emerged from the Calvinist Puritan pattern of order. The heart of Puritan thought rested in its advocacy of a new basis for obedience and a new form of authority. Out of its Calvinist heritage, it introduced a conception of social life with profoundly disruptive implications for English society, a conception that had certain affinities with the characteristics of the spirit of capitalism.[23]

The implications for English society that Little mentions focus on the role of fathers in the family. In Defoe's day the legal power of the father in nuclear families in English society was very strong. According to Susan Amussen:

> The moral and disciplinary authority of fathers, common to all western Europe, was strengthened by the English legal system. After the passage of the Stature of Wills in 1540, there were almost no restrictions on the distribution of property by the father to his children.[24]

Political and religious theory emphasized the moral authority of the father. Nevertheless, Calvinist theology provided a limitation on paternal authority. Amussen notes the tension between these two positions:

> Most household manuals were written by puritan clergymen. For them the family was a spiritual institution. The father was a king, but he

---

[22] Watt, *Rise of the Novel*, 68.

[23] Little, *Religion, Order, and Law*, 30.

[24] Susan Amussen, "Gender, Family, and the Social Order, 1560-1725", in *Order and Disorder in Early Modern England*, eds Anthony Fletcher and John Stevenson, Cambridge, 1985, 198.

> was also in some way a minister to it .... The puritan belief in the
> spiritual equality of the elect existed in tension with assumptions
> about social hierarchy.[25]

The Protestant reformation had made every home into a center of Christian education, and Defoe was part of that movement. As we have seen, Defoe wrote his *Family Instructor* for the market in instruction manuals on how to carry out Christian education in the home. Hunter lists seven typical texts in this genre published between 1690 and 1704. He reports, "when the Williamite concerns about a reformation of manners had their most powerful impact, worry about the decay of family religion became heated".[26] Defoe had published the first volume of that series in 1715, and the second volume in 1718. A third volume would come out in 1727. The second volume concentrated on "the behavior of fathers, especially in their responsibility for spiritual guidance in their extended households".[27]

The father's duties, however, had to do with young children. Defoe did not think that a father should have the power to order the life of an adult son. Critics who see Robin's father as a god-like figure in the story seem to assume that for Defoe the ideal father was someone who dominates his children. Critic James Maddox, who allows for some distance between Defoe and Robin, nevertheless says, "it is striking that every major relationship Crusoe has in this novel falls into a paternal-filial pattern .... Another way of putting the matter is to say that every relationship Crusoe enters is a rigidly binary relationship of dominance and submission."[28] But reading more closely, we can see that many of Robin's relationships with his foster fathers are relationships of partnership or trust. Defoe realized that the abuse of paternal authority could lead to tyranny. There were religious and practical limits on the authority of fathers, as on the authority of kings.

The topic of fatherhood in the early eighteenth century is heavy with political overtones. By making Robin's father an unquestioned moral authority, abridgers not only removed a clue to Robin's immaturity, but also changed an important political theme. The issue

---

[25] *Ibid.*, 201.

[26] Hunter, *Before Novels*, 266.

[27] Backscheider, *Daniel Defoe, His Life*, 424.

[28] James H. Maddox Jr, "Interpreter Crusoe", *English Literary History*, LI/1 (Spring 1984), 36.

of how long a father's authority over his children extends had been a matter of public debate in England, in political as well as in social terms. Locke's *Second Treatise on Civil Government* had argued for parental rather than paternal power, and for limits on the time of parental power: "The *power*, then, *that parents have* over their children, arises from that duty which is incumbent on them, to take care of their off-spring, during the imperfect state of childhood."[29]

Locke's analysis of government power informed the political arguments of Defoe's earlier long poem, *Jure Divino*.[30] The role of a father was commonly an analogy for the role of kings in their country. In *The Life and Strange Surprising Adventures* Robin links the ideas of family and kingdom in a joke just before he sees the footprint and discovers that cannibals use his island for their feasts:

> It would have made a Stoick smile to have seen, me and my little Family sit down to Dinner; there was my Majesty the Prince and Lord of the whole Island; I had the lives of all my Subjects at my absolute Command. I could hang, draw, give Liberty, and take it away, and no Rebels among my Subjects.[31]

Defoe did not think that a king had the right to govern without the people's consent. Robin's ironic linkage of "my Majesty" with his power to "hang, draw, give Liberty, and take it away" from his "Family" is consistent with his later care to secure oaths of voluntary submission and loyalty from all the people he welcomes to his island. The idea of a king as father would soon have colonial implications, as European colonists decided that native peoples of one tribe or another were like children. The tensions between dominance and distance in Robin's deliberations on what he should do to the cannibals and the tensions between dominance and distance in his relationship to Friday made questioning the idea of colonial paternalism into a theme of the first volume of the series.

Heathcot's fatherless frame

One early abridgement did not see father Crusoe as a representative of

---

[29] John Locke, *The Second Treatise of Government* (1689), ed. Peter Laslett, Cambridge, 1969, 324 (emphasis in the original).

[30] Daniel Defoe, *Jure Divino: A Satryr in Twelve Books* (1706), Library of English Literature Microfiche, 1976. Fiche 1570.

[31] Defoe, *The Life and Strange Surprising Adventures of Robinson Crusoe*, 108.

God. In fact, it deleted Robin's father from the story. This was the newspaper serial version of the first two volumes of the *Robinson Crusoe* series.[32] The serial began running in October 1719, after Gildon's pamphlet had appeared, but before Cox's angry public letter denying any involvement in piracy. As mentioned earlier, Dahl suggests that Defoe himself may have approved of the serial abridgement since Heathcot directed his readers to Taylor's shop for the unabridged texts.

Dahl reports this striking editorial change as a feature of the Heathcot serial abridgement:

> What Heathcot does in his serialization is remarkable since his version of the text withholds an entire group of ideas from the reader. These are all the places in the text that concern Robinson's relationship – both present and past – with his parents. The feelings of guilt which grow in Robinson over his defiance and disobedience and which, according to his understanding, make a second cause – along with his unbelief – for his punishment are thus eliminated. Heathcot begins this process at the start of the novel. There he does not mention Robinson's conversation with his father and the immediately following talk with his mother. Since Robinson thinks about both these conversations later, Heathcot is forced to erase these memories as well. In total Heathcot erases this kind of text material seven times and thereby eliminates all the places that link back to the relationship between Robinson and his parents.[33]

This change takes away the issue of whether or not Robin was being punished for his disobedience to his father. If, as I suggest, Defoe originally intended Father Crusoe's advice to Robin to be wrong and his curse to be impotent tyranny, then Robin's extravagant guilt is dramatic irony. The reader is supposed to see its folly. The Amsterdam Coffee-House and "O" abridgements show that many

---

[32] Daniel Defoe, *The life and strange adventures of Robinson Crusoe of York, Mariner: who lived eight and twety [sic] years alone in an uninhated [sic] island on the coast of America, near the mouth of the great river Oroonoque; having been cast on shore by shipwreck, wherein all the men perished but himself. With an account how he was al last strangely delivered by pyrates. Written by himself,* London: the *original London Post,* or *Heathcot's Intelligence,* Numbers 1125-289, 7 October 1719-20 October 1720. Hereafter I will refer to this abridgement as the Heathcot abridgement.

[33] Dahl, *Die Kürtzungen,* 110-11.

readers missed the irony. The Heathcot abridgement may represent Defoe's attempt to correct the misinterpretation of Robin's father.

Robin's material circumstance

The complicated narrative of Robin's fluctuating mental state during his twenty-eight years on the island seemed long-winded to abridgers. The Amsterdam Coffee House abridger explained that his abridgement had improved the original by focusing on "material Circumstance" and "Matters of Fact".[34]

The abridgers wanted to give readers the account of industrious activity, happy solitude, and horrifying cannibal contacts. The Amsterdam Coffee House text modified the account of Robin's first ten months on the island by cutting down the accounts of his emotional distress in these first months. It simplified Robin's spiritual anguish by limiting his sense of guilt – linking it simply to his disobedience to his father. It simplified Robin's personality by cutting out important passages that indicate his self-irony as a storyteller both in the initial ten-month pre-conversion section and in the later narrative.

In the Amsterdam Coffee House abridgement, Robin feels himself to be saved as soon as he struggles ashore onto the island, but Defoe's Robin says "I had a dismal Prospect of my Condition".[35] This abridgement also re-writes crucial segments of the text to improve Robin's attitude to the island. In Defoe's text, Robin does not see the island as a garden until after his 4 July conversion. Defoe has Robin describe the island in neutral or negative terms before his conversion. He makes his camp "on the Flat of the Green just before this hollow Place".[36] However, the Amsterdam Coffee House text says the place "being Green all over was like a pleasant Garden".[37] Defoe does not give Robin a sense of blessedness until after his religious awakening. The most he can recognize is a lessening of fear and grief. Defoe has Robin list "Comforts " and "Miseries" in his analysis of his situation.[38] The Amsterdam Coffee-House abridgement has him

---

[34] Amsterdam Coffee House, Preface.
[35] Defoe, *The Life and Strange Surprising Adventures of Robinson Crusoe*, 46.
[36] *Ibid.*, 48.
[37] Amsterdam Coffee House, 44.
[38] Defoe, *The Life and Strange Surprising Adventures of Robinson Crusoe*, 44.

record his "Blessings" and "Miseries".[39] Defoe's Robin makes the best of things in a bad situation: "Having now brought my Mind a little to relish my condition, and giving over looking out the Sea to see if I could spy a Ship … began to apply my self to accommodate my way of Living, and to make things as easy to me as I could."[40] The Amsterdam Coffee House abridger is eager to have Robin happy on the island: "My mind being thus brought to relish contentedly the State I was in, I neglected looking out to Sea for a sail; and thinking that Time misspent, I began to adjust my manner of living and make everything as easy to me as possible."[41] The effect of the abridgement is to minimize Robin's conversion by making Robin seem happy on the island well before his conversion.

The Amsterdam Coffee House abridgement simplifies both Robin's pre-conversion state of mind and his spiritual discernment. When Robin lists his sins as part of his religious awakening, in the abridged text he lists only one: "the many dangerous Circumstances of my Life, were so many Punishments for my Undutifulness to my Parents."[42] In Defoe's text, Robin lists several sins. The first one is his "rebellious Behaviour against my Father". He goes on to list others that indicate a developing view of Providence: his failure to be thankful for being rescued by the Portuguese captain and his failure to be thankful for surviving the shipwreck.[43]

Robin's despair

Defoe's text allows the reader to track Robin's spiritual and mental growth during the first ten months of his time on the island. Robin tells the story of his first few weeks twice, and Defoe makes a significant difference between the accounts. This duplication, however, led Defoe's critics to condense the journal account.

Robin's arrival on the island first appears as an immediate narrative. The second account is a copy of Robin's journal. In the overall structure of the narration, these first ten months get as much space as the next fourteen years after his conversion. During these ten months he works energetically to salvage as much as he can from the

---

[39] Amsterdam Coffee House, 48.
[40] Defoe, *The Life and Strange Surprising Adventures of Robinson Crusoe*, 50.
[41] Amsterdam Coffee House, 50.
[42] *Ibid.*, 69.
[43] Defoe, *The Life and Strange Surprising Adventures of Robinson Crusoe*, 65.

ship, and then he makes himself a place to live. Nevertheless, he is not happy on the island. He moves from frenetic activity to sober unhappiness. The account of these ten months is repetitious, chaotic, and desperate. When he first struggles ashore, Robin is energetic: "I walked about on the shore, lifting up my hands, and my whole being, as I may say, wrapt up in the contemplation of my deliverance, making a thousand gestures and motions which I cannot describe."[44]

Robin does not spend much time thinking. He is all activity. He reports that in the first eleven days he made thirteen trips to the wrecked ship so that when a storm carried it off he can congratulate himself: "I was a little surprised, but recovered myself with this satisfactory reflection, viz., that I had lost no time, nor abated no diligence, to get everything out of her that could be useful to me, and that indeed there was little left in her that I was able to bring away if I had had more time."[45] He does not waste time celebrating. He goes right to work to analyze the terrain, choose a site for his settlement, and begin building a homestead.

The details of his activity come quickly. He is working as hard and as fast as he can. The language keeps the reader focused on the present moment. Typical paragraph beginnings use the adverbs of time "now", and "soon": "I now gave over any more thought of the ship"; "My thoughts were now wholly employed about securing myself"; "I soon found the place I was in was not for my settlement."[46] Simple paragraphs focus on short segments of activity and combine active verbs with clear descriptions: "I found"; "I consulted several things"; "I resolved"; "I drew"; "I pitched." Robin's narration catches the reader's attention with its intensity.

Robin is working so hard that he has no time to analyze what he is doing. He describes his consternation when a lightening bolt makes him realize that if he stores his gunpowder all together inside his tent, he might lose it all. As he looks back on those frantic times from a later narrative vantage point he mocks himself. He points out the irony: "I was nothing near so anxious about my own danger; though had the powder took fire, I had never known who had hurt me."[47]

This kind of action-orientated narration covers the first month or so

---

[44] *Ibid.*, 51.
[45] *Ibid.*, 63-64.
[46] *Ibid.*, 44.
[47] *Ibid.*, 45.

of Robin's time on the island. Next Robin begins to think about his situation. In this more reflective mode, Robin tells the story of his first weeks on the island all over again in the form of a journal. Defoe has Robin make an explicit transition between action and reflection:

> But I must first give some little Account of my self, and of my Thoughts about Living, which it may well be suppos'd were not a few. I had a dismal prospect of my Condition .... I had great Reason to consider it as a Determination of Heaven, that in this desolate Place, and in this desolate Manner, I would end my Life. The Tears would run plentifully down my Face when I made these Reflections, and sometimes I would expostulate with my self, Why Providence should thus completely ruine its Creatures.[48]

These comments begin an account of Robin's journal writing during his first months on the island. The way Defoe explains this journal shows how concerned he was to trace the development of Robin's mental and spiritual life. From the perspective of Defoe's critics, the way Defoe presents Robin's possession of pen, ink, and paper reveals Defoe's slapdash writing method. When Robin had a breathing space after his first few hyperactive days on the island, he made a calendar cross on which he notched a mark for each day so that he would not "lose my Reckoning of Time for want of Books and Pen and Ink".[49] In the next paragraph he says he had got "Pens, Ink, and Paper" from the ship. Robin also notes that he had "three very good Bibles which came to me in my Cargo from England, and which I had pack'd up among my things". These Bibles would prove central to the later conversion scene.

The Amsterdam Coffee House abridger re-wrote this section to clarify it: "But this [the calendar cross] I had begun before I knew what I had gotten from on Board in Parcels as yet not opened, so that I afterwards found among the Captain's Mate and Gunner's stores several Compasses" and pen, ink, and paper.[50] The re-written version makes explicit the suppositions of a sympathetic reading. It does not change the main focus of Defoe's text on Robin's use of writing, since Robin realizes that he is keeping track of his thoughts as a way to control them: "I drew up the State of my Affairs in Writing; not so

---

[48] *Ibid.*, 46-47.
[49] *Ibid.*, 48.
[50] Amsterdam Coffee House, 47.

much to leave them to any that were to come after me ... as to deliver my thoughts from daily Pouring upon them and afflicting my Mind."[51]

Writing the self

Robin's introduction to his journal develops his character into a person with a sense of self-irony. The Amsterdam Coffee-House abridgement regularly reduces this aspect of the text. Robin decides that he will write the journal in a fictional mode – as if he had been writing it as soon as he reached the island – so that it covers all the building, constructing, sorting, and planning he has already described. Defoe exploits contemporary familiarity with the conventions, style, and motivations of journal writing by letting Robin play with the form. Having already told us how he had walked the shore after struggling out of the sea, Robin now gives the reader two more versions. The first one he presents to the reader as a mock entry – the journal entry he is not going to write:

> After I got to shore, and had escaped drowning, instead of being thankful to God for my deliverance, having first vomited with great quantity of salt water which was gotten into my stomach, and recovering myself a little, I ran about the shore, wringing my hands, and beating my head and face, exclaiming at my misery, and crying out, I was undone, till, tired and faint, I was forced to lie down on the ground to repose but durst not sleep, for fear of being devoured.[52]

The second version demonstrates a self-consciously literary style:

> *September* 30, 1659. I, poor miserable Robinson Crusoe, being shipwrecked, during a dreadful storm, in the offing, came on shore on this dismal unfortunate island, which I called the Island of Despair, all the rest of the ship's company being drowned, and myself almost dead.
>
> All the rest of that day I spent in afflicting myself at the dismal circumstances I was brought to, viz., I had neither food, house, clothes, weapon, or place to fly to .... At the approach of night, I slept in a tree for fear of wild creatures, but slept soundly, though it rained all night.[53]

---

[51] Defoe, *The Life and Strange Surprising Adventures of Robinson Crusoe*, 49.
[52] *Ibid.*, 51.
[53] *Ibid.*, 52.

The abridgers thought Robin's duplications were redundant. The Amsterdam Coffee House abridgement, for example, deleted the mock journal entry. Modern critic Peter Hulme takes the triple account of Robin's arrival on the island very seriously but does not understand it as Defoe's irony. Hulme seems to see the double journal entry as an indication of Defoe's difficulty in writing the story. He says it highlights "the desperate difficulties the text has in composing Crusoe's self, an activity, as the word indicated, every bit as much scriptive as it is psychological".[54] James Maddox, another critic who takes the triple account seriously, thinks Defoe is showing us how Robin creates his own story. He reminds us that Crusoe's narration is a constant recreation of what happened. Maddox suggests that "Crusoe prefers the version that most clearly shows his ability to dominate his fate".[55]

Late in his stay on the island, years after his discovery of the cannibal feasts on the island, Robin gets a companion. Their relationship does not fit any one category that Robin has for relationships. Robin rescues a native whom the cannibals intend to eat: "It came now very warmly upon my thoughts, and indeed irresistibly, that now was my time to get me a Servant, and perhaps a Companion, or Assistant; and that I was call'd plainly by Providence to save this poor Creature's Life."[56] He names this man "Friday", after the day of the week on which he was rescued. By introducing the character of Friday, Defoe not only gives Robin a spiritual companion but he also introduces an exotic figure with its own claim on the English readers. The Amsterdam Coffee House text preserves much of the detail Defoe gives of Robin's fascination with Friday. The close relationship between Robin and Friday is symbolized by Robin's giving Friday access to his weapons. The original and the abridged accounts are virtually identical.[57]

Friday's rescue proves to be much more like the adoption of a son than the acquisition of a servant. Robin comes to love Friday and depend on his companionship in ways that cannot fit into the social and political categories available to Defoe. Although Robin's relationship with Friday is not a relationship between peers, Friday is

---

[54] Hulme, *Colonial Encounters*, 193.
[55] Maddox, "Interpreter Crusoe", 57 n2.
[56] Defoe, *The Life and Strange Surprising Adventures of Robinson Crusoe*, 146.
[57] *Ibid.*, 173; Amsterdam Coffee House, 195.

a spiritual companion in a way that his foster fathers or the English sea captain were not.

The Amsterdam Coffee House abridgement, however, makes a significant alteration in Robin's description of his attempt to explain Christianity to Friday. Defoe preserves and even emphasizes the spiritual challenges of preaching to the heathen, while the Amsterdam Coffee House smoothes over the difficulties.

Defoe has Friday enter into serious theological discussion with Robin, just as native American converts were doing in New England. "Friday as a Convert", Hunter's essay on native conversion accounts, makes it clear that Defoe would have known about such dialogue from the reports New Englanders regularly made to British Dissenters. Hunter reminds us that during his schooldays in his Dissenter Academy and in church Defoe would have heard the missionaries' reports. These reports cited the Indians' questions as proof of their serious interest in the Gospel. Friday asked Robin why the all-powerful God did not simply kill the devil. Hunter says, "Apparently this kind of question bothered pagans everywhere, and in 1719 Defoe, as well as his readers, might fairly be expected to know the fact".[58]

The question stumps Robin during his Bible study sessions with Friday. In the original text, Robin tells how he evades the question: "I therefore diverted the present Discourse between me and my Man, rising up hastily, as upon some sudden Occasion of going out; then sending him for something a good way off." The Amsterdam Coffee House abridgement deletes this evasion. In Defoe's text when Robin is unable to answer Friday he prays for wisdom for himself as evangelist: "I seriously prayed to God that he would enable me to instruct savingly this Creature, to receive the Light of the Knowledge of God in Christ, reconciling him to himself, and would guide me to speak so to him from the Word of God as his Conscience might be convinc'd, his Eyes open'd, and his soul sav'd."[59] In the Amsterdam Coffee House version Robin simply prays for Friday: "I broke off Discourse, and retir'd to Pray to God to enlighten his Mind, and give him his saving Knowledge, thro' Christ."[60]

---

[58] Hunter, "Friday as a Convert", 245.
[59] Defoe, *The Life and Strange Surprising Adventures of Robinson Crusoe*, 158.
[60] Amsterdam Coffee House, 194.

Robin's deliverance

Defoe makes a radical difference between Robin's state of mind before his conversion experience and afterwards. The Amsterdam Coffee House abridger blurs that distinction. Robin's journal keeping brings him to a more reflective state of mind, but it does not bring him peace. The pivotal event, his conversion, is a mental reorganization resulting in a changed vocabulary. He carefully records this event as happening on 4 July 1660. Robin is sick with what seems to be malaria. He sees a vision of a man "as bright as a Flame".[61] Hearing a voice pronouncing doom, Robin staggers over to one of the sea chests he had salvaged and takes out one of the English Bibles that he had mentioned earlier. He opens the Bible at Psalm 50:15: "Call on Me in the day of trouble, and I will deliver, and thou shalt glorify Me." These words echo in his heart, because deliverance from the island is what he has been hoping for.

Defoe had salted the preceding narrative with the word deliverance, but Robin did not notice how often he had been delivered. When he first comes to the island he uses the word twice in his account: "my whole being wrapt up in contemplation of my Deliverance" and a paragraph later "in a word I had a dreadful Deliverance".[62] When he picks out a place to make his fortress he says that he need a "View to the Sea, that if God sent any ship in sight, I might not lose any Advantage for my Deliverance, of which I was not willing to banish all my Expectation yet".[63] After his conversion when he is re-thinking his experience, he uses the word "deliverance" twenty-eight times within three pages.[64] Finally on the momentous fourth of July, his mind is stirred "to construe the words mentioned above, 'Call on Me and I will deliver you' in a different Sense from what I had ever done before".[65] He sees that he has been delivered physically, but what he must be delivered from is his spiritual, not physical, isolation. This revelation has a miraculous effect in liberating Robin from his sense of being imprisoned on the island.

The Amsterdam Coffee House abridgement blurs this moment of insight by adding at least one use of the word "deliverance" to the

---

[61] Defoe, *The Life and Strange Surprising Adventures of Robinson Crusoe*, 64.
[62] *Ibid.*, 35.
[63] *Ibid.*, 44.
[64] *Ibid.*, 69-71.
[65] *Ibid.*, 71.

early narrative. When Robin is contemplating his condition (quoted above) he feels sure that he will never be rescued. The Amsterdam Coffee-House abridgement has Robin recognize that he has been delivered from death: "my Memory afresh brought to mind the many Dangers I had run thro' before the Deliverances I had receiv'd."[66]

In Defoe's text, Robin's story-telling style changes after his religious conversion. He is happy on the island. He begins to describe the land, and he starts enjoying new projects besides his day-by-day survival. Without giving us transcripts of his devotional life, he tells us that after his conversion he instituted daily times of Bible study and prayer.[67] He is no longer in prison with his thoughts looping constantly back on himself, but he has come into a period of communion with God.

In this new settled frame of mind, he starts exploring the island and discovers that it is beautiful. He finds that it is full of "divers other Plants, which I had no Notion of", and on further exploration finds "Mellons upon the Ground in great Abundance, and Grapes upon the Trees". The inland meadow is so attractive that he stays all night. The next day, he finds a valley "so fresh, so green, so flourishing, everything being in a constant Verdure or Flourish of *Spring*, that it looked like a planted Garden".[68] Defoe makes Robin a representative European colonialist, whose expressions of delight include seeing the land as something that he could own. The pattern of European reaction to the Americas, as revealed in written accounts, is noted by recent critical works. Stephen Greenblatt's *Marvellous Posessions*[69] introduces and analyzes these early documents, noting the feminization of the land as it welcomes the masculine explorer. Robin's thoughts, however, are tinged with self-irony: "this was all my own; ... I was King and Lord of all this Country indefeasibly, and had a Right of Possession; and, if I could convey it, I might have it in Inheritance as completely as any Lord of a Manor in England."[70]

For Defoe, Robin's religious awakening changes him from a solitary prisoner to an energetic participant in God's Providence. The

---

[66] Amsterdam Coffee House, 45.

[67] Defoe, *The Life and Strange Surprising Adventures of Robinson Crusoe*, 71, 83, 84.

[68] *Ibid.*, 73.

[69] Stephen Greenblatt, *Marvellous Possessions: The Wonder of the New World*, Chicago, 1991.

[70] Defoe, *The Life and Strange Surprising Adventures of Robinson Crusoe*, 73.

radical change in narrative style distinguishes a before and after. The Amsterdam Coffee House abridgement of August 1719 blurred this distinction by presenting Robin's time on the island as a happy deliverance well before his fourth of July religious awakening. For the abridger, the point of the story is Robin's successful taming of the island. All he needs for that task is his English common sense. This abridgement exemplifies not only the kinds of changes made, but also the contemporary attitude to Defoe's story.

Robin's kingdom

Robin's new frame of mind is creative and productive. The story of his post-conversion fourteen years focuses on his one-man development of the island as his home. This material is fully and accurately represented in the Amsterdam Coffee House abridgement. Robin develops a second home – a place to live inland. He figures out the climate of the island, so he can grow crops. He makes bread – from seed to loaf. He makes pottery, and he makes a canoe. This part of the story is Rousseau's game of Robinson Crusoe. It celebrates at once the complexity of civilization and the ability of ordinary human beings to make and do things. Robin starts to think of his cats and dog as his "Family".[71] He captures a parrot, and he starts teaching the bird to call him by name.[72]

The largest part of the attraction of *The Life and Strange Surprising Adventures of Robinson Crusoe* is certainly due to this part of the story. Robin's energy and invention are what the Spanish castaway will admire when he praises Robin as a typical Englishman. Robin does more than survive; he re-creates the development of western material culture. He is a hunter-gatherer; he is a farmer; he is a boat-builder, carpenter, potter, thresher, and baker. The omni-competence of the ordinary man is part of Defoe's theme. Robin states this idea explicitly several times. "[I] improved myself in this time in all the mechanic Exercises which my Necessities put me upon applying to, and I believe I could, upon Occasion, make a very good *Carpenter*", he boasts.[73] Earlier he had explained his assumptions: "I must needs observe, that as Reason is the Substance and Original of the Mathematics, so by stating and squaring everything by Reason,

---

[71] *Ibid.*, 108.
[72] *Ibid.*, 104.
[73] *Ibid.*, 105 (italics in the original).

and by making the most rational Judgment of things, every Man may be in time Master of every mechanic Art."[74]

Robin also philosophizes in the vein of Locke: "'Tis a little wonderful, and what I believe few People have thought much upon, viz., the strange multitude of little Things necessary in the Providing, Producing, Curing, Dressing, Making, and Finishing this one Article of Bread."[75] But Defoe knew that people had already remarked on it. Locke, for example, in his 1698 *Second Treatise on Government*, a book Defoe knew well, had pointed out the immense social organization needed to produce a loaf of bread: "for it is not barely the plough-man's pains, the reaper's and the thresher's toil, and the baker's sweat, is to be counted into the *bread* we eat."[76] Robin's delight in his ability to reproduce all the crafts of society is the complement of Locke's analysis of social cooperation. Defoe's imaginative proof of Everyman's ability to do mechanical work reinforces the idea that social cooperation is voluntary and reciprocal. Robin's naïve delight in his own accomplishment is contagious. The alert reader, however, remembers that Robin had brought raft-loads of tools and other English artifacts from the wrecked ship. His ability to organize himself is wonderful, but he is not a self-made man.

This kind of narrative was what the Amsterdam Coffee House abridger took to be the point of the story, so he made few alterations to Defoe's text in this section of the book. The abridged version of Defoe's story thus juxtaposes contradictory stories: Robin is wrong to have gone to sea; yet, his punishment – being imprisoned alone on an island – is an exciting adventure. The original version with its frame narrative that examines a father's duties in the burgeoning world of English international trade presents a much more complex picture. Even though the abridgers did not understand Defoe's analysis of a father's duties, they could admire Robin's energy and ingenuity. Although the Amsterdam Coffee House abridger said the story demonstrated the value of submission, the story itself conveys the value of innovation and adventure.

Analysis of the original text of *The Life and Strange Surprising Adventures of Robinson Crusoe* reveals amazing complications,

---

[74] Defoe, *The Life and Strange Surprising Adventures of Robinson Crusoe*, 51 (italics in the original).
[75] *Ibid.*, 86.
[76] Locke, *The Second Treatise of Government*, 316.

which, nevertheless, were easily omitted in the pirated versions. The book's title, the segmented narrative, the dramatic scenes, and the complicated development of Robin's character enabled pirate publishers to re-write Defoe's text quickly and easily. When Defoe saw what they had done, he responded with another story. In this second volume, *The Farther Adventures of Robinson Crusoe*, he worked deliberately to tell a story about the international trade he wanted England to develop. When that failed to persuade, he spelled out his views as essays in a third volume.

CHAPTER SEVEN

A WORLD UNITED BY TRADE

In *The Farther Adventures of Robinson Crusoe*. Defoe strengthens an important theme of his first volume: the rational potential of all humankind. He also reinforces themes that the abridgers had failed to see in the first volume: how to discern the voice of Providence and the value of trade. As Defoe had planned when he finished the first volume, Robin returns to his island. He tries to set it up as a self-sufficient society, forgetting that he himself had run away from home to avoid such a static life. He sails away on a trading expedition, but his adventures illustrate the dark side of world trade more dramatically than they show the joy of travel. Robin's account of his island's history and his engagement in trade underscore the unity of humankind and the providential function of trade.

Robin is the protagonist in *The Farther Adventures of Robinson Crusoe* as he is in *The Life and Strange Surprising Adventures of Robinson Crusoe*. Abridgers were able to make Robin into a heroic Everyman in the first volume. That transformation proved impossible for the second volume. Defoe modifies popular genres that promoted nationalistic individualism as the ideology of world trade, but he casts Robin as a bumbling innocent. Robin is more clown than hero.

The rise and fall of Robin's colony

The story of *The Farther Adventures of Robinson Crusoe* consists of three segments connected by Robin's voice. His emotional and intellectual commitment to the activity of trade and his pleasure in human community tie the events of the narrative together. The first segment tells what had happened on Robin's island after he sailed away. It gathers up all the threads of that story, at least briefly. The second describes Robin's crew's engagement in a massacre on Madagascar. The third completes Robin's voyage round the world by taking him to China and back to London overland via Siberia and a Baltic seaport.

Unlike Rogers, Cooke, and other travelers, Robin does not promote a national mission, but his trading voyage does start off with the complicated and nearly successful attempt to found a colony. To picture this transformation of an uninhabited island into a settled colony, Defoe imagines how a stable society could emerge on the island. Next he tries to imagine what would happen to such a society in the world of expanding empires. The kind of colony Robin sets up can feed itself, but it can thrive only if it is part of an international trading network. Robin fails to help his colony become part of the world trading system. As a result the colony fails.

The story of the relations that had been established between the Europeans on the island during Robin's seven-year absence sounds like a demonstration of Locke's theory of the origins of civil society. There had been a murderous struggle between three groups of European settlers, but these three groups – the Spanish, the English rogues, and the English marooned sailors – had learned to work together for their mutual defense. The English men have taken wives from the South American natives. In Locke's terms, the Europeans have formed a social unit: "a community for their comfortable, safe, and peaceable living one amongst another, in a secure enjoyment of their properties, and a greater security against any, that are not of it."[1] Nevertheless, the island is still not a unified society. The inhabitants live in three separate and unfriendly camps. These three groups do join to repel invasions.

Robin plans to leave the islanders after delivering the manufactured goods he has brought them, and after he has settled the handyman whom he has brought from England to live on the island. When a French priest – one of the shipwreck survivors Robin rescues *en route* to the island – demands that Robin organize Christian wedding ceremonies between the Englishmen and the Native American women with whom they are living, Robin sees only an inconvenient delay in the departure date. In order to enter Christian marriages the men have to convert their partners to Christianity. This, in turn, means that the men have to explain the Christian gospel to the women. All this spiritual rearrangement will take more time than

---

[1] Locke, *The Second Treatise of Government*, 349.

Robin has available. He is merely a passenger on the trading ship commanded by his nephew. He is not in control of the ship's schedule.

This conversion assignment, however, becomes the engine of dynamic social transformation. The native women find Christianity very attractive, as had Friday in *The Life and Strange Surprising Adventures of Robinson Crusoe.* The mechanism for the transformation is the conversion of Will Atkins, the British mutineer, rogue, and reprobate – the son of a Protestant clergyman – who had been left on the island at the end of the first volume.

Will's conversion galvanizes Robin. Robin operates under the colonial fiction that since he was the first European settler, he owns the island. After Will Atkins' conversion, Robin integrates the three settlements into a cooperative society by formally giving away the land to its inhabitants. He has Will Atkins draw the property lines so that every family has land. Robin tells the Europeans to include not only the native wives, but also the band of thirty-seven natives whom they had penned up on a peninsula of the island. These natives, says Robin, may choose whether they will be farmers or servants, and the settlers must explain Christianity to them. In contrast to the actual British colonial sugar plantation economy of the Caribbean Robin's plans are radically egalitarian.

Friday is a lose thread in this story. He is left over from *The Life and Strange Surprising Adventures of Robinson Crusoe.* Once Robin does not need him as a companion, Defoe has no more use for him. Friday's bear-baiting antics during Robin's travel through the Pyrenees in the first volume are hard to explain in terms of either trade or adventure. His only contribution to *The Farther Adventures of Robinson Crusoe* is his death in a grotesque scene that stands out in the narrative in the way the bear-baiting stood out at the end of *The Life and Strange Surprising Adventures of Robinson Crusoe.*

Friday's final appearance is part of an encounter between the trading ship and a large flotilla of hostile natives in canoes. Robin sends Friday to speak to the natives from the prow of the ship. Unfortunately Friday does not know the local language: "as soon as he had call'd to them, six of them, who were in the foremost or nighest Boat to us, turns their Canoes from us; and stooping down, shew'd us their naked Backsides, just as if in *English*, saving your Presence, they had *bid us kiss------*."[2]

Robin refuses to interpret this action: "whether this was a Defiance or Challenge, we know not; or whether it was done in meer Contempt, or as a Signal to the rest." What happens next is that Friday is killed, much to Robin's grief and anger. But Robin reiterates his claim that the natives' action is not susceptible to his interpretation:

> The ill Manners of turning up their bare Backsides to us, gave us no great Offence; neither did I know for certain, whether that which would pass for the greatest Contempt among us, might be understood so by them, or not; therefore in Return, I had only resolv'd to have fir'd four or five Guns at them with Powder only, which I knew would fright them sufficiently: But when they shot at us directly with all the Fury they were capable of, and especially as they had kill'd my poor *Friday*, who I so entirely lov'd and valu'd, and who indeed so well deserv'd it; I not only had been justify'd before God and Man, but would have been very glad, if I could to have overset every Canoe there, and drown'd every one of them.[3]

This scene appears to be Defoe's attempt at a reduction to absurdity of Locke's claim that all cultures were different. It also takes Friday off stage permanently. Now, alone again, Robin is set to become a trader, some thirty-five years after first leaving his father's house.

A massacre on Madagascar

The initial episode in Robin's trading voyage is the breakdown of trading relations with the natives on Madagascar. Defoe gives the story a central place in the action of the volume. Although the events take only two days, the account occupies thirty pages in the center of the 354-page volume. The event and Robin's subsequent quarrel with the sailors and the captain cut Robin off from his nephew and his ship.

Robin describes the massacre in excruciating detail. While the ship is idled off Madagascar, nine members of the crew decide to sleep on shore. Robin, who is sleeping in the ship's boat, hears the shore party's signal of distress. One sailor has been killed, and another has gone missing, but Robin manages to rescue seven of the men. Their assailants are an angry crowd of three or four hundred natives, who

---

[2] Defoe, *The Farther Adventures of Robinson Crusoe*, 208.
[3] *Ibid.*, 210.

are avenging the rape of a local woman by the missing sailor. Three nights later Robin leads a group of sailors on shore to see if they can find their comrade.

Robin has no control over the sailors, although he is supposed to be leading them. The men propose attacking a nearby village; "where these Dogs as they call'd them dwelt … and if they could find, them as still they fancy'd they should, they did not doubt getting a good Booty, and it might be, they might find *Tho. Jeffry* there, that was the Man's Name we had lost."[4] Eager for plunder and looking for their missing shipmate, Thomas Jeffry, they go to the sleeping village where they set the place on fire and kill the people as they come out of their houses.

The scene stretches over a long night filled with confrontation and horror. When most of the search party chooses to follow the boatswain in search of plunder, Robin comes along to watch. He describes the scenes of terror and madness, calling the sailors "Butchers" and talking about their rage as something not human: "in short, there were such Instances of a Rage altogether barbarous, and of a Fury, something beyond what was human, that we thought it impossible our Men could be guilty of it, or if they were the Authors of it, we thought they ought to be every one of them put to the worst of Deaths."[5]

The sailors find the body of their comrade and see that his throat has been cut. Then they decide to exterminate the natives. Robin's nephew the ship's captain, who has come ashore to see what is going on, joins the men in their murderous rampage. Robin tries to protect a small group of natives, but in the end he gives up and retreats to the ship: "I, seeing it quite out of my Power to restrain them, came away pensive and sad; for I could not bear the Sight, much less the horrible Noise and Cries of the poor Wretches that fell in their Hands."[6] All the sailors and Robin's nephew, the Captain, make it back safely to the ship, and they leave the island before the natives can mount an attack on the ship.

Robin reprimands his nephew for joining the men in their rampage. He tells the men that he considers them guilty of murder:

I always, after that Time, told them, God would blast the Voyage; for I

---

[4] Defoe, *The Farther Adventures of Robinson Crusoe*, 227.
[5] *Ibid.*, 234.
[6] *Ibid.*, 238.

> look'd upon all the Blood they shed that Night to be Murther in them:
> For tho' it is true, that they had kill'd *Tho. Jeffry*, yet it was as true,
> that *Jeffry* was the Aggressor, had broken the Truce, and had violated,
> or debauch'd a young Woman of theirs who came down to them
> innocently, and on the Faith of their publick Capitulation.

To Robin's surprise, both his nephew and the boatswain defend their
actions. The nephew says that the sight of Tom Jeffry's corpse filled
him with a passion he could not govern. The boatswain argues the
same case: "[Although the] poor Man had taken a little Liberty with a
Wench, he ought not to have been murther'd, and that in such a
villanous Manner, and that they did nothing but what was just, and
what the Laws of God allow'd to be done to Murtheres." [7]

The ship becomes a debating forum for Robin and the boatswain as
it proceeds up the coast of Africa. When Arab traders seize five of the
crew and make them slaves, Robin tells the crew that this is God's
judgment on the men. He is a little taken aback to discover that the
five who were captured had not been part of the massacre perpetrators.
Robin and the boatswain argue the case till the ship reaches Bengal.
There the boatswain takes advantage of Robin's sightseeing trip on
shore to organize a rebellion of the crew. They insist that if Robin
comes back on the ship, they will all desert. Defoe describes the scene
vividly, with the crew shouting in chorus "One and All" at the
boatswain's signal.

The resemblance to a dramatic scene may be both historical and
literary. Peter Linebaugh and Marcus Rediker describe a London play
published in 1649, *The Rebellion of Naples*. The play depicts a
contemporary proletarian rebellion in Naples, but Linebaugh and
Rediker say that its author echoes English levelers: "the first words
from the crowd ... are the sailor's abiding principle of solidarity and
the particular cry heard during the mutinies of 1626: 'One and all, One
and all, One and all'." [8]

Rolling with the world

Just as piracy by rebellious sailors had helped Robin get off his island
in the first volume, so this sailors' rebellion serves to move Robin
from one activity to another in the second volume. Robin idles ashore

---

[7] *Ibid.*, 240.
[8] Linebaugh and Rediker, *The Many-Headed Hydra*, 114.

in Bengal for nine months. Then he forms a partnership with another Englishman, and they begin a very profitable ten-year trading career. Robin discovers that he enjoys trade and is good at it, but his career comes to an abrupt end when he and his partner come under suspicion of being pirates themselves. They have bought a ship that turns out to have been pirated by her crew. An impromptu vigilante navy of Dutch and English traders chases Robin in the Gulf of Cambodia. Robin's fear of these Dutch and English vigilante captains leads him to abandon his ship and his trading enterprise.

After leaving his ship and partner, Robin spends several months in China, visiting Nanquin and Peking. Aware that Europe thinks highly of Chinese civilization, Robin decides that such admiration must have been founded on low expectations, rather than on observation of Chinese society. He does admire the good order he sees in Nanquin, but most of his other observations are negative: "But when I come to compare the miserable People of these Countries with ours, their Fabricks, their Manner of living, their Government, their Religion, their Wealth, and their Glory (as some call it), I must confess, I do not so much as think it is worth naming, or worth my while to write of, or any that shall come after me to read."[9]

Robin devotes only sixteen pages to his survey of China before he joins a camel caravan overland through the deserts to the territories ruled by Russia. The journey is full of the same kinds of semi-military adventures that marked Robin's return to England from his island in *The Life and Strange Surprising Adventures of Robinson Crusoe*. This time instead of being attacked by wolves, he and his party are surrounded by hordes of Tartars whom they escape by trickery.

The longest, most detailed and most significant of these adventures is Robin's destruction of a Tartar idol. This enterprise occupies some thirteen pages of the text, and forms a counterpoint to the massacre on Madagascar. Robin witnesses a group of seventeen Tartars worshiping their idol:

> ... there stood out upon an old Stump of a Tree, an idol made of Wood, frightful as the Devil, at least as any Thing we can think of to represent the Devil can be made; it had a Head certainly not so much as resembling any Creature that the World ever saw; Ears as big as Goats Horns, and as high; Eyes as big as a Crown-Piece, a Nose like a crooked Ram's Horn, and a Mouth extended four Corner'd like that of

---

[9] Defoe, *The Farther Adventures of Robinson Crusoe*, 296.

> a Lion, with horrible Teeth, hooked like a Parrot's under Bill; it was
> dressed up in the filthiest manner that you could suppose; its upper
> Garment was of Sheeps-skins, with the wool outward, a great *Tartar*
> Bonnet on the Head, with two Horns growing through it, it was about
> eight Foot high, yet had no Feet or Legs, or any other Proportion of
> Parts.[10]

In a comic scene, Robin reacts to this sight of people reduced to idol
worship by attacking the idol with his sword. When two or three
hundred of the idol's supporters spring to its defense Robin runs back
to his caravan and hides. That evening Robin recruits two Scotsmen,
fellow travelers in the caravan, to destroy the idol as a religious
testimony to the heathen.

One of the Scots merchants does not see how burning the idol will
advance the "Honour of God", so Robin suggests that he will leave the
Tartars a note explaining that this attack is designed to demonstrate
the idol's impotence. His fellow-iconoclast points out that the Tartars
cannot read. Robin does not give up, but simply hopes his message
will get across to the Tartars: "Perhaps Nature may draw Inferences
from it to them, to let them see how brutish they are to worship such
horrid Things."[11] Robin and his friends ambush the pagan priests as
they come out of their hut. Robin insists that the idol's priests not be
killed, but be tied up and forced to watch their idol burn.[12] He thinks
such a sight will discredit the idol. As it happens, all it does is enrage
the Tartars. Only a trick by a sharp-witted caravan guide prevents an
attack by avenging Tartars the next day.

The rest of Robin's journey is through territory controlled by
Moscow, and Robin's main interest is in observing the Russian failure
to preach the Christian faith to their Siberian and Tartar subjects:

> I also found, which I observ'd to the *Muscovite* Governours who I had
> Opportunity to converse with, that the poor Pagans are not much the
> wiser or the nearer Christianity for being under the *Muscovite*
> Government, which they acknowledg'd was true enough, but, as they
> said, was none of their Business: That if the Czar expected to convert
> his *Siberian*, or *Tonguese*, or *Tartar* Subjects, it should be done by
> sending Clergy-men among them, not soldiers; and they added, with

---

[10] *Ibid.*, 329.
[11] *Ibid.*, 332.
[12] *Ibid.*, 337.

more Sincerity than I expected, that they found it was not so much the Concern of their Monarch to make the People Christians, as it was to make them Subjects.[13]

Robin winters in Siberia, among the Russian noblemen who have been sent there for opposing the Tsar. Robin smuggles a nobleman's son out of Russia in his entourage, but the main plot of Robin's story loses energy at the end of *The Farther Adventures of Robinson Crusoe*. Readers of this volume knew quite well that Defoe was the author of this tale. Naturally, the readers cared more about Robin's return to his island than Defoe's derivative descriptions of China and Russia. Since Robin's return did not produce a thriving island-kingdom, it is not surprising that *The Farther Adventures of Robinson Crusoe* fell out of circulation.

Robin affirms human unity

In this second volume of his *Robinson Crusoe* series Defoe develops some of the themes that had been overlooked by readers of the first volume and discarded by abridgers. The universality of human rationality is the most striking of such themes. In *The Life and Strange Surprising Adventures of Robinson Crusoe* Robin is not much of an anthropologist. That role is left to the reader. Robin is too worried about being attacked by wild animals or cannibals to notice that all the animals are harmless and the cannibals are not looking for him. Modern critics have seen Robin's fears, not as Defoe's irony, but as Defoe's participation in a pattern of European psychosis. Peter Hulme points out that Robin's fears are out of all proportion to his experiences on the island: "the extent and persistence of Crusoe's fear … proves to be psychotic inasmuch as it constantly disavows all contradictory evidence."[14]

In the first volume Robin simply assumes his own intellectual and practical superiority to Friday and to the Spanish soldiers he proposes to rescue. He is surprised by Friday's intellectual and spiritual gifts. Defoe gives readers evidence that the Spanish castaway is a decent man and that Friday is much more loving to his father than Robin is to his own. Robin himself does not seem to notice. In *The Farther Adventures of Robinson Crusoe*, however, Robin is not so paranoid.

---

[13] *Ibid.*, 346-47.
[14] Hulme, *Colonial Encounters*, 194.

He is able to encounter other people without being threatened. Nevertheless, he is still the impetuous, foolish Robin.

The action in the second volume involves people from many different races and nations. Defoe frequently casts the story into exchanges of dialogue that resemble play scripts, although he conveys all the action and dialogue through Robin's experiences. This dramatic form gives an implicit answer to two questions raised by global exploration: are all human beings the same? And how should Europeans relate to the people of other cultures? Defoe's answer is simple: trade with them. The people he meets are all able to enter into trading relationships. From the initial voyage to his island across the Atlantic till the winter in Siberia with Russian political prisoners, Robin finds trade a universal language: empirical, egalitarian, and non-violent.

Robin's stance in *The Farther Adventures of Robinson Crusoe* is that of an observer, rather than an advocate of human unity. Even so, Robin's intellectual detachment and emotional engagement make him an effective witness. Robin starts his anthropological analysis at the start of the second volume during the crossing to his island colony. He acts with compassion in ordering the ship to rescue two sets of distressed mariners. His reflections center on his observation of the effects of extreme emotion on human beings. Robin explains that what he has done: "[It is] nothing but what Reason and Humanity dictated to all Men and that we had as much Reason as he to give Thanks to God who had bless'd us so far as to make us the Instruments of his Mercy to so many of his Creatures."[15] This analysis echoes Locke's *Second Treatise on Government*, where Locke reasons as follows:

> [The] Law of Nature ... willeth the Peace and *Preservation of all Mankind* .... In transgressing the law of Nature, the Offender declares himself to live by another Rule than that of *reason* and common Equity, which is that measure God has set to the actions of Men.[16]

By giving Robin the role of a witness, Defoe stakes out a position in the contemporary debate between proponents of natural hierarchy and proponents of a more egalitarian model of humanity. This idea of an inclusive human community differs from the classical idea of a

---

[15] Defoe, *The Farther Adventures of Robinson Crusoe*, 23.
[16] Locke, *The Second Treatise of Government*, 289-90.

community. In an analysis of differences between Locke and Hobbes, Joshua Mitchell argues "Christianity and not ancient political thought is the pedigree of the modern notion of the equality of all under the one, in whatever its manifested form".[17]

Defoe's interests go well beyond those of most of his immediate contemporaries. When we compare *The Life and Strange Surprising Adventures of Robinson Crusoe* and *The Farther Adventures of Robinson Crusoe* to the travel narratives of Dampier, Rogers, and Cook, we can see that Robin is more personally engaged in theological anthropology and moral complexity than the narrators of these standard works. The second volume carries Robin around the world as an observer and judge of other cultures. Even the first volume discusses native religion, mission work, Providence, and honesty throughout the volume.

Defoe's *The Farther Adventures of Robinson Crusoe* projects Robin's interests beyond the age of nation-states and national churches to the age of Protestant missions and to what we now call the global economy. Benedict Anderson's study of the development of nationalism in eighteenth-century Europe, *Imagined Communities*, suggests that print culture encouraged people to experience community along nation-state lines rather than along religious lines. Anderson says, "in Western Europe, the eighteenth century marks not only the dawn of the age of nationalism but the dusk of religious modes of thought".[18]

Defoe's work, however, mixes nationalism, internationalism and religion. Defoe writes self-consciously to create England as an imagined community, but, for him, national interests also imply international concerns, and he certainly thinks in religious terms. In this regard, Defoe's narrative is quite unlike that of travel writers such as Dampier, Cooke, or Rogers. Robin's explorations bring English imperialism into question. Defoe pushes Englishmen to imagine a global community. This perspective was taking shape already in the first volume with Robin's discussion of pagan morality. It comes to a bizarre climax with Robin's confrontation of idol worship in the second volume.

Robin takes instruction from the most unlikely sources in the most unlikely circumstances. His radical re-education begins when he is

---

[17] Joshua Mitchell, *Not By Reason Alone*, Princeton: NJ, 1992, 144.
[18] Anderson, *Imagined Communities*, 11.

tutored about native society by Will Atkins, the violent English mutineer left on the island at the end of *The Life and Strange Surprising Adventures of Robinson Crusoe*. Will has become a leader of the island community. From Will Atkins, Robin learns that the supposedly savage natives are remarkably similar to Englishmen in their customs and values. They have a god, they value marriage, and they refrain from marrying near relatives.[19] The possibility of their keeping human beings as a food supply does not even enter the conversation. Here Will's testimony implies a contradiction of the report Robin had received through the Spanish Captain of how the English sailors had tried to escape the island but had come back with native slaves who had been given to them for food by friendly natives on the mainland.[20] At one point when Robin and Will are negotiating the attempt to convert Will's woman into a Christian wife, Robin voices his naive English prejudice about savage morality, and Will sets him straight:

> *W.A.* Why, I first told her the Nature of our Laws about Marriage, and what the reasons were, that Men and Women were oblig'd to enter into such Compacts, as it was neither in the Power of one or other to break; that otherwise, Order and Justice could not be maintain'd.

> *R.C.* [how] could you make her understand ... they know no such Thing among the savages, but marry any how without regard to Relation, Consanguinity, or Family; Brother and Sister, nay ... even the Father and Daughter and Son and the Mother.

> *W.A.* I believe, sir, you are misinform'd, and my wife assures me of the contrary, and that they abhor it ... she tells me they never touch one another in the near Relations you speak of.[21]

Earlier in this conversion narrative Robin is literally dumb. The French priest speaks with the moral authority and decisiveness Robin lacks. The second voice of the dialogue is that of Will Atkins, the mutineer turned colonist. When the priest demands that the Englishmen preach to their wives, Will is appalled:

---

[19] Defoe, *The Farther Adventures of Robinson Crusoe*, 176.
[20] *Ibid.*, 81.
[21] *Ibid.*, 176.

Lord! Sir, says Will Atkins, How should we teach them Religion? Why we know nothing our selves; and besides, Sir, said he, should we go to talk to them of God, and Jesus Christ, and Heaven and Hell, 'twould be to make them laugh at us and ask us, What we believe our selves? And if we should tell them we believe all the things that we speak of to them, such as of good People going to Heaven, and wicked People to the Devil, they would ask us Where we intend to go our selves, that believe all this, and are such wicked Fellows, as we indeed are? Why, sir, 'tis enough to give them a Surfeit of Religion at first Hearing: Folks must have some Religion themselves before they pretend to teach other People.[22]

The words appear in the text as though they were lines in a drama. Robin serves as the priest's translator (from French) during the dialogue in which the priest persuades Will to repent and thus enable himself to preach repentance and mercy to his wife. Later Robin and the priest hide in the bushes to watch Will talk to his wife. The rebel Will is converted by what in Defoe's work is the paradigmatic pre-conversion vision: seeing one's-self from the outside – a version of the educational banter he tried to use in *The Shortest-Way with the Dissenters*. Here Will has to confront himself in the mirror of his wife's eyes. After this conversion he becomes one of the moral leaders in the community, as well as a military leader. All of his character traits – his energy, his will power, and his persistence – become virtues.

The educational experiences that Defoe constructs for Robin build on Locke's view of human unity but contradict Locke's idea that travel narratives had revealed radical dissimilarity between cultures. In the first volume of his *Essay on Human Understanding* Locke had cited travel literature to prove that, while the capacity to form laws is innate, elementary or basic concepts and social laws are not universal and therefore cannot be innate.[23] If there are no innate ideas, Locke thought, all people are equal. Robin's travels do not attempt to discover innate ideas, but they do argue that human cultures have the same concept of justice all over the world. Early accounts had invented more differences than existed.

In *The Life and Strange Surprising Adventures of Robinson Crusoe* Robin had found cannibalism and savagery among the natives of

---

[22] *Ibid.*, 161-62.
[23] Locke, *An Essay Concerning Human Understanding*, 46-48.

South America. He also found generosity and affection among the natives, and cruelty among the English. The idea that all people share ideas of justice and God's law comes up over and over again in *The Farther Adventures of Robinson Crusoe*, more explicitly than it had in the first volume. Robin's belief in common human rationality and morality underlies his response to the settlers on his island. It supports the trading conventions in Madagascar, conventions Defoe had met in travel narratives:

> [The group who wants to trade sets up a symbolic fence of three poles]: a Mark in the Country, not only of Truce and Friendship, but when it is accepted, the other Side set up three Poles or Boughs, which is a Signal, that they accept the Truce too but then, this is a known Condition of the Truce, that you are not to pass beyond their three Poles towards them, nor they to come past your three Poles or Boughs ... and all the Space between your Poles and theirs, is allow'd like a Market, for free Converse, Traffick and Commerce. When you go there you must not carry your Weapons with you; and if they come into that Space, they stick up their Javelines and Launces, all at the first Poles and come on unarm'd but if any Violence is offer'd them, and the Truce thereby broken; away they run to the Poles, and lay hold of their Weapons, and then the Truce is at an End.[24]

Later this belief makes him reluctant to kill Cambodian natives who think his ship is their rightful salvage:

> But as we got this Victory without any Blood shed, except of that Man the Fellow kill'd with his naked Hands, and which I was very much concern'd at; for I was sick of killing such poor Savage Wretches, even tho' it was in my own Defence, knowing they came on Errands which they thought just, and knew no better; and that tho' it may be a just Thing because necessary, for there is no necessary Wickedness in nature, yet I thought it was a sad Life, which we must be always oblig'd to be killing our Fellow-Creatures to preserve, and indeed I think so still; and I would even now suffer a great deal, rather than I would take away the Life, even of that Person injuring me: And I believe, all considering People, who know the Value of Life, would be of my Opinion, at least they would, if they entered seriously into the Consideration of it.[25]

---

[24] Defoe, *The Farther Adventures of Robinson Crusoe*, 220.
[25] *Ibid.*, 271.

Still later Robin is so happy to find a logical court system in Mongolia that he does not complain when he loses his case.[26] His passionate belief in human rationality comes to its fullest expression near the end of the second volume when Robin sees Tartars engaged in idol worship. He is enraged:

> To see God's most glorious and best Creature, to whom he had granted so many Advantages, *even by Creation*, above the rest of the Works of his Hands, vested with a reasonable Soul, and that Soul adorn'd with Faculties and Capacities, adapted both to Honour his Maker; and be honoured by him, sunk and degenerated to a Degree, so more than stupid, as to prostrate it self to a frightful Nothing, an meer imaginary Object dress'd up by themselves, and made terrible to themselves by their own Contrivance.[27]

Providence and the circulation of trade

The corollary of Robin's affirmation of universal human rationality is his dawning conviction that there is a Providential plan to unite humanity in a network of trade. Robin's gradual awareness of such a plan is the second major theme of the second volume. As a much younger man, Robin had struggled with the notion that God's Providence was caring for him. He comes to think of the idea of Providence as a way to interpret what happens to him, but certainly not as something that guides his decisions. In the second volume of the series, Providence takes on an external, practical role. Robin's search for Providential leadership unites the economic Defoe with the spiritual Defoe. Indeed, taking a cue from David Little, I argue that for Defoe an important aspect of spiritual life consists of discerning the working of Providence in the currents of economic life.

During the course of *The Life and Strange Surprising Adventures of Robinson Crusoe*, Robin came to suspect that Providence was leading him to travel. As *The Farther Adventures of Robinson Crusoe* proceeds, Robin begins to understand trade as part of God's Providence for humanity. Early in the story of this second volume Defoe hints that Robin's desire to revisit the island may be from God, not from the Devil. Robin's wife explains his dreams of the island as a message from Providence. After his wife's death, Robin himself

---

[26] *Ibid.*, 319
[27] *Ibid.*, 330.

thinks that the coincidence of his dreams and his nephew's offer of passage to the island is evidence of God's design, and he plans to set the island colony up as a self-supporting community.

As was the case in *The Life and Strange Surprising Adventures of Robinson Crusoe*, the reader wants Robin to travel. The reader shares Robin's interest in finding out what happened to the assortment of people left on the island at the end of the first volume. Readers might even judge that Robin had some responsibility to the men he had left behind. The intellectual and emotional tug of war between the treadmill of prudential wisdom and Robin's desire for adventure persists throughout the volume.

Robin needs more than activity to keep him happy. After he marries, he and his wife take up farming, and he turns his English farm into a focus of contented activity. The death of his wife pushes Robin back into the larger world, a world he judges morally repulsive because of its economic inequity. When Robin comes to London after his wife's death he sees a stultifying closed system that is worse than his experience of life alone on the island:

> I saw the World busy round me, one Part labouring for Bread, and the other Part squandering in vile Excesses or empty Pleasures, equally miserable, because the End they propos'd still fled from them; for the Man of Pleasure every Day surfeited of his Vice, and heap'd up Work for Sorrow and Repentance; and the Men of Labour spent their Strength in daily Struggles for Bread to maintain the vital Strength they labour'd with, so living in a daily Circulation of Sorrow, living but to work, and working but to live, as if daily Bread were the only End of wearisome Life, and a wearisome Life the only Occasion of daily Bread. This put me in Mind of the Life I liv'd in my Kingdom, the Island; where I suffer'd no more corn to grow, because I did not want it; and bred no more Goats, because I had no more Use for them; Where the Money lay in the Drawer 'till it grew mouldy, and had scarce the Favour to be look'd upon in 20 Years.[28]

Robin keeps wondering what God wants him to do; eventually he realizes that not only his needs but also his desires might give him an answer. The voice of God comes to him through his dreams, through the French priest he befriends, and through events and chance encounters on his travels. This new perspective, which was emerging

---

[28] *Ibid.*, 9.

already in the first volume, comes to open expression when Robin is abandoned in Bengal. He joins up with another Englishman who suggests that by trading they would be joining God's work, "the whole World is in Motion, rouling round and round, all the Creatures of God, heavenly Bodies and earthly are busy and diligent. Why should we be idle?"[29]

When Robin first ran away from home and later when he learned to survive on his island he challenged the patriarchal social pattern of obedience as well as the classical disrespect for manual labor. Robin's spiritual challenge on his island was to recognize the hand of Providence and to celebrate ordinary life. John Richetti points out Robin's integration of penitential introspection and joyful practical activity: "Crusoe's eventual integration of these two states of being makes him a secular saint whose blessedness flows from his achievement of ideological equilibrium."[30] Even so, the island was a detour for Robin. He had wanted to be a trader; he is the creature of his author Defoe, the apostle of trade.

Defoe's essays in his journal *The Review*, written years before *The Life and Strange Surprising Adventures of Robinson Crusoe*, expound the spiritual and moral value of trade. He makes a case for trade as a divinely ordained mechanism weaving together all the different people on the globe. In *The Review* of 3 February 1713, Defoe writes that there is "a kind of Divinity in the Original of Trade" and again, "Providence has adapted Nature to Trade, and made it subservient in all Parts to the several necessary Operations of Commerce".[31] All nations can be enriched through trade. Defoe argues that raw materials and manufacturing capabilities were concentrated in different parts of the world so that the circulation of goods could give employment to everyone.

Defoe did not invent this argument, nor was he the only one who used it. The classical figure of the "circulation" of trade was a common contemporary figure of speech. Dryden used it in *Annus Mirabilis*.[32] Defoe is known as one of his time's most vocal supporters of such exchange, as David Porter notes in his essay "A Peculiar but

---

[29] *Ibid.*, 248.
[30] Richetti, *Popular Fiction Before Richardson*, 94.
[31] Defoe, *Review*, IX, 54, 107.
[32] John Dryden, "Annus Mirabilis" (1665), in *The Poetical Works of Dryden*, ed. George R. Noyes, Boston, 1950, 51.

Uninteresting Nation":

> Defoe devotes an entire issue of his *Review* to the topic of 'Circulation in Trade' and a vigorous defense of the proposition that 'circulation is the life of general commerce: Like blood flowing though the body, the perpetual motion of trade goods over England's highways sustains and enriches the nation.[33]

The emphasis on the word "round" in the titles of the travel literature takes on additional significance in the context of this argument.

Robin takes a long time to recognize his vocation as a trader. He keeps on trying to interpret the designs of Providence to himself and to his companions, but he is never quite sure that he has it right. Finally in the second volume of his story, when he and a partner have several successful voyages, he finds happiness in his work. This period of ten years takes up very little space in the narrative. His trading career is cut short by his being mistaken for a pirate, but Defoe has more work for Robin to do in the service of international trade.

Robin ends his travels as a scornful visitor to China and a fugitive in Mongolia. He epitomizes China by describing a mandarin whom he observes. This man has himself carried by servants; he sports fingernails so long he cannot feed himself; he is dressed in brocade made filthy by the food spilled by the servant who feeds him. Robin leaves China in disgust. He joins a caravan traveling to Russia through Mongolia. He converts the profits of his years of trading into diamonds, and he sews these diamonds into the seams of his garments. He comes home to England with the fruits of trade, not with captured treasure. This end to his career makes him less attractive to readers than privateer writers who often came home with a ship full of Spanish plunder.

Critique of non-trading peoples

Human equality and trade are crucial factors in two social systems Robin describes. The first is his description of his dream for his island. It shapes his analysis of how and why the island colony fails. The second is Robin's description of China. Both stories hinge on the

---

[33] David Porter, "A Peculiar but Uninteresting Nation: China and the Discourse of Commerce in Eighteenth-Century England", *Eighteenth-Century Studies*, XXXIII/2 (Winter 2000), 186.

failure to engage in international trade. The colony's future is based on the egalitarian patterns set up by Robin's enthusiastic response to the Christianizing of his island settlement. For both Robin and Will, conversion involves accepting the natives as intellectual and spiritual equals. This acceptance is the mechanism Defoe sets up for the transformation of detached groups into a society based on cooperation. The Christianization of these Caribbean natives, like the Christianization of Friday and his father, seems simply a matter of explaining Christianity. Defoe himself would have known that native conversions were not so easy, but Robin, the eternally restless and curious traveler and trader, is not a deep thinker. Even Robin, however, will come to question his initial European assumptions of moral superiority.

By the time Robin leaves the island, it is a model community of different types of people. Robin assumes the society will be self-sustaining. He has forgotten how isolation ate at his spirit in his island exile, and he does not realize that the island can again become a kind of prison. Further along in his account of the voyage, Robin tells us that the promising young island society did not succeed. The settlers became homesick and sent Robin a letter: "they begg'd ... me, to think of the Promise I had made, to fetch them away, that they might see their own Country again before they dy'd."[34]

The colony's failure, says Robin, is due to his failure to build links to European power, and thus to international trade. He had felt proud of himself as an enlightened monarch when he left the island. He had left them in charge of making their own laws: "As to the Government and Laws among them, I told them I was not capable of giving them better rules, than they were able to give themselves."[35] After the colony fails, he tells us what he should have done to make the island society workable:

> [I should have] gone to the Plantation from England with a small vessel loaded with supplies .... Taken a Patent from the Government here to have secur'd my Property, in Subjection only to that of *England* .... Carried over Cannon and Ammunition, servants and People to plant. Taking Possession of the Place, fortify'd and strengthen'd it in the Name of *England,* and encreas'd it with People

---

[34] Defoe, *The Farther Adventures of Robinson Crusoe,* 217.
[35] *Ibid.,* 192

> ... settled myself there and sent the Ship back loaded with good Rice
> in six Months Time and order'd my Friends to have fitted her out
> again for our Supply ....[But] I pleas'd myself with being the Patron of
> those People I plac'd there and doing for them in a kind of haughty
> majestick Way, like an old Patriarchal Monarch; providing for them,
> as if I had been Father of the whole Family, as well as of the
> Plantation. But I never so much as pretended to plant in the Name of
> any Government or Nation.[36]

The dream of a community built on cooperation is the attractive
core of Robin's island both in *The Life and Strange Surprising
Adventures of Robinson Crusoe* and *The Farther Adventures of
Robinson Crusoe*. In the earlier story, he sketches it as a joke:

> My island was now peopled, and I thought my self very rich in
> Subjects; and it was a merry Reflection which I frequently made ... we
> had but three subjects, and they were of three different Religions ....
> However, I allow'd Liberty of Conscience throughout my
> Dominions.[37]

In the second volume the self-contained colonial society has no
interest for Robin, and we should not be surprised that it became a
dead-end for the settlers there.

The final section of the second volume includes Robin's visit to
China, a country whose resistance to trade Robin sees as an affront to
Providence. It was well known in England that China was not eager
for trade with Europe. The Chinese rejected European trade goods,
forbade the teaching of Chinese to foreigners, and restricted trade
contact between Chinese and foreigners. These restrictions and the
European attitude to China's refusal of trade are the topic of David
Porter's article on the eighteenth-century English attitude to China.
Porter cites many late eighteenth-century accounts of China. He
devotes several pages of his article to Robin's visit to China, though
he seems not to be aware of Defoe's sources. Porter says:

> Crusoe's story, with its frequent references to trade and measures of
> economic prosperity, echoes the commercialist orientation Defoe had
> developed in the *Review* ten years before. And yet the themes that

---

[36] *Ibid.*, 217.
[37] Defoe, *The Life and Strange Surprising Adventures of Robinson Crusoe*, 174.

emerge in the passages on China also anticipate with uncanny precision those of the real-life travelers who would follow Defoe's intrepid wanderer.[38]

While the English Tories admired the stability of Chinese government, more egalitarian English thinkers found the Chinese trade restrictions and Chinese social hierarchy annoying.

Both admiring and critical accounts of China were readily available in London. Defoe based his account of China on the *Memoirs* of Louis Daniel Le Comte, a Jesuit whose letters about his travels in China were in a second edition.[39] The first translation of these Letters was published in 1679. A *Second Edition very much corrected, with the Addition of a Map of China and a Table* was published in London in 1698. Defoe's library sale catalogue shows several works on China, including one French text of a LeComte letter.[40] Defoe echoes Le Comte's disparaging comments on both Chinese astronomy and the Great Wall. Robin thinks European soldiers would have no difficulty blowing it up. He scorns Chinese military defenses, thinking that European forces could easily conquer Chinese cities.[41] On this theme Robin resembles Swift's Gulliver, who appalls the King of Brobdingnag with his bloodthirsty and destructive demonstration of gunpowder as the highest glory of British culture. Swift's Gulliver would not appear on the public stage until 1727, seven years after Defoe described Robin's trip to China. It seems fair to suggest that Swift, like Defoe before him, was responding to the school of thought Robin here represents.

Robin sums up his attitude to Chinese culture by comparing the Chinese to the savages of America:

> The Pride of these People is infinitely great, and exceeded by nothing but their Poverty, which adds to that which I will call their misery, and I must needs think the naked Savages of *America* live much more happy because, as they have nothing, so they desire nothing whereas

---

[38] Porter, "A Peculiar and Uninteresting People", 194.

[39] Louis Le Comte, *Memoirs and Observations Topographical, Physical, Mathematical, Mechanical, Natural, Civil and Ecclesiastical. Made in a late Journey through the Empire of China, and Published in several Letters by Louis Le Comte, Jesuit* (1679), 2nd edn. trans., London, 1698.

[40] Payne, *Libraries*, Item 1290b.

[41] Le Comte, *Memoirs*, 73; Defoe, *The Farther Adventures of Robinson Crusoe*, 298.

these are proud and insolent, and in the main are meer Beggars and Drudges; their ostentation is inexpressible, and is chiefly shew'd in their Cloths and Building, and in the keeping Multitudes of Servants or Slaves, and, which is to the last Degree ridiculous, their Contempt of all the World but themselves.[42]

Narrator's voice and spiritual autobiography

Robin's voice in the second volume flouts the conventions of spiritual autobiography that demanded a self-absorbed repentant speaker. Although Defoe begins the volume with Robin's passionate desire to revisit his island, Robin's suffering is not the heart of this volume. Contemporary readers of *The Life and Strange Surprising Adventures of Robinson Crusoe* enjoyed Robin's emotional suffering and his triumph. Far from finding Robin ridiculous or foolish, the readers sympathized with him in his troubles. Looking back on this time, the introducer to the 1722 Midwinter abridgement of all three volumes recalls the public sentiment:

> When the book first appeared in the world how delightful, how ravishing did it seem to every Reader? Here the Passions of the Mind were so beautifully exprest, both in the Nature of his Adversity and Prosperity, that melted every heart with tender Sympathy and Compassion. Robinson Crusoe was in every Reader's Mouth as much as in the mouth of Pretty Poll. [43]

In *The Farther Adventures of Robinson Crusoe*, Robin cannot be cast as a suffering sinner in need of repentance. The mistakes he makes are not easily re-written as disobedience. His errors come from his lack of political understanding and his lack of self-understanding. He makes a mistake in setting up the government of his island, but he does not repent it as a sin. In an unheroic manner he does gain some self-knowledge in the course of his travels: "I might perhaps say with some Truth, that if Trade was not my Element, Rambling was, and no

---

[42] Defoe, *The Farther Adventures of Robinson Crusoe*, 301.

[43] Thomas Gent, Introduction to *The life and Most Surprizing Adventures of Robinson Crusoe, of York, who Lived Edith and Twenty Years in an Uninhabited island on the Coast of America, Lying Near the Mouth of the Great River of Oroonoque: Having been Cast on Shore by shipwreck, Wherein All the Men were Drowned but Himself: As Also a Relation How He was Wonderfully Deliver'd by Pyrates, The Whole three Volumes Faithfully Abridged, and Set Forth With Cuts Proper to the Subject*, 2nd edn, London, 1722.. References to this text will use the term Midwinter Abridgement.

Proposal for seeing any Part of the World which I had never seen before could possibly come amiss to me."[44] Before deciding to return to England, he goes on to discover that he does enjoy trade and is good at it.

Robin is not a repentant sinner, but neither is he a saint. Robin is never self-critical of his youthful involvement in slavery. Charles Gildon's response to the first two volumes of the *Robinson Crusoe* series makes a telling criticism of Robin's moral discernment: "tho' he afterwards proves so scrupulous about falling upon the Cannibals or Men-Eaters, yet he neither then nor afterwards found any check of Conscience in that infamous Trade of buying and selling of Men for Slaves; else one would have expected him to have attributed his *Shipwreck* to this very Cause."[45] Defoe could not have read Gildon's criticism before writing *The Farther Adventures of Robinson Crusoe*, but he keeps Robin out of slave trading, even though British Caribbean colonies all relied on slave labor. Defoe not only has Robin set up his colony without slavery, he has Robin's trading voyage violate the normal direction of English trading voyages. Robin goes from England to South America and then to the East, rather than making the slave-trading voyage from England to West Africa to South America and then back to England.

Occasionally Robin speaks with a strong moral voice, but he himself does not seem to learn much from his experiences. During the course of the voyage in *The Farther Adventures of Robinson Crusoe*, which lasts some ten years, Robin comes to affirm and even brag about positions he had earlier judged wrong. Robin had refused to take part in his shipmates' massacre of natives on Madagascar. He retreated to the ship when he was unable to stop the sailors in their rampage. Yet, years later, when he proposes burning the Tartar idol, he seems to brag about the massacre: "… *says I*, I'll tell you a Story, so I related the Story of our Men at *Madagascar*, and how they burnt and sack'd the Village there, and kill'd Man, Woman and child, for their murthering one of our Men, just as it is related before; and when I had done, I added, that I thought we ought to do so to this Village."[46] A reader who affirms his first position is left gasping by Robin's change of attitude.

---

[44] Defoe, *The Farther Adventures of Robinson Crusoe*, 249.
[45] Gildon, *The Life and Strange Surprizing Adventures of Mr D…..De F..*, 14.
[46] Defoe, *The Farther Adventures of Robinson Crusoe*, 333.

Not only is Robin powerless to affect the larger world, he also is unable to govern himself. Right from the start of *The Farther Adventures of Robinson Crusoe*, when he takes the reader into his confidence, he acts from impulse rather than by plan. Unlike narrators of the authentic voyages, Robin dithers. He is impetuous, confused, and inconsistent, just as he was at the beginning of *The Life and Strange Surprising Adventures of Robinson Crusoe*. Then he was eighteen years old. Now at age fifty-four, he again presents himself as an adolescent who can't resist an adventure:

> Yet all these things [rational considerations of his responsibilities to his family] had no effect upon me, or at least, not enough to resist the strong Inclination I had to go Abroad again, which hung about me like a chronical Distemper; particularly the Desire of seeing my new Plantation in the Island, and the Colony I left there, run [*sic*] in my Head continually.[47]

The Farther Adventures and the culture of the privateer narrative

Defoe explicitly evokes the contemporary privateer travel narrative not only in the format of the second volume, but also in the text itself. As mentioned earlier in Chapter Five, Robin refers to the conventions of the genre when he announces that he will not follow them. Defoe seems to evoke the privateer narrative only to burlesque its most significant features. The format of *The Farther Adventures of Robinson Crusoe*, with its introductory letters and map, makes it look like privateer narrative, but the narrator's voice has none of the assurance of Dampier, Cooke, or Rogers. These men write as representatives of English strength, and they embody the calm control of men who take charge of a chaotic world. By contrast, Robin emphasizes his violation of conventional wisdom and his indecision in moments of crisis.

By imitating travel narrative and violating its conventions, Defoe makes *The Farther Adventures of Robinson Crusoe* not only a critique of the genre but also a judgment of the enterprise on which it was based. Unlike the privateer narrative, Robin's story stages a series of dramatic scenes. As Robin tells his story, he talks about people rather than geography and about human relationships rather than natural history. He gives the picture of a dynamic world full of opportunity

---

[47] *Ibid.*, 2.

and danger. Robin manages to navigate this world of constant motion, but he cannot control it. He often has to run for his life, but he survives. The developing system of international trade has room for lively individuals, though it is plagued by piracy and the kind of vigilante justice piracy breeds.

Robin's story highlights the violent activities of the English privateers who can barely be distinguished from pirates. The voyage with his nephew is destroyed before it is well begun by the sailors' violence on Madagascar. The crew ejects Robin from the ship in Bengal when he dares to criticize them. Robin's naive narrative calls into question the ideological divisions between enemy and friend, Protestant and Catholic, Christian and pagan, pirate and merchant in the English imperial enterprise. The Madagascar episode mimics a familiar feature of privateer journals: the attack on a Spanish town. In Defoe's parody, however, the English sailors attack a native town, and the English sailors are just as bloody and violent as any Spanish conquistadors. The sailors "kill'd or destroy'd about 150 People, Men, Women and Children, and left not a House standing in the Town".[48]

We have already seen that contemporary privateer travel narrative minimized accounts of English attacks on native villages. People killed on such raids were usually assumed to be Spanish troops or officials, and they appear in the text as "the enemy". Sometimes the privateers describe an inept Spanish force that disintegrates under attack. The English sailors are more than a match for large numbers of Spanish opponents. Captain Sharp, an early associate of Dampier's, describes being attacked by 250 Spanish soldiers. He and his group of privateers "vigorously repulsed" the attack.[49] Robin's account, however, makes both victims and killers visible. He engages the reader's sympathy for the victims, horror at the sailors, and frustration with Robin's lack of power.

The story of this massacre on Madagascar shows Robin as a man who cannot lead. He cannot control the men in his search party. He has no economic or moral authority, or even consistency. His reactions and arguments shift ground during the narration. During the massacre, he tries to stop the sailors by reminding them of their duty to the ship owners. As the massacre proceeds, he says that seeing

---

[48] *Ibid.*, 240.
[49] Captain Sharp, *Captain Sharp's Journal of His Expedition* in *A Collection of Voyages in Four Volumes*, London, 1729, IV, 70.

Jeffries' corpse nearly moved him to revenge as well. Later on he reprimands the sailors on the grounds that Jeffry's violation of the truce compact, and the rape of a young female trader provoked that the natives' murder of Jeffry.

After witnessing lawlessness behavior he sees among the European explorers Robin decides that the South American cannibals are less frightening than violent Europeans. His later use of the savage Amerindians noted in his description of China shows Defoe's effort to link all of humankind to one moral law. Robin thinks of being captured by the Dutch and English vigilante sea captains as worse than being captured by cannibals:

> ... it were much better to have fallen into the Hands of the Savages, who were Man-Eaters, and who, I was sure, would feast upon me, when they had taken me; than by those who would perhaps glut their Rage upon me, by inhuman Tortures and Barbarities ... for the Savages, give them their due, would not eat a Man till he was dead, and kill'd them first, as we do a Bullock; but that these Men had many Arts beyond the cruelty of Death.[50]

Such an analysis separates the second volume of *Robinson Crusoe* from the first and from the European fear of the Caribbean cannibals.

The Madagascar massacre account demonstrates the dangers to trade from violence and lawlessness. These threats are a human problem, not simply a Spanish or pagan defect. By showing how important the long arm of British law is to the world, the massacre also illustrates the way society can cope with such violence. London justice is the standard and the final certainty for Robin, but this does not mean that he thinks the standards of justice vary with the country and culture. When Robin and a partner are being pursued as pirates by angry English and Dutch ship captains, Robin's first thought is to return to Bengal where they had bought their ship and where they could "bring it before the proper Judges [and] have some Justice and not be hang'd first and judg'd afterward".[51] After that he thinks of getting British justice: "If ever they [the English captains] came to England and I lived to see them there, they should answer for it if the Laws of my country were not grown out of Use before I arrived

---

[50] Defoe, *The Farther Adventures of Robinson Crusoe*, 286-87.
[51] *Ibid.*, 263.

there."[52]

The Life and Strange Surprising Adventures of Robinson Crusoe exploits many features of the spiritual autobiography genre, but readers and abridgers were able to transform Defoe's tale of conversion into a story about a successful individual colonist. The second volume builds on features of contemporary privateer travel narration, but it both cites the conventions and flouts them. It becomes a critique of privateering itself.

The story line of the second volume drops many of the elements that made the first so attractive to readers and abridgers. The most obvious difference from the first volume is Robin's mobility. Although the episodes of *The Farther Adventures of Robinson Crusoe* demonstrate the unity of humanity and the universal power of trade, there is no single focus of Robin's activity. Robin's confinement to the Island had unified the plot in the first volume and limited the cast of characters. Abridgers had been able to sharpen the focus of Robin's constant activity to the physical improvement of his life on the island. In the second volume Defoe satisfies readers' curiosity about subsequent events on the island, but he refuses to construct a prosperous utopia. When Robin fails to attach the island to the rest of the world, the colony starts to die even though Robin and the reader do not find this out until some years later.

Robin's increasing loneliness is the most remarkable reversal of patterns from the first volume. Rather than ending with a circle of friends as he had in *The Life and Strange Surprising Adventures of Robinson Crusoe*, Robin loses all his companions over the course of his travels. Robin becomes a social castaway. In the first volume, Robin defines himself in nationalistic terms, and he finds friends from all nations. The second volume, however, shows Robin at sea in a world of villains and predators – many of them English.

The second volume of the *Robinson Crusoe* series has little of the clear coherence of the first volume. The shifts of focus from island politics to trading voyages and finally to religion seem to make the second volume a contrast rather than a continuation of the first. The three segments do not build to a dramatic ending. They address the contemporary roles of Englishmen as colonists, traders, and travelers,

---

[52] *Ibid.*, 280.

but Robin the Englishman is not heroic. His return to London is not a triumph.

None of the individual segments of *The Farther Adventures of Robinson Crusoe* provides the kind of dramatic satisfaction that the island section of *The Life and Strange Surprising Adventures of Robinson Crusoe* achieved. There is nothing in Robin's relationship with Will Atkins in the return to the island to match the emotional bond between Robin and Friday that had proved to be such a strong element in the original story. Nor is there anything to match the simple physical triumph of setting up a home. In the second volume Robin's survival and return to London with diamonds and sables is not a disaster, but it is the end of his adventures. His island kingdom has failed. Madagascar, India, and China have spit him out. From barbarous Russia he has escaped with his life and his wealth. A castaway and solitary traveler, he is alone and is ready to discuss solitude. An observer of the world, he turns a critical traveler's eye on British society and religion. Defoe delivers Robin's thoughts in his third volume – *Serious Reflections of Robinson Crusoe*.

CHAPTER EIGHT

SERIOUS REFLECTIONS

The third volume of Defoe's *Robinson Crusoe* series is structured as if it were a series of interlocking pamphlets. Like pamphlets, the chapters are designed to engage in debate or provoke a reaction from readers, though the chapters are long-winded, and the prose is often turgid. The volume has only one dramatic scene. That scene is funny, but it is not enough to enliven the whole volume. *Serious Reflections During the Life and Surprising Adventures of Robinson Crusoe* did not sell well, and we can see why.

Defoe returns to Robin's story to emphasize themes that the public missed in the first two volumes. He also responds to the specific alterations made in the Amsterdam Coffee House abridgement of *The Life and Strange Surprising Adventures of Robinson Crusoe* and to Charles Gildon's pamphlet attack on the first two volumes of the series. Nevertheless, Defoe does more than repeat himself in this volume. He develops Robin's awkward and bumbling attempts at missionary work into a two-pronged plan: an overseas campaign to expose the folly of pagan religion and religious reformation in England. In *Serious Reflections During the Life and Surprising Adventures of Robinson Crusoe* Defoe comes close to identification with his fictional hero. Although he frequently refers back to his supposed earlier travels, Robin seems to have become something of a scholar in his old age. He says, "I resolved to travel over the rest of the world in books".[1] He is liberal with quotations and allusions. He even includes some verses of his own in these essays. The impetuous activist Robin is hard to recognize behind the prolix, diffuse, and pompous voice of the narrator. Only in the one narrative incident – his

---

[1] Defoe, *Serious Reflections During the Life and Surprising Adventures of Robinson Crusoe*, 143.

conversation with an "ancient gentlewoman" – is he still our hero, the enthusiastic, energetic, uneducated mariner from York.

Pamphlet structure of *Serious Reflections*

In August 1720, just a year after the publication of *The Farther Adventures of Robinson Crusoe*, Defoe published his final installment of the series. He called it *Serious Reflections During the Life and Surprising Adventures of Robinson Crusoe, with His Vision of the Angelick World*. William Taylor, the same publisher who had brought out the first two volumes, published it and advertised it in Heathcot's *Intelligence*, where a serialized abridgement of the first two volumes was running.

This third volume is a collection of seven essays that interpret Robin's travels as told in the first two books. Only the first two essays and the last make good use of the adventures described earlier, but they all demonstrate that Defoe's Robin is better at storytelling than at reflecting. Ian Watt dismisses the volume as having been "put together to cash in on the great success of the first part of the trilogy".[2] Watt's evaluation is most convincing with respect to the essay "Of the Immorality of Conversation and the Vulgar Errors of Behaviour". This is the kind of writing Defoe was doing in the 1690s when he was a member of the London Society for the Reformation of Manners.[3] The essay's references to King William ("the king now his wars are over") and Queen Mary ("the late Queen Mary of heavenly memory") date it between Queen Mary's death in 1695 and King William's death in 1702.[4] In the chronology of Defoe's story, it would have been possible for the fictional Robin to have written this essay at the end of the time when he was farming in England between 1687 and 1695, when he leaves to go trading after his wife dies. Most of the chapter has nothing to do with Robin's travels – except the very end, which takes up – yet again – the difference between "lying" and writing a "parable".

Serious Reflections During the Life and Surprising Adventures of Robinson Crusoe looks as though it was designed as a challenge to all the readers who preferred action to reflection. As we have seen, all the

---

[2] Watt, *The Rise of the Novel*, 89.
[3] Backscheider, *Daniel Defoe, His Life*, 236-37.
[4] Defoe, *Serious Reflections During the Life and Surprising Adventures of Robinson Crusoe*, 81.

abridgers agreed that Robin was an action hero. They cut out Robin's moral analysis, and they streamlined the account of his pre-conversion mental distress on the island. Defoe insisted that "they strip it of all those Reflections, as well religious as moral, which are not only the greatest Beautys of the Work, but are calculated for the infinite Advantage of the Reader".[5] His third volume is all Robin's reflections with virtually no action.

Serious Reflections During the Life and Surprising Adventures of Robinson Crusoe was such a failure that Taylor's heirs could not sell the copyright in 1723. At the same time, the copyright to the first volume was divided in half to collect more from its sale.[6] Critics are wrong, however, to assume that the absence of narrative indicates lack of purpose. The topics Defoe tackles in this volume spring from the public's misreadings of Robin's story. The readers had missed what Defoe had to say on several topics: the difference between being alone and being alone with God, the meaning of "honesty" in family and business relations, and the task of living a reasonable Christian life in a largely pagan world.

Robin's rich solitude
When he recapitulates his travels in *Serious Reflections During the Life and Surprising Adventures of Robinson Crusoe*, Defoe restates the moral of the story in terms that contradict both the Amsterdam Coffee House abridger and Charles Gildon. He does not imply submission to one's father or to one's station in life as a moral. Instead he recommends patience, application, and resolution: "Here is invincible Patience recommended under the worst of Misery; indefatigable Application and undaunted Resolution under the greatest and most discouraging Circumstances; I say, these are recommended, as the only Way to work through these Miseries."[7]

The first topic Robin takes up is "Solitude". In this sixteen-page essay he explains the difference between the loneliness he experienced on the island before his religious awakening and the solitude he experienced afterwards. Robin says, "there are many good Reasons why a Life of Solitude, as Solitude is now understood by the Age, is

---

[5] Defoe, *The Farther Adventures of Robinson Crusoe*, Preface.
[6] Hutchins, *Robinson Crusoe and Its Printing*, 122.
[7] Defoe, *Serious Reflections During the Life and Surprising Adventures of Robinson Crusoe*, xii.

not at all suited to the life of a Christian or of a wise Man". Robin tries to build a positive spiritual meaning for the word "solitude" rather than let it simply refer to the state of being physically alone. He develops the terms "retirement" and "forced retreat" to describe two different ways of being alone. He will recommend "retirement" into one's self as a spiritual discipline. When he was a castaway, Robin had no option. He endured a forced retreat. But in his *Serious Reflections* Robin insists "I enjoy much more Solitude in the Middle of the greatest Collection of Mankind in the World, I mean, at London, while am writing this, than ever I could say I enjoyed in the eight and twenty Years' confinement to a desolate Island".[8]

Like his contemporary Locke, Robin explores individual self-awareness as a defining human condition.[9] Robin admits, "All reflection is carried Home, and our dear self is in one Respect, the End of Living. Hence Man may be properly said to be alone in the Midst of the Crowds and hurry of Men and Business."[10] Pope explores the same idea when he says: "Two Principles in human nature reign; / Self-love, to urge, and Reason, to restrain."[11] Robin's version of this theme picks up his image of life as circular motion, but Defoe also makes this idea literal by imagining Robin alone on his island. In his *Serious Reflections* Robin tries to universalize his experience: "it seems to me that Life in general is, or ought to be but one universal Act of Solitude .... Every Thing revolves in our Minds by innumerable circular Motions, all centering in our selves."[12] At the end of his life, Robin argues that a mental solitary state is not necessarily linked to physical isolation. Introversion is normal and healthy for human beings.

---

[8] Defoe, *Serious Reflections During the Life and Surprising Adventures of Robinson Crusoe*, 5.

[9] Locke says "to find wherein personal identity consists, we must consider what 'person' stands for; which, I think, is a thinking intelligent being, that has reason and reflection, and can consider itself as itself, the same thinking thing, in different times and places" (Locke, *An Essay Concerning Human Understanding*, 246).

[10] Defoe, *Serious Reflections During the Life and Surprising Adventures of Robinson Crusoe*, 4.

[11] Alexander Pope, *Essay on Man* (1733), II, 53-54, ed. Maynard Mack, London, 1951, 62.

[12] Defoe, *Serious Reflections During the Life and Surprising Adventures of Robinson Crusoe*, 4.

Confused and agonized loneliness is what Robin experiences when he first comes ashore in the island. This loneliness is not the mental state he defines as "solitude" in his *Serious Reflections During the Life and Surprising Adventures of Robinson Crusoe*: "Confinement from the Enjoyments of the World, and Restraint from human Society … was no Solitude; indeed no part of it was so, except that which, as in my Story, I apply'd to the Contemplation of sublime Things, and that was but a very little, as my Reader will know, compar'd to what a length of Years my forced retreat lasted." Positive solitude is not a matter of physical isolation, but a matter of spiritual communication: "What then is the silence of Life? And, How is it afflicting, while a Man has the Voice of his Soul to speak to God, and to himself?" asks Robin.[13]

It cannot be a coincidence that Robin's discussion echoes Steele's description of Alexander Selkirk's regret at leaving the island of Juan Fernandez. Steele talks about Selkirk's reluctance to leave "the Tranquility of his Solitude".[14] Robin cautions his readers against idealizing isolation. At this point we hear Defoe, the man loyal to his Dissenter fellowship and committed to public worship services react to Steele's flippant suggestion that absence of people would produce spiritual excellence:

> Solitude, therefore, as I understand by it, a Retreat from human Society, on a religious or philosophical Account, is a mere Cheat; it neither can answer the End it proposes, or qualify us for the Duties of Religion, which we are commanded to perform, and is therefore both irreligious in itself, and inconsistent with a Christian Life many Ways. Let the Man that would reap the Advantage of Solitude, and that understands the Meaning of the word, learn to retire into himself. Serious Meditation is the Essence of Solitude.[15]

In *The Life and Strange Surprising Adventures of Robinson Crusoe*, Robin is always talking and planning. In his essay "On Solitude" he analyzes the radically different kinds of interior conversation he experienced. In his first few months on the island he

---

[13] Defoe, *Serious Reflections During the Life and Surprising Adventures of Robinson Crusoe*, 3-4.

[14] Steele, *The Englishman*: see n.66 in Chapter Two above (page 47).

[15] Defoe, *Serious Reflections During the Life and Surprising Adventures of Robinson Crusoe*, 12-13.

is alone, but he has no "solitude". His thought for months circled endlessly upon himself without any connection to God. For Robin these were not happy times. Curtis points out how Robin acts out this introversion:

> One of Crusoe's major activities during the island portion of his narrative is fortification, or the construction of walls and enclosures. These structures are described as circles and fences.[16]

The caves he constructs or finds are the threatening form of these enclosures. As noted earlier, abridgers tried to make this period pleasant, contrary to Defoe's text. In this time Robin suffered a painful isolation. After his religious awakening Robin enjoys solitude, but that is destroyed by his fear of the cannibals. In the final section of *Serious Reflections During the Life and Surprising Adventures of Robinson Crusoe*, in the essay called "A Vision of the Angelick World", Robin confesses that before he rescued Friday he was prey to ideas that his island was haunted by the devil: "what with ruminating on the Print of a Foot upon the Sand, and the Weight of the Devil upon me in my Bed, I made no difficulty to conclude that the old Gentleman really visited the Place."[17]

All this was, he says, "Imagination raised up to disease" which did not stop until he had Friday to talk to. His companionship with Friday gives him back the ability to meditate and pray. Defoe's Friday speaks pidgin English, but his questions challenge Robin's dulled piety. Clearly Friday is a foil for Robin, not an anthropologically accurate native. Nevertheless, Defoe gives Friday some independence and some moral ascendancy over Robin. Friday is also affectionately connected with other people. Friday loves his father and he wants to preach to his fellow countrymen. On the journey to London from Portugal, Friday reveals a sense of play quite different from Robin's self irony.

Charles Gildon's attack

Charles Gildon published his critical pamphlet of the first two *Robinson Crusoe* volumes in autumn 1719, within weeks of the

---

[16] Curtis, *The Elusive Daniel Defoe*, 74.
[17] Defoe, *Serious Reflections During the Life and Surprising Adventures of Robinson Crusoe*, 256.

publication of *The Farther Adventures of Robinson Crusoe*.[18] Gildon's biographer, Paul Dottin, says that Gildon had a practice of making pamphlet attacks on famous authors in hopes of eliciting a direct response and boosting his own sales.[19] Gildon's ploy worked. Although Defoe did not respond to Gildon by name, Gildon's pamphlet attack on Defoe went into three editions that year, and its success increased sales of Gildon's other works. This kind of dialogue between author and critic is the same kind of dialogue we can see in Defoe's political writing.

Gildon's pamphlet is made up of three disjointed segments, all expressing his personal animus against Daniel Defoe. The three sections were printed together, but they show the stages of their composition during the period between April 1719 and August 1719 when the first two volumes of the *Robinson Crusoe* series were first published together and discussed. Dottin suggests there may be a simple physical explanation for the Gildon pamphlet's ungainly shape. By 1718 Gildon was blind. He probably wrote his pamphlet in three stages, as Defoe's books came out and his assistant read Defoe's book to him. Gildon may not have revised his own pamphlet because he was in a hurry to capitalize on Robinson Crusoe's popularity.[20]

The first segment of the pamphlet is a dramatic skit – a clever, abusive, imaginary encounter between Defoe and his two characters Crusoe and Friday. The next two sections are cast as "an Epistle" to Defoe. Gildon works his way through *The Life and Strange Surprising Adventures of Robinson Crusoe* and *The Farther Adventures of Robinson Crusoe*. He comments on whichever details of Defoe's work catch his attention and arouse his anger. Gildon pays special attention to Defoe's Preface to *The Farther Adventures of Robinson Crusoe* in which Defoe complains about the pirate abridgements and justifies his story-telling practices. Gildon's pamphlet attacks Defoe's patriotism, his piety, and his literary theory. It lists Defoe's grammatical and factual errors, quarrels with his storytelling techniques, and defends the practice of making abridgements.

---

[18] Paul Dottin, "Introduction to Gildon's Pamphlet", in *Robinson Crusoe Examin'd and Criticis'd: or A New Edition of Charles Gildon's famous Pamphlet now published with an Introduction and Explanatory Notes together with an Essay on Gildon's Life*, London, 1923, 57.

[19] Paul Dottin, "The Life of Charles Gildon", in *ibid.*, 67.

[20] Dottin, "Introduction to Gildon's Pamphlet", in *ibid.*, 55-57.

Gildon's farce sets an imaginary encounter on the way to Defoe's house at Newington Green. It mocks Defoe as a coward:

> *A Dialogue betwixt D-----F—e Robinson Cruso and his Man Friday.*
>
> *Scene: a great Field betwixt Newington-Green and Newington Town, at one a Clock in a Moon-lit morning. Enter DF with two pocket Pistols.*[21]

The two islanders, dressed in their goatskin caps, intercept Defoe on his way home to Newington Green. After complaining about the way he has portrayed them, they force him to eat both volumes of the story. They then toss him in a blanket until he loses control of his bowels. The drama takes up eighteen pages of the pamphlet, but is paginated with small Roman numerals as if it were an introduction.

After the dramatic skit, Gildon writes in the style of an open letter to Defoe. This section of the pamphlet is separately paginated with Arabic numbers. This letter may have been started very soon after *The Life and Strange Surprising Adventures of Robinson Crusoe* appeared, since Gildon pretends to be tentative about Defoe's having written the book. He addresses his letter with pretended caution: "An Epistle to D------ D'Foe The Reputed Author of Robinson Crusoe."[22] For the first twenty-nine pages Gildon discusses material from *The Life and Strange Surprising Adventures of Robinson Crusoe*. At page 29 he notes that he has just been told that the second volume is out. From pages 30 to 44, Gildon responds to the Preface of *The Farther Adventures of Robinson Crusoe* in a section he calls Postscript.

The terms of Gildon's attack testify to the broad appeal of *The Life and Strange Surprising Adventures of Robinson Crusoe*. Gildon has his farcical Daniel protest to the Crusoe character:

> Hold, hold, dear Son Crusoe, hold, let me satisfy you first before any more come upon me. You are my Hero, I have made you, out of nothing, fam'd from Tuttle-Street to Limehouse-hole; there is not an old woman that can go to the Price of it, but buys thy Life and Adventures and leaves it as a Legacy, with the Pilgrims Progress, the

---

[21] Gildon, *The Life and Strange Surprizing Adventures of Mr D.....De F...*, vi, in *ibid.*, 67.

[22] *Ibid.*, 81.

Practice of Piety, and God's Revenge against Murther, to her
Posterity.[23]

Dottin notes that these two streets bracket London, and he points
out, "Though this is intended to ridicule De Foe's book, it is a striking
acknowledgment of its extraordinary popularity in London".[24]
Gildon's pamphlet also suggests that there may have been early
abridgements that have not survived. Gildon's pamphlet-character
Crusoe berates Daniel for making him a chapbook hero:

> Your Mob Hero! Your Pyecorner Hero on a foot with Guy of
> Warwick, Bevis of Southampton or the London Prentice. For M..w..r
> has put me in that Rank, and drawn me much better.[25]

Dottin identifies these three figures as chap-book heroes, and explains
their stories. The M.w.r. reference looks very like a reference to the
publisher E. Midwinter.

What prompted Gildon's personal attack?

Defoe and Gildon were old acquaintances and old antagonists. Their
textual exchange over the Robinson Crusoe series fits the pattern of
London pamphlet wars both of them were used to. By the time of *The
Life and Strange Surprising Adventures of Robinson Crusoe*, Gildon
and Defoe had been in different political camps for years. They also
lived in different physical circumstances. Defoe lived in a fine house
in Newington Green with his large family, while Gildon lived in a
small rented room in London. In his pamphlet Gildon alludes to every
scandal about Defoe he can remember or invent. Clearly he was
jealous of Defoe's success and clearly he had been keeping track of
Defoe.

Although Gildon and Defoe both earned their living by writing,
they differed in class, culture, religious tradition, and lifestyle. Both
had gone to schools intended to train non-Anglican clergy, but Gildon
was a Roman Catholic and Defoe was a Dissenter. Defoe set out to
become a London merchant and citizen, while Gildon aimed at a

---

[23] *Ibid.*, ix-x.
[24] Paul Dottin, *The Life and Strange Surprising Adventures of Daniel Defoe*, trans.
Louise Ragan, London, 1929, 183.
[25] Gildon, *The Life and Strange Surprizing Adventures of Mr D.....De F...*, vi, in
Dottin, *Robinson Crusoe Examin'd and Criticis'd*, 72.

career in letters. When Defoe was fighting bankruptcy and writing his early populist political pamphlets, *The True-Born Englishman* (1700) and *Legion's Memorial* (1701), Gildon was frequenting the salon of Aphra Behn. Later he would bring out an edition of her complete plays and novels.[26] He became a Deist – before a public transition to the Anglican Church.[27] He wrote on international politics, English grammar, and poetry.[28]

As young men, Defoe and Gildon must have been acquainted. Defoe contributed a poem to the *History of the Athenian Society* edited by Gildon in 1692.[29] Eleven years later, however, Defoe included a dismissive reference to Gildon in *More Reformation*, the poem he wrote in 1703 from Newgate while waiting to stand in the pillory for *The Shortest-Way with the Dissenters*. Defoe said,

> G---writes Satyr, rails at Blasphemy,
> And the next Page, lampoons the Deity;
> Exposes his Darinda's Vicious Life,
> But keeps six whores
> And starves his modest wife ...[30]

The two men moved in different social, intellectual, and religious circles. Defoe remained a member of Dissenter congregations all his life, dreamed up projects to improve the conversation and manners of society, and worried about England's role in the world. The government subsidized his writing about trade and politics. Gildon made a pamphlet copy of his own biography – his move from the Roman Catholic Church to Deist circles and then to the Anglican

---

[26] Aphra Behn, *All the Histories and Novels Written by the Late Ingenious Mrs Behn*, ed. Charles Gildon, London, 1699.

[27] As a Deist he first edited the works of Charles Blount, a noted Deist, then wrote his own book, *The Deist Manual: Or a Rational Enquiry into the Christian Religion*, London, 1705.

[28] Charles Gildon, *The Golden Spy*, London, 1709; *A Grammar of the English Tongue*, London, 1711; *The Complete Art of Poetry*, London, 1718.

[29] Backscheider, *Daniel Defoe, His Life*, 55.

[30] Defoe, *More Reformation. A Satyr upon himself. By the author of the true born English-man*, London, 1705.

Church.[31] He tried to become a member of the artistic elite patronized by the nobility.[32]

Gildon's dishonest reading

Both Gildon and the abridgers claimed to understand Defoe's hero. The abridgers claimed to love Defoe's story, whereas Charles Gildon despised both the book and its author whom he identified as Robinson Crusoe. Gildon's criticism of Defoe was rooted in the deep religious and political differences between the two men. The structure of Gildon's text makes it difficult to summarize his criticism, but three topics recur through his pamphlet: style, patriotism, and religion. Gildon thought that Defoe's writing was bad in conception and bad in execution. He said that removing the "clumsy and tedious Reflections" might improve the fable, if the story itself were not so flawed. As far as Defoe's patriotism and religious views were concerned, Gildon found Defoe "as bad an *Englishman* as Christian".

The deep political chasm between Gildon and Defoe means that Defoe's patriotism looks to Gildon like disrespect. Defoe's attempt to imagine cooperation between Catholics and Protestants in preaching to the savages looks to Gildon like currying favor with Rome. Defoe's attempt to explore new ways of understanding human psychology and his attempt to discuss the theological conundrum of Divine Providence seem to Gildon to be superstition.

Gildon casts himself as a literary policeman, reprimanding Defoe for violations of long-established rules of genre and style in *The Life and Strange Surprising Adventures of Robinson Crusoe* and its sequel. According to the rules, says Gildon, a well-written fable should have a clear moral, but "this of Robinson Crusoe, you plainly inculcate, is design'd against a publick good".[33] Gildon assumes – or pretends to assume – that Defoe had intended to write a sermon on obedience to parents. Instead, says Gildon, the tale of Robin's adventures is a warning against going to sea. Gildon spends six pages elaborately proving that it was no crime for Robin to go to sea. He states his case: "I dare believe that there are few men who consider justly, that would

---

[31] Dottin, "The Life of Charles Gildon", in *Robinson Crusoe Examin'd and Criticis'd*, 22.

[32] *Ibid.*, 26.

[33] Gildon, *The Life and Strange Surprizing Adventures of Mr D.....De F...*, vi, in *ibid.*, 2.

think the Profession of a Yorkshire attorney more innocent and beneficial to Mankind than that of a seaman, or would judge that Robinson Crusoe was so very criminal in rejecting the former, and chusing the latter."[34] Gildon's jealousy makes him a close reader. At the same time it prevents him from understanding Defoe's intention. He realizes that Robin's going to sea is not a terrible crime, and he notices that Robin comes home a rich man. He thinks that he has uncovered a contradiction in Defoe's plot, because he assumes that Defoe is trying to teach young boys to listen to their fathers. He is unable to acknowledge the irony in Defoe's depiction of Father Crusoe.

Defoe's Chapter on "Honesty", the fifty-two-page-long second chapter in *Serious Reflections During the Life and Surprising Adventures of Robinson Crusoe*, was written after Defoe had read Gildon and after he had seen what the Amsterdam Coffee House abridgement did to exaggerate Robin's guilt for running away from home. The section called "Relative Honesty" explains that the good father is obliged to provide his sons with vocational as well as spiritual leadership. Robin explains that the virtue of honesty governs not only business dealings, but also family relationships: "A wife and children are creditors to the father of the family, and he cannot be an honest man that does not discharge his debt to them."[35] These duties to children include not only providing education but also "studying the genius and capacities of their children". Fathers have a duty to establish their sons in careers for which they are suited. Robin's father has not done this, so Robin's rebellion is not surprising. This point is set up in the first section of the story in the first volume, as I have argued. Gildon's dislike of Defoe prevented him from perceiving that Defoe was writing ironically, or perhaps, made him pretend to take Defoe's story as a parable against disobedience.

God and grammar in Robin's voice
Even the dispute about style represents the two men's different religious perspectives. Robin embodies Defoe's Dissenter attitude towards religious authority. He does not need a church or priest to shape his religion, nor does he need a grammar book to correct his

---

[34] *Ibid.*, 3.
[35] Defoe, *Serious Reflections During the Life and Surprising Adventures of Robinson Crusoe*, 66.

style of writing. He expects God to talk to him, and he talks to God through Bible-study sessions on the island. He sees the work of Providence in the events of his life. Gildon has different ways of relating to God. As a member of the Established church, Gildon is concerned to uphold established rules and established institutions both in writing and in religion.

Gildon objects to Defoe's grammar, his vocabulary, his characterization of Friday's Pidgin English, and his way of writing a fable. Gildon complains about "the frequent Solecism, Looseness and Incorrectness of stile, Improbabilities and sometime Impossibilities".[36] Later on in his pamphlet Gildon becomes more technical: "How, friend D-n! ... I thought, that beyond the superlative Degree there was nothing ... perhaps he had it from his House Learning, with all the other false Grammar, which is to be found almost in every page, particularly the *Nominative Case* perpetually put for the *Accusative*."[37]

Gildon goes much further than the Amsterdam Coffee House abridger in criticizing Defoe's story-telling style. Where the abridger simply implies that Robin's reflections are superfluous, Gildon quotes the terms Defoe uses to characterize the story in the Preface to *The Farther Adventures of Robinson Crusoe*, and charges Defoe with lying: "what you mean by *Legitimating*, *Invention*, and *Parable*, I know not; unless you would have us think, that the matter of your telling a Lie will make it a Truth."[38]

Defoe answered Gildon's charge briefly in the preface to *Serious Reflections During the Life and Surprising Adventures of Robinson Crusoe* and in the chapter on "Conversation and Behaviour", but his broadest response is this long chapter, "An Essay upon Honesty". He brings up yet again Gildon's charge that inventing stories is a form of lying as he concludes the chapter. In trying to distinguish lying from truth, he cites examples: "Such are the historical Parables in the Holy Scripture, such the Pilgrim's Progress, and such, in a Word, the Adventures of your fugitive Friend, *Robinson Crusoe*."[39]

Defoe's reference to *Pilgrim's Progress* echoes Gildon's pamphlet sneer at his book's popularity. Defoe turns the charge of dishonesty

---

[36] Gildon, *The Life and Strange Surprizing Adventures of Mr D.....De F...*, 2.

[37] *Ibid.*, 23.

[38] *Ibid.*, 33.

[39] Defoe, *Serious Reflections During the Life and Surprising Adventures of Robinson Crusoe*, 115-16.

back on his critics when he defines what it means to write and read honestly:

> I desire to speak plainly and sincerely …. likewise the same Sincerity is required in the Reader, and he that reads this Essay without Honesty, will never understand it right. *She must, I say be view'd by her own Light.* If Prejudice, Partiality, or private Opinions stand in the Way, *The man's a reading Knave.* He is not honest to the Subject; and upon such an one all the Labour is lost. This Work is of no Use to him, and by my Consent, the Bookseller should give him his Money again.[40]

Nevertheless, Defoe still seems to need to justify his storytelling. Shortly after this manifesto, Robin challenges his critics:

> If any Man object here that the preceding Volumes of this Work seem to be hereby condemned …. I demand in Justice such Objector stay his Censure till he sees the End of the Scene. [41]

Honesty as a citizen ethic

Speaking in the voice of Robin, Defoe broadens the concept of honesty from simple repayment of debt to generous concern for others. Defoe would have known that such a broad interpretation of "debt" is thoroughly rooted in the New Testament, as in Romans 13:8: "Owe no man anything except to love one another." Robin refers back to the network of trade contacts he had made as a young man: "One time as I was upon my inquiries into the happy concurrence of the causes which had brought the event of my prosperity to pass, as an effect, it occurred to my thoughts how much of it all depended, under the disposition of Providence, upon the principle of honesty which I met with in almost all the people whom it was my lot to be concern'd with in my private and particular affairs."[42] This section makes it clear that in Defoe's mind *The Life and Strange Surprising Adventures of Robinson Crusoe* was about trade and spiritual growth. The frame story was not just a mechanism for getting Robin to his island.

Robin's essay carries on in the tradition of the Elizabethan trade epic. He discusses the difference between reasonable business loans,

---

[40] *Ibid.*, 25, 27.
[41] *Ibid.*, 118.
[42] *Ibid.*, 219.

which include taking a risk, and loans that involve fraud because the borrower never plans to repay. Robin argues that honesty, not social position, should be the basis of public trust. This egalitarian code was based on the shift in values from feudal hierarchy to egalitarian individualism implicit in the Protestant theology of John Calvin and his followers. It fitted the national self-image that the Hakluyt collection had developed. It provided a rationale for a society in which wealth could be earned by commerce, not by collecting rent from hereditary estates. Charles Taylor, in his study *Sources of the Self*, points out the continuity between the old and new ethic: "The citizen ethic was in some ways analogous to, and could at times even partially fuse with the aristocratic ethic of honour in which willingness to risk life was the constitutive quality of the man of honour."[43] But Taylor also points out that the citizen ethic was needed for a society engaged in trade since "In some societies, engaging in trade was considered a derogation of aristocratic status".[44]

An ethical code based on the concept of honesty could be a code for an expanding economic system in which entrepreneurs borrowed capital in a plan to make a profit. Non-commercial relationships between people, too, could be governed by mutual confidence rather than by aristocratic or paternalistic assertion of hierarchical status.

Defoe's global consciousness

Gildon's most telling charge, judging from Defoe's response, is that Defoe's idea of Providence is like "the Papists in the Legends of their Saints".[45] In *The Life and Strange Surprising Adventures of Robinson Crusoe* and *The Farther Adventures of Robinson Crusoe* Defoe shows how Providence works through Robin's observations, dreams, emotions, and impulses in the first and second volumes. To Gildon, such means are irrational. They are beneath the dignity of "the eternal Divine Wisdom!".[46] Gildon complains: "What you call Religion, is only to mislead the Minds of Men to reject the Dictates of Reason, and embrace in its Room a meer superstitious Fear of I know not what *Instinct* from unbodied Spirits."[47]

---

[43] Taylor, *Sources of the Self*, 214.

[44] *Ibid.*, 214.

[45] Gildon, *The Life and Strange Surprizing Adventures of Mr D.....De F...*, 47.

[46] *Ibid.*, 37.

[47] *Ibid.*, 33.

The four essays "The Present State of Religion", "Of Listening to the Voice of Providence", "Of the Proportion between the Christian and Pagan World", and "A Vision of the Angelick World" that make up two thirds of the volume, answer Gildon's charge of irrational superstition, by going far beyond Gildon's trivial complaints. In these chapters Defoe faces two contemporary challenges to Christian teaching: a geo-political challenge and an epistemological challenge. Both arise from fifteenth- and sixteenth-century travelers' tales. The reading public was becoming aware of how big the world is and how various human cultures are. In *Serious Reflections During the Life and Surprising Adventures of Robinson Crusoe* Robin comes to terms with the realization that Christians are a minority in the world.

Robin tries to combine the religious doctrine of God's Providence with Lockean epistemology and with the information on the world brought back by travelers. Using introspection as a method of inquiry, Locke had argued that some human ideas connect by "a natural correspondence and connexion one with another" but others are combined "voluntarily or by chance".[48] Robin, however, insists that observable events are not products of chance, but represent the voice of Providence to the individual who is willing to listen.

Defoe's contemporaries refused to take him seriously as a philosopher or theologian. But Defoe had intellectual pretensions, as his early political poem *Jure Divino* (1706) had demonstrated. The fate of that twelve-book poem in heroic couplets, however, showed the limits of Defoe's skill and the limits of the London public's desire to listen to him philosophize. Defoe not only read Locke on the value of introspection, he took the next step in opening his character's interior monologue and his later reflections for public discussion. If we take Defoe's own account of his work seriously, we can see that his creation of Robin is just as ambitious as his early poem had been. Defoe's account of Robin and his voyage round the world was a philosophical treatise analogous to those of Locke and Montaigne – who also used travelers' tales to validate their opinions.

Travel literature was the seventeenth- and eighteenth-century vehicle for the study of human psychology and political philosophy, and it was a way to voice criticism of one's own culture. Besides relying on introspection to discover patterns of knowledge, the new

---

[48] Locke, *An Essay Concerning Human Understanding*, 316.

epistemology relied on travelers' reports to find out facts about the world and its peoples. Travel narrative had given Locke the evidence that proved, he thought, that there are no innate ideas. He cites travelers' tales about the Caribs and the Indians of Peru as "Instances of enormities practiced without remorse".[49] However, Montaigne's essay "On Cannibals" implies universal human values as it criticizes French society from the imagined perspective of South American visitors.[50] We are fairly certain that Defoe was familiar with both these essays: Montaigne's essays had been available in English since 1603, when John Florio translated them, and Defoe's library lists a French three-volume edition published in 1724.[51]

Robin's critique of religion in England

Defoe's early pamphlets and his journal *The Review* developed a method of argumentation by indirection. As already noted in relation to *The True-Born Englishman* and *The Shortest Way With the Dissenters*, Defoe regularly practices an ironic mode of writing that echoes the ideas he dislikes and calls on the reader to react rather than agree. Defoe's presentation of Robin in the first two volumes of the *Robinson Crusoe* series has this same kind of banter style. Robin is admirable for his persistence and his effort. He is a hero who points out problems, not a hero who can always solve them. The essays on religion in *Serious Reflections During the Life and Surprising Adventures of Robinson Crusoe* follow Defoe's patterns of argument by indirection.

Each essay in *Serious Reflections During the Life and Surprising Adventures of Robinson Crusoe* leads Robin back to himself and his culture. He looks at both critically. The word "reflections" becomes a pun as Robin's thoughts become a mirror for Englishmen to use in looking at themselves and their religion. He says that all of his imagined adventures in the first two volumes have been allegorical descriptions of actual events. The travels are an opportunity for the readers to identify with the main character and see themselves from

---

[49] *Ibid.*, 30.
[50] Michel de Montaigne, "Of Cannibals" (1575), in Montaigne, *Selected Essays*, ed. Blanchard Bates, trans Charles Cotton and W. Hazlitt, New York, 1949, 83: "We may, then, well call these people barbarians in respect to the rules of reason, but not in respect to ourselves, who, in all sorts of barbarity, exceed them."
[51] Payne, *Libraries*, Item #537.

the outside. His writing is a mirror for the narrator and the reader, and as he said then, it is "a test for fools".[52]

In *Serious Reflections During the Life and Surprising Adventures of Robinson Crusoe*, Robin's thoughts become fixed on religious questions. In order to read them well, we must remember that in the first two volumes Defoe goes out of his way to show Robin's spiritual weakness. Robin's religious awakening after his first ten months on the island is impressive and liberating, but it does not last. When he cowers in his cave after seeing a strange footprint in the sand, he makes a point of telling how fear cancelled his faith. Robin is selfish. He has little or no interest in preaching to the savages. Robin explains the Christian faith to Friday more for his own comfort than for Friday's good. If the *The Life and Strange Surprising Adventures* of *Robinson Crusoe* is seen as a testimony to individual survival, Robin's fickle spirituality can be taken as a sign of health. Paula Backscheider points out that spiritual growth slips out of the main focus in the last sections of the book, and she thinks this is a virtue of the book: "Once he has worked out his relationship to God, his religion is no more intrusive than most men's."[53] When Robin returns to the Island in *The Farther Adventures of Robinson Crusoe*, it is the French priest who worries about preaching to the savages, not Robin. Robin feels embarrassed by his lack of zeal, but not embarrassed enough to change. Robin shows a persistent interest in questions of religion on his voyage round the world, but his actions are farcical. His method of combating idol worship simply causes political trouble for the Muscovy outpost.

Several times in the first two volumes of the series Robin comes up against religious questions that he cannot solve by his common-sense logic. His pattern in this situation is to outline the problem and dismiss it. We see this pattern when Robin wonders why "it has pleas'd God to hide the life saving Knowledge from so many Millions of Souls".[54] He reassures himself, and quickly returns to more practical matters of teaching Friday English. The same kind of confrontation happens when Friday points out the contradiction between God's omnipotence and the Devil's power.[55] In *The Farther Adventures of Robinson*

---

[52] Defoe, *The True-Born Englishman*, 43.

[53] Backscheider, *Daniel Defoe, His Life*, 45.

[54] Defoe, *The Life and Strange Surprising Adventures of Robinson Crusoe*, 115.

[55] *Ibid.*, 157.

Crusoe Will's wife wonders why a supposedly omnipotent God does not punish Will for cursing, and Robin cannot answer.[56]

In the middle of *Serious Reflections During the Life and Surprising Adventures of Robinson Crusoe*, Defoe writes one scene in which Robin again is caught off guard by someone else's religious perception. This scene, the single new narrative incident in the book, is comic. Robin is flattered to see an "old Gentlewoman" listening to him tell about his travels "with a great deal of attention and, as I thought, with some pleasure".[57] She asks Robin "What have you observed to be the principal business of mankind?". For the next five pages of text she interrogates Robin relentlessly. She rejects Robin's evasions and his suggestions of "eating and drinking" and preying on each other, asking finally, "is not religion the principal business of mankind in all the parts of the world?".[58] She backs up her claim by referring to Robin's own adventures – the stories of what he learned about native culture from Friday and from Will Atkins' wife. Then she goes away, leaving Robin to his own agitated thoughts. He starts thinking, turns to reading, and then writes "An Essay on the Present State of Religion in the World" and "Of the Proportion between the Christian and Pagan World". These two chapters on world religion alternate with his chapters expounding his rational Christianity, "Of Listening to the Voice of Providence" and "A Vision of the Angelick World".

Robin's procedure in his survey of world religion is remarkably similar to the procedure used fifty years later by William Carey in a pamphlet that triggered an explosion of British missionary activity. Carey's 1792 Enquiry precipitated the formation of numerous missionary efforts: "the London Missionary Society (1795), the Scottish and Glasgow Missionary Societies (1796), the American Board of Commissioners for Foreign Missions (1810), and the General Missionary Convention of the Baptist Denomination (1814)."[59] Carey estimated the world population at about 731 million, of which 420 million are "still in pagan darkness" even though "they

---

[56] Defoe, *The Farther Adventures of Robinson Crusoe*, 187.
[57] Defoe, *Serious Reflections During the Life and Surprising Adventures of Robinson Crusoe*, 120.
[58] *Ibid.*, 113.
[59] Keith E. Eitel, Introduction, in William Carey, *An Enquiry into the Obligations of Christians to Use Means for the Conversion of the Heathen* (1792), ed. John Pretlov, Dallas: TX, 1988, xv.

appear to be as capable of knowledge as we are".[60] Carey's pamphlet led him to become a missionary-translator in India. Robin, however, is no William Carey. Robin does nothing more than mentally retrace his route, estimating the population of the countries he has visited and commenting on their religion. Robin's primary focus continues to be on England.

Robin's survey raises only his familiar questions about Divine Providence. Robin acknowledges the logical dilemma posed within Christendom by the seeming incompatibility between the conviction that God is good and the conviction that rejection of Christ leads to Hell:

> What the Divine Wisdom has determined concerning the Souls of so many Millions, it is difficult to conclude … if they are received to Mercy in a future State … then their Ignorance and Pagan Darkness is not a Curse, but a Felicity: and there are no unhappy People in the World, but those lost among Christians for their sins against revealed Light …. On the other Hand, if all those Nations are included under the Sentence of eternal Absence from God … then what becomes of all the skeptical Doctrines of its being inconsistent with the Mercy and Goodness of an infinite and beneficent Being to condemn so great a Part of the World, for not believing in him of whom they never had any Knowledge or Instruction?

Just as in the previous volumes, Robin raises the problem in its strongest form and evades any solution: "But I desire not to be the Promoter of unanswerable Doubts in matters of Religion … and therefore I only name Things."[61] In this case, as in most of the cases where Robin raises religious questions, the questions turn a mirror on himself and his culture.

Robin's survey of world religions

Robin's survey of world religion begins with his travels, but Defoe spends more time on Europe and England than he does on pagan lands. This sixty-seven-page essay devotes only about thirty pages to religion outside Europe. In the first part of the survey Robin spends

---

[60] Carey, *An Enquiry into the Obligations of Christians to Use Means for the Conversion of the Heathen*, 49-50.
[61] Defoe, *Serious Reflections During the Life and Surprising Adventures of Robinson Crusoe*, 127.

nine pages on China. In this volume he quotes his source, Father LeComte, by name. Perhaps Defoe was responding to Gildon's jibe at his ignorance of China. The world survey gives nearly the same space (six pages) to a criticism of the English peace celebrations. The following eleven pages on "Differences in Religion" focus almost completely on European religious quarrels. The last section on "negative religion" is a long-winded wandering complaint about people who pride themselves on their own virtue by comparing themselves with others.

Robin proposes to judge the religions of the world for their effects on the worshipers and for the governments associated with the religions. The key terms of the paradigm he will use to judge all people are terms he considers universal: "justice", "mercy", "unselfishness", "self-control", and "rationality". Robin's goal is to show that Christianity is a civilizing influence on a nation. Even though many subjects of a nation state such as England may not be Christian, Christianity may civilize them. Defoe enunciates this idea to explain his simultaneous criticism of and confidence in his own society:

> Wherever Christianity has been planted or profess'd nationally in the World, even where it has not had a Saving influence, it has yet had a Civilizing Influence: It has operated upon the Manners, the Morals, the Politics, and even the Tempers and Dispositions of the People: It has reduc'd them to the Practice of Virtue, and to the true Methods of Living, wean'd them from the Barbarous Customs they had been used to, infusing a Kind of Humanity and softness of disposition into their very Natures; civilizing and softening them, teaching them to love a Regularity of Life, and filling them with Principles of generous Kindness and Beneficence one to another.[62]

Robin's crusade

The least-known portion of Defoe's Robinson Crusoe series is Robin's final proposal for a "Crusado".[63] The proposal repays examination as an example of Defoe's failed banter, coming as it does as part of his essay "Of the Proportion between the Christian and

---

[62] *Ibid.*, 129.

[63] "This is my crusado, and it would be a war as justifiable, on many accounts, as any that was ever undertaken in the world; a war, that would bring eternal honour to the conquerors, and an eternal blessing to the people conquered" (*ibid.*, 253).

Pagan World". Robin's survey of the position of Christianity in the world has convinced him that Christians are in a minority and that they have no effective mission program. In his distress, Robin suggests that the Christians of the world unite to send a crusade into non-Christian countries: "This is just but a very sad Account of the small Extent of Christian knowledge in the World: and were it considered as it ought, would put the most powerful Princes of Europe upon thinking of some Methods, at least, to open a Way for the spreading Christian Knowledge."

Robin admits "I am not much of the Opinion, indeed, that Religion should be planted by the Sword".[64] Nevertheless he thinks a military alliance could "beat Paganism out of the World" and "beat the very Name of Mahomet out of the World". To modern ears, the proposal is so outrageous that ignoring it is more reasonable than attacking it. We can only judge the contemporary response by the fact that there was none.

The "crusado" is a puzzle because it is difficult to imagine what Defoe might have been trying to do with it. The fact that Gildon's pamphlet ridicules Robin's friendship with Roman Catholics and singles out the iconoclastic raid for special attention suggests that this crusade might be an attempt to develop the only story elements that had aroused response. This proposed crusade, however, received no eager affirmation, no indignant refutation, and no somber consideration from readers in its day.

The shortest way with the pagans
Robin's crusade is only loosely linked to Robin's travels. In the very last paragraph he makes reference to "all my Travels and Illuminations".[65] The proposed crusade, however, is closely tied to Robin's criticism of European Christianity. The chapter has three arguments for a crusade. None of them has any positive force. First, God can bring good out of evil; second, a war against pagans would be more just than a war between Christians; and third, Christians go to war with each other constantly over trade. Each argument gives Robin an occasion to speak against problems he sees in Christian Europe. Since Robin was not in a position to lead a crusade, and since, as we have seen, *Serious Reflections During the Life and Surprising*

---

[64] *Ibid.*, 250.
[65] *Ibid.*, 270.

Adventures of Robinson Crusoe focuses on Europe, it seems reasonable to suggest that Robin's proposed crusade is another instance of Defoe writing a banter.

If we consider Robin's proposal to be one more of Defoe's failed jokes it makes some sense. The new crusade is a proposal laced with absurdities, inconsistencies, and factual errors. It is designed to explode in the hands of anyone who picks it up. Refuting the proposal, however, might make Christians pay attention to the shocking lack of Christian unity in England. Only when the proposal's implications elicit an indignant repudiation does its logic speak to Defoe's concerns. This proposal repeats the strategy Defoe used in *The Shortest-Way with the Dissenters* in 1702. Defoe here has Robin playing the fool by suggesting a violent and absurd crusade, one that Defoe expects the discerning reader to reject.

This crusade does sound like something Robinson Crusoe would suggest. Robin enjoys military demonstrations, but he does not have the ability to foresee trouble. Robin is not a reliable spiritual or intellectual leader. It sounds like Robin's suggestion because it is so impractical and so theatrical. The more fundamental question is whether a crusade sounds like something Daniel Defoe would have suggested in his own voice.

The challenge of distinguishing Defoe from the narrators of his works has tantalized and defeated generations of Defoe biographers, as P.N. Furbank and W.R. Owens demonstrate in their study of the history of Defoe scholarship. The distinction between author and narrator has been especially hard to draw in the case of the *Robinson Crusoe* series. Defoe wrote a polemic introduction to *Serious Reflections During the Life and Surprising Adventures of Robinson Crusoe* in which he seems to identify his life with that of Robinson. At the same time he affirms the story of Don Quixote as his model.

The European problems that drive Robin's crusade proposal certainly troubled Defoe. He often expressed distress at the spectacle of Christian disunity. He had suffered from the antagonism in England between the Church of England and Dissenters. In European affairs, he deplored the divisions between Christians that led some of them to make alliances with the Muslim Turks. In his *Review* of 21 August 1707 he warns against the Protestants calling in the Turks against the Hapsburg Emperor: "it is not a light thing to call the Turks into Europe, and I would fain have those that are so forward, to call the

Turks down upon the Emperor, examine a little what would be the condition of Europe, if the Turk should reduce the Empire, take Vienna, establish a Vizer there, and possess all the lower Austria."[66]

Defoe's experiences as a member of a persecuted minority in Christian England made him aware of how ugly fighting religious battles could be. His life as a Dissenter also put him in contact with the one Protestant mission experiment active in his lifetime: the mission to the Indians in North America. Defoe was twenty-one in 1681 when he took notes on John Collins' sermons on "the Great Commission". John Collins moved to England from America and preached a series of six sermons in London on the Biblical text in Mark 16:15-16:

> Go ye into all the world and preach the Gospel unto every creature. He that believeth and is baptized shall be saved but he that believeth not shall be damned.

Defoe thought these sermons interesting enough to make a point of attending them and copying his notes into a special exercise book. Collins preached once a month on this theme, and Defoe heard five of the six sermons, making a note in his book that he had not been able to listen to one of them "being absent in the country". This topic was obviously important to him as a young adult.[67]

For the rest of his life he remained a member of Dissenting assemblies, in spite of the political inconveniences he suffered for this allegiance. He kept track of the efforts to convert the Native Americans to Christianity and of the difficulties colonists suffered in their conflict with the Native Americans. His library included works by Increase Mather and Mary Rowlandson. The Olive Payne sale catalogue lists one copy of Rowlandson's captivity narrative and two copies of Increase Mather's *A Brief History of the Indian Wars*.[68] These particular books deal with the wars that followed such radical attempts at Indian evangelization as the establishment of special Indian villages where the Indians could be weaned away from their pagan social customs. By the time Defoe wrote The *Serious*

---

[66] Defoe, *Review*, IV, 312.

[67] Daniel Defoe, unpublished notes 1680-1681. *Writings of Daniel Defoe*, ed. J.R. Moore, Ann Arbor, MI: University Microfilms, number 1.

[68] Payne, *Libraries*, Item LO565.

Reflections During the Life and Surprising Adventures of Robinson Crusoe, the failure of these methods had become clear. It is not likely that any of the Dissenters would have supported Indian wars as a crusade, or that Daniel Defoe would have suggested one. There were hideous Indian wars in the Americas, but they were not done in the name of evangelism.

One notable textual clue to the nature of the proposal comes in the matter-of-fact description of what the crusade would involve. When challenged for practical details of his proposal by "Men of good Judgment" Robin imagines attacking an "infinitely populous" island, like Japan, inhabited by "a most sensible sagacious People under excellent Forms of Government, and capable more than ordinarily of receiving Impressions, supported by the Argument and example of a virtuous and religious Conqueror".[69] Robin argues that sensible people, once overcome "by a moderate, and, as far as in them lies, a bloodless Conquest" would admire the restraint of their Conquerors and "embrace that Truth which dictated such just Principles to those who espoused it".[70] Naturally, there would be a strong element of coercion for those who did not submit:

> In Case any rejected the Instruction of religious Men and adhered obstinately to his Idolatry, and would not be reclaimed by gentle and Christian Usage, suitable Methods are to be taken with such, that they might not make a religious Faction in the Country and gain others to side with them in order to recover their Liberty, as they might call it, to serve their own Gods, that is to say, Idols.[71]

The switch to passive voice and euphemism is chilling. This is a "Shortest Way" for pagans.

Modern readers who see the proposal as a bad joke must admit that Robin's suggestion was prophetic. The economic and political system being developed by European trade, did exactly what Defoe proposed. It discredited ethnic religions. Seventy years later when the English missionary William Carey went to India as a translator and teacher English churches supported him. In fact, Carey also had military backup, since India by then had been declared a part of the British Empire.

---

[69] Defoe, *Serious Reflections During the Life and Surprising Adventures of Robinson Crusoe*, 264.

[70] *Ibid.*, 252

[71] *Ibid.*, 267.

Providence: submission and dialogue

"Listening to the Voice of Providence" pulls together many of the theological and epistemological questions about God's Providence that run through the narrative volumes. Robin turns Gildon's charge of superstition back onto English culture. He attacks what he calls the "felony or robbery ... the treason" of ordinary Englishmen who set up "hap, luck, chance" as idols "more inconsistent than those I mentioned among the Chinese".[72]

Charles Gildon is not the only Christian who considers that a proper respect for God's Providence should mean submission to authority – in society, in family relations, in logic, in life's events. This has been a common, if mistaken, interpretation of the Protestant idea that God is sovereign.[73] In his essay "On Listening to the Voice of Providence" Defoe has Robin undercut the formal categories and syllogistic method of argument that Gildon thought God's dignity demanded. That syllogistic style of argumentation had led to the logical impasses that Friday, Will Atkins' native wife, and Robin himself had noticed: If God is all powerful and just and good, why does he allow evil? And why has God kept his plan secret from so many people? The questions are unanswerable, as Robin had demonstrated. Defoe's solution re-focuses the role of Providence from a logical premise to a personal communication. This solution pictures a way to respect Providence by active listening. Defoe's Providence does not require submission, but conversation.

Robin argues that communication with God should be reasonable, imaginative, and dynamic. The language of Providence is not a human language of sounds, words, and grammar, but a language of event, action, and motivation for action. He postulates a speaker, God, who desires to communicate with beings capable of perceiving the words and grammar of this language. Defoe was working creatively within his own theological tradition that told him that God speaks in two different ways: through experience (the world) as well as through direct revelation (the Word). As the 1646 Westminster Confession of Faith puts it: "Although the light of nature; and the works of creation;

---

[72] *Ibid.*, 233.

[73] Charles Partee's recent study, *The Theology of John Calvin,* Louisville: KY, 2008 addresses this issue: "While Calvin firmly believes in God's universal providence he focuses on special providence because he thinks more in experiential and personal terms than in logically impersonal categories" (114).

and providence; do so far manifest the goodness, wisdom, and power of God, as to leave men inexcusable; yet are they not sufficient to give that knowledge of God and of His will, which is necessary unto salvation."[74] Robin declares that he has put himself under the discipline of listening to the voice of God in his work – as distinguished from his word.[75]

God works through reason, says Robin, but not only by argument and logic. Reason involves observation of events and desires. God has arranged events into patterns of cause and effect, and God intends people to notice these patterns. The main evidence of Providential design is open to inspection: "events shall attend upon causes in a direct chain, and by an evident necessity, and has doubtless left many powers of good and evil seemingly to ourselves, and, as it were, in our hands as the natural product of such causes and consequences."[76] Here Defoe echoes the traditional Christian formulation which had been reaffirmed in the sixteenth-century Reformation in testimonies such as this from John Calvin:

> This skillful ordering of the universe is for us a sort of mirror in which we can contemplate God, who is otherwise invisible. The reason why the prophet attributes to the heavenly creatures a language known to every nation (Ps 19.2) is that therein lies an attestation of divinity so apparent that it ought not to escape the gaze of even the most stupid tribe.[77]

Robin suggests that people hear the voice of Providence through perception and reflection. Robin claims that the correct chain of cause and effect is to be found in "the silent voice ... of His managing events and causes", and the sequence of "visible Punishments follow[ing] visible Crimes".[78] Even in less obvious ways, he says, incidents form coincidences – a "Concurrence between the Actions of Men which it

---

[74] Westminster Confession, Chapter 1 "Of the Holy Scriptures" (1689) (http://www.vor.org/truth/1689/1689bc01.html).

[75] Defoe, *Serious Reflections During the Life and Surprising Adventures of Robinson Crusoe*, 225.

[76] *Ibid.*, 211.

[77] John Calvin, *The Institutes of the Christian Religion* (1559), ed. John T. McNeill, trans. Ford Lewis Battles, Philadelphia, 1960, 52-53.

[78] Defoe, *Serious Reflections During the Life and Surprising Adventures of Robinson Crusoe*, 216, 217.

does not approve or does approve, and the Reward of these Actions in this World".

Robin thinks there is a second kind of communication in the world: God's clock on which significant events coincide in the calendar. This Divine chronology is usually invisible, but men can read it.[79] Careful readers will remember Robin's sense of awe at noticing that he had been shipwrecked on the very day of the year he had taken his first sea voyage from Hull. This kind of coincidence implies, Robin says, that in God's chronology all the events are happening on schedule. At the end of this sequence Robin lists the kind of "secret hints" that Gildon had called "the Dregs of Popery".[80] These are "hints, impulses, allegories, mysteries" which "He expected we should take notice of, and take warning by".[81] How much Defoe agrees with Robin here is not clear.

Robin's use of human language as a metaphor for God's work in governing the world is generally orthodox and traditional. Nevertheless, Defoe's argument undercuts the readers who thought that Robin had learned "Submission to the Divine Will".[82] Defoe's picture of submission is the kind of active energetic dialogue with God that Robin demonstrates on his island after his conversion. Max Weber and his generation of modern scholars explain Puritan economic dynamism as built on a sense of duty, but Weber could not explain Puritan individualism.[83] David Little's re-working of Max Weber's analysis provides an explanation that sees the Puritans as radical revolutionaries who were building a society based on dynamic and voluntary obedience to God, not passive obedience to rules and commandments.[84] This energy permeates Robin's discussion of Providence, and corrects both Gildon's reading and Cox's reading of Robin's life.

Robin pictures reciprocal action between God and man. God "expected" human beings to notice cause and effect, rewards and

---

[79] *Ibid.*, 219.

[80] Gildon, *The Life and Strange Surprizing Adventures of Mr D.....De F...*, 26.

[81] Defoe, *Serious Reflections During the Life and Surprising Adventures of Robinson Crusoe*, 212.

[82] Amsterdam Coffee House Preface.

[83] Little, *Religion, Order, and Law*, 30.

[84] *Ibid.*, 40.

punishments, and even intimations of results.[85] People who listen to the voice of Providence are those who learn its language. They are not "supinely and unconcernedly passive" but are active and alert. People are intended to "converse with the acting part of Providence".[86] Robin says that Christian submission is not to be stupid, lethargic, or passive as if Christians were outside of God's care:

> To be utterly careless of ourselves in such cases and talk of trusting Providence, is a lethargy of the worst nature; for as we are to trust Providence with our estates, but to use, at the same time, all diligence in our callings, so we are to trust Providence with our safety, but with our eyes open to all its necessary cautions, warning, and instructions, many of which Providence is pleased to give us in the course of life for the direction of our conduct.[87]

Submission to Providence is part of the learning process, but in Robin's mouth even submission becomes active. For him, the verb "submit" is a transitive verb not a reflexive one: Robin encourages Christians to be active – in submitting "all events to Providence"[88] for analysis and discussion.

---

[85] Defoe, *Serious Reflections During the Life and Surprising Adventures of Robinson Crusoe*, 212.
[86] *Ibid.*, 231.
[87] *Ibid.*, 221.
[88] *Ibid.*, 211.

CHAPTER NINE

THE END OF THE DEBATE

The popularity of the pirate abridgement published by Edward Midwinter In 1722, just two years after Defoe published his third volume of the series, shows that Defoe had both won and lost the struggle over his text. According to Erhard Dahl, this Midwinter abridgement would be the basis for forty subsequent abridgements before 1819.[1] Defoe had won. The public loved *Robinson Crusoe* and rejected Gildon's attacks on the story. But Defoe lost the argument over interpretation. Robin the quixotic trader had become Robinson the heroic survivor.

Defoe's interactive epistemology

During his lifetime Defoe participated in changes in publishing and reading changes, but he could not control those changes. He was a victim of his own success. Recent studies of this period, such as Nancy Armstrong and Lawrence Tennenhouse's *The Imaginary Puritan*, emphasize the power of the text in shaping readers:

> We have insisted all along that fiction was instrumental in producing a new imagined community that was the basis for both a nation and a new ruling class. Daniel Defoe's *Robinson Crusoe* provides a partial fable for the emergence of the modern middle class .... In this respect, the novel might be called an instrument as well as a model of the process we want to articulate.[2]

Armstrong and Tennenhouse see *The Life and Strange Surprising Adventures of Robinson Crusoe* as an agent of social change. They

---

¹ Dahl, *Die Kürtzungen*, 197.
² Armstrong and Tennenhouse, *The Imaginary Puritan*, 184.

argue that novels as well as newspapers formed readers into new groups linked by shared experiences of reading. Their view incorporates Benedict Anderson's insight that new ways of publishing and reading texts created new ways of experiencing one's self. Anderson's emphasis on the unifying effect of a shared print culture echoes Robin's self-identification as a representative Englishman in the first volume of the series: "The convergence of capitalism and print technology on the ... diversity of human language created the possibility of a new form of imagined community, which in its basic morphology set the stage for the modern nation."[3] I argue that Defoe's experience with the *Robinson Crusoe* series demonstrates the reciprocal nature of this process. Sometimes the community's reading of texts shapes the texts.

The eighteenth-century revolution in popular literacy, sketched earlier in Chapter Two, grew out of a religious and epistemological revolution. Journal-keeping Protestants put into everyday practice the inductive reasoning recommended by Francis Bacon and the introspection practiced by John Locke. The new patterns of private record keeping were developed in Protestant spiritual life to help people recognize the patterns of Providential communication. These habits also enabled the journal keepers to recognize psychological patterns. They became alert to patterns of interpretation as well as to patterns of cause and effect.

The reception of early novels also grew out of a culture of face-to-face social interaction, both in families and in the towns and cities of England. Jürgen Habermas reminds us that novels often were read aloud in a family setting, and that they elicited discussion as they were read.[4] Reading novels out loud in a family setting made it normal for family members to discuss characters' motives and self-awareness. Such reading made discussion of the characters' self-knowledge part of the enjoyment of the text.

As we have seen, in telling the story of Robin's first days on the island, Defoe demonstrates that the events of our lives can receive varying interpretations. The activity of interpretation itself becomes part of the action of reading *The Life and Strange Surprising Adventures of Robinson Crusoe*. Defoe shows us that individuals may

---

[3] *Ibid.*, 46.
[4] Habermas, *The Structural Transformation of the Public Sphere*, 83.

not recognize the patterns in their own lives. It takes Robin a long time to realize that he has been "delivered", though readers see how often the term appears in his account. In Robin's final word, the "Vision from the Angelick World" at the end of *Serious Reflections During the Life and Surprising Adventures of Robinson Crusoe*, Robin emphasizes his earlier spiritual blindness by pointing out how wild and frantic his thoughts had become before he rescued Friday near the end of his stay on the island.[5]

Defoe's banter technique

By the time he wrote *The Life and Strange Surprising Adventures of Robinson Crusoe* Defoe had been a journalist for fifteen years. He was used to writing for readers who varied greatly in intellectual sophistication. His pamphlets and journals appealed to a mass market and were designed to elicit immediate response. Nevertheless, his readers often failed to pick up on his use of irony. Frequent instances of public anger and misunderstanding marked the reception of his work. Why did Defoe keep on using this kind of irony if he was aware of the danger of misinterpretation?

One possibility is that he was driven by motives he did not understand and control. Some critics take this approach. We have seen this explanation used in the case of his pamphlet *The Shortest Way With the Dissenters*, discussed in Chapter Three. Laura Curtis explains Defoe as a man driven by psychological forces he could not analyze. Curtis finds that in Defoe's *Review* writing "the ultimate aim of his ordering was to construct an ideal world of peace and of clarity".[6] Defoe's other personality, says Curtis, "is irresistibly drawn to a real world of disorder and impulse". In this disordered world, Curtis thinks, "Elements from the ideal and the real world are present in Defoe's fiction and in his non-fiction, and frequently the mixture is unstable".[7] Curtis asks us to think of him as "a worldly, even cynical man with a rather peculiar sense of humour" when he was writing

---

[5] Defoe, *Serious Reflections During the Life and Surprising Adventures of Robinson Crusoe*, "Vision", 12. The "Vision from the Angelick World" section of this volume has separate pagination.
[6] Curtis, *The Elusive Daniel Defoe*, 59.
[7] *Ibid.*, 8.

Moll Flanders.[8] She identifies Defoe with Moll: "the fear of others expressed by [Moll's] secretiveness found its vent, in Defoe as well as in Moll, in making fools of other people." Curtis thinks that Defoe's need to make fools of others "occurs only intermittently in the ideal world of *Robinson Crusoe* where fear of others is overcome through long and patient toil and prayer performed in isolation from society".[9]

My explanation for Defoe's use of irony is that he was trying to provoke his readers to make them examine their own ideas. He thought that he knew the readers' frames of reference. He thought the things he wanted to say required the kind of two-stage recognition elicited by ironic speech in order to have the effect he wanted. This analysis of Defoe's writing as attempted dialogue takes seriously the idea that a written text is the kind of written speech act whose success depends on its readers' perception and co-operation.

Defoe's participation in pamphlet exchanges had established him as a professional writer. In two early exchanges, discussed in Chapters Two and Three, he developed his idea of "banter" to identify and label his kind of indirect argumentation. He tried to provoke his readers into self-analysis. This tactic is one he would use frequently. When he was trying to persuade his fellow Englishmen that France was a dangerous opponent, for example, he entitled his newspaper *A Review of the Affairs of France*. Some of his readers thought he was praising France to the harm of his own nation. To readers who accused him of glorifying the enemy, he said: "My design is plain: to tell you the strength of your enemy that you may fortify yourselves in due proportion, and not go out with your ten thousands against his twenties."[10] In short, he hoped to provoke his readers to listen to his praise of France, look back at their own country, and try to make whatever changes were necessary to outdo the French.

If the readers failed to pick up Defoe's implication he would respond in his next pamphlet or in his next edition of the *Review*. This ironic mode of communication is fraught with possibilities for miscommunication. Audiences who fail to perceive irony often

---

[8] *Ibid.*, 147.

[9] *Ibid.*, 149.

[10] Defoe, *Review*, Volume I, Preface, February 1705, in *The Best of Defoe's Review*, ed. William L. Payne, New York, 1951, 4.

become angry. In fact, some of Defoe's contemporaries did become angry with him. As we have seen, they accused him of lying.

Defoe's negotiations of genre

Defoe's introductions to the three volumes of his *Robinson Crusoe* series carry on a dialogue with his critics and provide directions on how his story is to be read. In all of these prefaces Defoe incorporates some of the interactive qualities of other popular print genres. These introductory essays also serve to add complexity to the character of Robin, the mariner from York. Defoe's identification with his character Robin is more ironic than many of his contemporary readers and most modern critics assume. By means of the misinterpretations and abridgements of his texts, readers persistently reduce that ironic distance.

Defoe was very conscious that he was dependant on the conventions of reading. As a writer of fiction, Defoe assumed the same interactive mode he used in his political pamphlets. His comments on his early pamphlets indicate that he calculated a dialogue with readers as part of the text. The same calculation is obvious in his polemic introductions to the second and third volumes of the *Robinson Crusoe* series. His writing presents London life as part of a global political drama, a drama in which he and his readers were both actors and audience. The fact that neither he nor most of the readers had direct political power did not prevent them from engaging in political debate, as Habermas explains: "From the outset those bourgeois strata of the Protestant middle class, involved in business and commerce (whose capitalist interests had been behind their substantial support of the Revolution, without now being represented in Parliament), formed something like a steadily expanding pre-parliamentary forum."[11]

Defoe and his readers were part of contemporary political discussion that regularly used satire and irony. Defoe, like many of his fellow writers, had polemic goals for all his work – including his first – person narratives. If these goals were not explicitly stated, they were implied. Nevertheless his readers emphasized other aspects of the text than its complex analysis of individuality, as the story of Defoe's text

---

[11] Habermas, *The Structural Transformation of the Public Sphere*, 62-63.

clearly shows. Contemporary abridgements indicate that Defoe's readers thought Robin's story celebrated independence from tradition and parental domination, at the same time as the narrator gave lip service to the importance of fatherhood and family duty.

The Farther Adventures of Robinson Crusoe and the essays in *Serious Reflections During the Life and Surprising Adventures of Robinson Crusoe* show Defoe attempting to point his readers toward the implications and context he had in mind for the story of Robin, the trader from York. The relative failures of both these volumes show that the story had slipped out of his control. Defoe's futile attempts to regain control over the text provide a unique window on the negotiation of authorial power.

Thomas Gent's admiring alchemy

As we have already noted in Chapter One, the 1722 Midwinter abridgement of the *Robinson Crusoe* series was actually written by Thomas Gent. The close relationship between the Preface to this abridgement and the editorial choices made in the abridgement itself make it likely that Gent wrote the Preface to the volume. Edward Midwinter and his associates published it. This abridgement is the only one that really attempts to treat all three of Defoe's volumes. The publisher presents Gent's work as a respectful treatment of Defoe's work, calling it a "very faithful abridgement", and promising "there is not one material Circumstance omitted neither is there any deprived of its most proper Observations".[12] Nevertheless, this abridgement ignores one very important political-religious theme Defoe introduces in *The Life and Strange Surprising Adventures of Robinson Crusoe* and carries through to *Serious Reflections During the Life and Surprising Adventures of Robinson Crusoe*: the difficulty of seeing Christianity as a world religion.

The Midwinter abridgement shows how the argument between Defoe and Gildon turned out. The abridger's Preface emphasizes the immediate and lasting popularity of Defoe's *The Life and Strange Surprising Adventures of Robinson Crusoe*. Gildon had said that only riff-raff, "the very *Canaille*", liked the book.[13] He was wrong. Nevertheless, Gildon was right to see that *The Farther Adventures of*

---

[12] Gent, *Midwinter Abridgement*, Preface.
[13] Gildon, *The Life and Strange Surprizing Adventures of Mr D.....De F...*, 32.

Robinson Crusoe was much less attractive than the first volume. The Midwinter abridgement acknowledges this difference by its proportions and its emphasis even though the book promises to be an abridgement of all three volumes.

Gent's Midwinter Preface sides with Defoe rather than Gildon in the argument over the literary status of the *Robinson Crusoe* series. The Midwinter Preface suggests that "the greatest Objection that many raise against these Surprizing Adventures is, by them supposing the Story to be fictitious: that there never was such a man as Robinson Crusoe". In answering this objection, Gent closely echoes "Robinson Crusoe's Preface" from *Serious Reflections*: "Granting the Relation is Allegorical, yet, I assure you, it is Historical too; and is in short a beautiful Representation of a Life of the most unprecedented and remarkable Contingence." For Gent, the heart of the first volume is Robin's anguish. As he sees it, Robin's story is not about colonies, trade, or travel, but about Robin's emotional suffering and his survival on the island. Gent seems very appreciative of Robin's reflections. He thinks the book offers solace to anyone in trouble: "you will find so many curious Moral Observations, so many Divine Reflections to comfort the afflicted Mind, and such a Heavenly Prospect of the wonderful Providence of God that scarce any who read it but may make some Application of it to themselves, and pleasingly be led to the knowledge of the Divine Blessings."[14]

Nevertheless, Gent's simplification of the story of the first volume rewrites it into a series of actions virtually without commentary. Gildon had complained that Robin was "a strange, whimsical, inconsistent Being".[15] Gent's version makes Robin a consistent character by continuing the process of consolidation and simplification that made the Robinson Crusoe story into a myth of survival. Such a reading of the first volume must have been as common already then as it is now. Pat Rogers summarizes the publication history: "The shipwreck and its aftermath in the days, weeks, and months immediately following clearly constitute the major point of interest for most compilers."[16] This interest explains why the first volume was a best-seller. All over the world other authors redid

---

[14] Gent, *Midwinter Abridgement*, Preface.
[15] Gildon, *The Life and Strange Surprizing Adventures of Mr D.....De F...*, viii.
[16] Rogers, "Classics and Cannibals", 39.

the story of an isolated shipwrecked European. That experience of isolation, with its challenges and suffering, was the paradigmatic tale that readers wanted.

Gent thinks that Robin is a believable and sympathetic character. His abridged version retains Robin's intense emotional swings and his active engagement in his own salvation. None of the abridgers could make Robin into someone who really should have stayed home and submitted to his father's advice. Nor could they make him a model of submission to the will of Providence. His story simply has too much action in it for such a reading. On the contrary, he becomes the model of a self-made man.

Gent's abridgement tries to say that one should submit patiently to the will of Providence. Gent removes most of Robin's self-criticism and doubts, but he does not cut out any of Robin's remorse over disobeying his father. As a result, Robin's shipwreck on his island becomes simply punishment for disobedience to a god-like father, as in some of the earlier abridgements.

The same kind of alteration shapes Gent's abridgement of *The Farther Adventures of Robinson Crusoe*. In Defoe's telling, when Robin is afraid he will be falsely accused of being a pirate and hanged by English and Dutch vigilante sea captains, Robin acts quickly to save himself and his partner. He is terrified and furious. He reflects that in this case he is innocent, though in most other cases he had been his own worst enemy.[17] Gent's Robin just feels sorry for himself. He thinks he is like "unhappy innocent Persons who, being over power'd by blasphemous and perjur'd evidences, wickedly resolve to take away their lives, or ruin their Reputation, have no other Recourse in this World to ease their unspeakable Sorrow but Sighs and Prayers and Tears."[18]

Gent thought Defoe's book was both religious and patriotic. One religious guideline in Gent's interpretation of the story shows very clearly in Robin's reaction to the loss of the wrecked ship when a storm carries it away. Defoe's Robin says, "I Lost no time ... [but] gave over any more thoughts of the Ship".[19] Gent's hero, by contrast,

---

[17] Defoe, *The Farther Adventures of Robinson Crusoe*, 265.
[18] Gent, *Midwinter Abridgement*, 307.
[19] Defoe, *The Life and Strange Surprising Adventures of Robinson Crusoe*, 67.

says "I comforted myself in the best manner and entirely submitted to the will of Providence".[20]

Gent's simplification of the action, his reduction of Robin's self-criticism, and his construction of an emotionally submissive Robin change the moral focus of the story. But Robin's actions resist being interpreted as submission. Robin suffered, but he did not give up. Since all the abridgers tried to keep the action of the story, they ended up with a story with an assumed moral but very little commentary. It is easy to see that the story of a triumphant European survivor was relevant to European colonizing culture. The fearless individual, who enjoys the challenges of survival and who transforms a wilderness into an English farm, seemed right to the abridgers and to the readers.

Robin, the exemplary Englishman

The Midwinter abridgement, like the Amsterdam Coffee House abridgement, makes Robin a paragon of specifically English endurance, ingenuity, and strength of character. As the worldwide popularity of Robin's adventures indicates, people everywhere could identify with Robin. Defoe makes Robin more alert to the unity of humankind in *The Farther Adventures of Robinson Crusoe*, whereas Gent's Robin is still a model Englishman in *The Farther Adventures of Robinson Crusoe*. The Spanish Governor of the Robin's island tells Robin, "Englishmen had, in their Distress, the greatest Presence of Mind than those of any other Country that he had met with".[21] Gent takes this directly from *The Farther Adventures of Robinson Crusoe*, but he deletes the next paragraph in which Defoe's Robin refuses the extraordinary credit: "I told them that their case and mine differ'd exceedingly ... [the] Supplies I had providentially thrown into my Hands by the unexpected driving of the Ship on Shore was such as would have encourag'd any Creature in the World to have apply'd himself as I had done."[22]

In order to preserve the moral stature of Englishmen, Gent had to modify Robin's story of the Massacre on Madagascar. Gent's abridgement includes the massacre but changes its emphasis. Instead

---

[20] Gent, *Midwinter Abridgement*, 30.
[21] Defoe, *The Farther Adventures of Robinson Crusoe*, 128; Gent, *Midwinter Abridgement*, 256.
[22] Defoe, *The Farther Adventures of Robinson Crusoe*, 127.

of plunder, the abridged version stresses revenge as the sailors' main motive. In both versions the sailors find their friend's corpse before they start their rampage, but Defoe's original stresses the sailors' hope of finding plunder: "When they went out, their chief Design was Plunder, and they were in mighty Hopes of finding Gold there; but a Circumstance which none of them were aware of, set them on Fire with Revenge, and made Devils of them all."[23]

The abridgement cuts down on Robin's expressions of horror. Phrases such as "what Devil it was possessed them"[24] do not appear, nor do some of the most vivid elements of Robin's descriptions – naked men and women running from their assailants. The abridged version refers to only one of the parallel massacres in the original text and focuses the guilt for that massacre onto Cromwell: "But surely never was such a Scene of Horror beheld, or more dismal cries heard before, except at the Time of that vile Traytor and Usurper Oliver Cromwell's taking of Drogheda in Ireland, where he neither spared Man, Woman or Child."[25] Defoe's original text cites two analogies and makes the sailors' violence appear common:

> … the Cries of the poor People were now of quite another Nature, and fill'd us with Horror. I must confess, I never was at the sacking of a City, or at the taking of a Town by Storm. I had heard of Oliver Cromwell taking Drogheda in Ireland, and killing man, Woman, and child: And I had read of Count Tilly, sacking the city of Magdeburgh, and cutting the Throats of 22 – of all Sexes: but I never had an Idea of the thing itself before, nor is it possible to describe it, or the Horror that was upon our Minds at hearing it.[26]

Such changes reduce similarities between English sailors and the Spanish conquistadors or Caribbean cannibals. The abridgement also omits the paragraph in Defoe's original that compares Robin's abandonment by his English nephew and the crew of English sailors to other acts of mutiny and piracy on European ships: "Here I had the particular Pleasure, speaking by Contraries, to see the Ship set sail

---

[23] *Ibid.*, 229.

[24] *Ibid.*, 236.

[25] Gent, *Midwinter Abridgement*, 292.

[26] Defoe, *The Farther Adventures of Robinson Crusoe*, 234.

without me, a Treatment I think a Man in my Circumstances scarce ever met with, except from Pirates running away with a Ship, and setting those that would not agree with their Villainy on Shore; indeed this was next Door to it, both ways."[27]

Gent's editorial slant

Gent takes a radical approach to abridging Defoe's *Serious Reflections During the Life and Surprising Adventures of Robinson Crusoe*. He does go to the trouble of preserving the outline of Defoe's third volume, but he cuts the essays ruthlessly. He reduces Defoe's essay "Upon Honesty" from fifty-six pages to a page and three quarters. Gent keeps Defoe's concept of generosity as honesty and he links honesty with the status of a "gentleman".[28] This is all that remains of Defoe's attempt to replace the aristocratic honor ethic with the middle-class ethic of honesty. Gone is the long opening discussion of the honesty Robin had met in his travels, and with that link goes Defoe's attempt to undercut the search for plunder as a motive for world travel. Also gone is the six-page section in which Robin explains that fathers are supposed to direct their children to careers the children will enjoy. This section was Defoe's determined attempt to redirect his readers from the simplistic interpretation of Robin as a prodigal.

Gent virtually reduces the volume to its final segment, renamed "Robinson Crusoe's Vision of the Angelick World". In Defoe's *Serious Reflections During the Life and Surprising Adventures of Robinson Crusoe* this final essay is the one in which Robin explores the way Providence can speak through imagination, dreams, coincidences and intuition. Gent's approach to abridging *Serious Reflections During the Life and Surprising Adventures of Robinson Crusoe* suggests his own interest in individual psychology rather than the analysis of world religions. He does not even notice Robin's proposed colonial crusade.

Although Gent cut out most of Defoe's second volume, he also added material. Defoe had not written a chapter on Robin's suffering. In fact, Defoe's Preface to *Serious Reflections During the Life and Surprising Adventures of Robinson Crusoe* speaks not of submission

---

[27] *Ibid.*, 247.
[28] Gent, *Midwinter Abridgement*, 340.

and suffering but of "Invincible Patience", "indefatigable Application", and "undaunted Resolution".[29] Gent, nevertheless, is sure he knows exactly how Robin feels. He has a poem of his own which fits the mood of *Robinson Crusoe* the way he reads it, so he supplies a short chapter on "Suffering Affliction", and he centers the chapter on his poem. The speaker here prays for death:

> My God! You see most injured Innocence,
> Trampl'd upon, as guilty of Ofence.
> Prisons and Chains do threaten me each Hour;
> False Friends and Enemies their Malice Shower.
> To thee alone, to stop impending Doom
> Look down in Pity on my Prayers and Tears
> And save me from the World's beguiling Snares.
>
> With Joy, they clap, as when the guileful Snare
> Intraps th'unwary Choristor of Air.
> No Friends I have, forlorn I'm left alone,
> When Malice now, conceal'd before, is shown
> If not, yet while in Suffering I implore,
> Comfort my Soul; O Lord! I ask no more
> At last (O Pardon my Delay!) I come.

Serious reflections on international issues

Defoe's final chapters of *Serious Reflections During the Life and Surprising Adventures of Robinson Crusoe* examine some of the psychological and political implications of the *Robinson Crusoe* series. Robin describes the strain of having to act without the security of traditional economic and social frameworks. The fate of his island colony points to the need for a legal framework for international trade. Robin's story provokes discussion of the religious and ethical implications of world trade. Gent deletes the focus of Defoe's political and economic interest by ignoring Robin's love of trade. He also deletes Robin's concern with the religions of the world and with the limited extent of Christian influence.

Robin's story had asked questions that arise when people are moving away from traditional guides for moral evaluation. If simple

---

[29] Defoe, *Serious Reflections During the Life and Surprising Adventures of Robinson Crusoe*, Preface.

obedience to a parent or a king is not an option, if new situations and experiences prompt new responses, how are people to guide their action? Gildon had an answer: Rational Religion and Common Sense,[30] certainly not Defoe's "silent messengers ... whether sleeping or waking, whether directly or indirectly, whether by hints, impulses, allegories, mysteries or otherwise, we know not".[31] Robin's recipe for action is dialogue with Providence. This dialogue requires rational observation of human affairs. It also requires prayer and respectful observation of one's own feelings, intuitions, dreams, and imaginations.

Gent saw what readers ever since have found in *The Life and Strange Surprising Adventures of Robinson Crusoe*. The publication history of the *Robinson Crusoe* series shows that both the original volume and many different abridgements have remained popular. Both the Amsterdam Coffee House abridger and Gent claimed to admire Defoe's *Robinson Crusoe*. The subsequent transformation of the story to a chapbook version about Robin on the island demonstrates that abridgers and most readers focused on the same elements. They read the story to emphasize Robin's suffering in solitude, his delight in overcoming practical problems, and his love of adventure.

The elements deleted from the book – its questions about God's Providence and colonial violence – were scraps to be swept aside. After appearing harmless for a very long time, these elements have come back to haunt modern readers of the story as we can see from such recent reinterpretations as Tournier's *Friday*, J.M. Coetzee's *Foe*, and Derek Walcott's "Pantomime".[32]

No matter how we measure the success or failure of Defoe's *Robinson Crusoe*, novel readers everywhere can thank Defoe for showing that survival is a matter of spirit and mind as much as a matter of physical prowess. We can thank him for trying to demonstrate that simple physical labor can be interesting and

---

[30] Gidon, *The Life and Strange Surprizing Adventures of Mr D.....De F...*, 25.

[31] Defoe, *Serious Reflections During the Life and Surprising Adventures of Robinson Crusoe*, 212.

[32] Michel Tournier, *Friday*, trans. Norman Denny, New York, 1969; J.M. Coetzee, *Foe*, New York, 1986; Dereck Wolcott, "Pantomime", in *Remembrance and Pantomime: Two Plays*, New York, 1980.

satisfying.

The history of the text shows Defoe's own survival skills. He adventurously explored the possibilities of fiction as an interactive writing exercise. Because of his "banter" mode of discourse, however, his ironic echo of contemporary thought was often mistaken for approval. Just as Robin abandoned his extra-large dugout when he could not get it into the water, so Defoe abandoned his ironic mode of writing fiction. Even so, this self-ironic character remains alive in his story and speaks to modern readers about the dangers and delights of individuality and global economics.

BIBLIOGRAPHY

PRIMARY

Behn, Aphra, *All the Histories and Novels Written by the Late Ingenious Mrs Behn*, ed. Charles Gildon, London, 1699.

---, "Epistle Dedicatory", *Oroonoko* (London, 1688), ed. Joanna Lipking, New York, 1977.

Calvin, John, *Institutes of the Christian Religion* (1559), ed. John T. McNeill, trans. Ford Lewis Battles, Philadelphia: PA, 1960.

Carey, William, *An Enquiry into the Obligations of Christians to Use Means for the Conversion of the Heathen* (1792), Introduction by Keith E. Eitel, ed. John Pretlov, Dallas, TX: Criswell, 1988.

Cooke, Captain Edward, *A Voyage to the South Seas and round the world, perform'd in the year 1708, 1709, 1710, and 1711*, London, 1712.

Dampier, William, *A New Voyage Round the World, Seventh Edition*, (1729), ed. N.M. Penzer, London, 1927.

Defoe, Daniel, *An Appeal to Honour and Justice* (1715), in *The Shortest-Way with the Dissenters and Other Pamphlets*, Oxford, 1974.

---, *A Brief Explanation of A late pamphlet, entitul'd The Shortest Way with the Dissenters, The Shortest Way with the Dissenters: [Taken from Dr Sach---ll's Sermon] or Proposals for the Establishment of the Church.* By the Author of the True-born English-Man, London, 1703: Library of English Literature Microfiche, 1976, Fiche 40136.

---, *An Essay upon Projects*, London, 1697.

---, *The Family instructor, in three parts; I. Relating to fathers and children. II. To masters and servants, III. To husbands and wives. The 8th edition, corrected by the author*, London, 1720.

---, *The Farther Adventures of Robinson Crusoe; Being the Second and Last Part of His Life, and of the Strange Surprising Accounts of His Travels Round Three Parts of the Globe. Written by himself*, London, 1719.

---, *A Hymn to the Pillory* (London, 1703), in *The Shortest Way with the Dissenters and Other Pamphlets*, Oxford, 1974.

---, *Jure Divino: A Satyr in Twelve Books*, London, 1706: Library of English Literature Microfiche 1976, Fiche 11570.

---, *Legion's Humble address to the LORDS, with an answer to it*, London, 1704.

---, *The Letters of Daniel Defoe*, ed. George Harris Healey, Oxford, 1955.

---, *The Life and Strange Surprizing Adventures Of Robinson Crusoe, of York, Mariner: Who lived Eight and Twenty Years, all alone in an un-inhabited Island on the Coast of America, near the Mouth of the Great River of Oroonoque; Having been cast on Shore by Shipwreck, wherein all the Men perished by himself. With an Account how he was at last as strangely deliver's by Pyrates. Written by Himself*, London, 1719.

---, *The Life and Strange Surprizing Adventures of Robinson Crusoe .... deliver'd by Pyrates. Written Originally by Himself, and Now Faithfully Abridg'd in Which Not One Remarkable Circumstance is Omitted*, London, 1719 [Amsterdam Coffee House Abridgement].

---, Meditac[i]ons, 1681, in *Writings of Daniel Defoe*, ed. John Robert Moore, Ann Arbor, MI: University Microfilms, number 1.

---, *More Reformation. A Satyr upon himself. By the author of the true born English-man*, London, 1703: Eighteenth-Century Collections Online (Y.1703) 1325658-1001.

---, *Review*, I/5, ed. A.W. Secord, New York, 1938.

---, *Review*, Volume I, Preface, February 1705, in *The Best of Defoe's Review*, ed. William L. Payne, New York, 1951.

---, *Serious Reflections During the Life and Surprising Adventures of Robinson Crusoe: with his Vision of the Angelick World. Written by Himself*, London, 1720.

---, *The Shortest Way to Peace and Union* (1703), in *The Writings of Daniel Defoe*, ed. John Robert Moore, Ann Arbor, MI: University Microfilms, number 57.

---, *The Shortest-Way with the Dissenters: Or, proposals for the Establishment of the Church*, London, 1702, in *The Shortest Way with the Dissenters and Other Pamphlets by Daniel Defoe*, Oxford, 1927.

---, *A Tour Through the Whole Island of Great Britain*, abridged and edited P.N. Furbank, W.R. Owens, and A.J. Coulson, New Haven: CN, 1991.

---, *The True-Born Englishman* (1700), in *The Shortest-Way with the Dissenters and Other Pamphlets by Daniel Defoe*, Oxford, 1927.

---, *A True Collection of the Writings of the Author of the True Born English-man*, London, 1703.

---, "Unpublished sermon notes", in *Writings of Daniel Defoe*, ed. John Robert Moore, Ann Arbor, MI: University Microfilms, number 1.

Dunton, John, *The Life and Errors of John Dunton citizen of London: with the Lives and Characters of More than a Thousand Contemporary Divines, and other persons of literary eminence to which are added, Dunton's Conversations in Ireland; selections from his other genuine works and a faithful portrait of the Author*, (1704), London, 1818.

Funnell, William, *A Voyage Round the World: containing an Account of Capt. Dampier's Expedition into the South-Seas in the Ship St. George. With his Various Adventures and Engagements &c. Together with a Voyage from the West Coast of Mexico to East India*, London, 1729.

Gent, Thomas, *The Life and Most Surprizing Adventures of Robinson Crusoe, of York, who Lived Edith and Twenty Years in an Uninhabited island on the Coast of America, Lying Near the Mouth of the Great River of Oroonoque: Having been Cast on Shore by shipwreck, Wherein All the Men were Drowned but Himself: As Also a Relation How He was Wonderfully Deliver'd by Pyrates, The Whole three Volumes Faithfully Abridged, and Set Forth With Cuts Proper to the Subject*, 2nd edn, London, 1722 [Midwinter abridgement].

---, *The Life of Mr. Thomas Gent, printer of York; written by himself*. Written 1746, ed. Joseph Hunter, London, 1832.

---, "Preface" to the Midwinter abridgment of all three volumes of Robinson Crusoe, London, 1724.

Gildon, Charles, *The Complete Art of Poetry*, London, 1718.

---, *The Deist Manual: Or a Rational Enquiry into the Christian Religion*, London, 1705.

---, *A Grammar of the English Tongue*, London, 1711.

---, *The Golden Spy*, London, 1709.

---, *The Life and Strange Surprizing Adventures of Mr D..... De F...*, *of London, Hosier who Has liv'd above fifty Years by himself, in the Kingdoms of* North *and* South Britain. *The various Shapes he has appear'd in, and the Discoveries he has made for the Benefit of his Country.* In a Dialogue between *him, Robinson Crusoe,* and his Man *Friday.* with Remarks serious and Comical upon the Life of Crusoe, London, 1719, in Paul Dottin, *Robinson Crusoe Examin'd and Criticis'd*, London, 1923.

Heathcot's Intelligence, Daniel Defoe, *The life and strange adventures of Robinson Crusoe of York, Mariner: who lived eight and twety* [sic] *years alone in an uninhated* [sic] *island on the coast of America, near the mouth of the great river Oroonoque; having been cast on shore by shipwreck, wherein all the men perished but himself. With an account how he was at last strangely delivered by pyrates. Written by himself,* London: the *original London Post,* or *Heathcot's Intelligence,* Numbers 1125-289, 7 October 1719-20 October 1720.

Johnson, Captain Charles, *A General History of the Robberies and Murders of the Most Notorious Pirates* (1724), ed. David Cordingly, New York, 1998.

Le Comte, Louis, *Memoirs and Observations Topographical, Physical, Mathematical, Mechanical, Natural, Civil and Ecclesiastical. Made in a late Journey through the Empire of China, and Published in several Letters by Louis Le Comte, Jesuit* (1679), 2nd edn, trans., London, 1698.

Locke, John, *An Essay Concerning Human Understanding* (1689), Amherst: MA, 1995.

---, *The Second Treatise of Government* (1689), ed. Peter Laslett, Cambridge, 1969.

Mather, Cotton, *Magnalia Christie Americana: or the ecclesiastical history of New England from its first planting in the year 1620 unto the year of our Lord 1698*, London, 1702.

Montaigne, Michel de, "Of Cannibals" (1575), in Montaigne, *Selected Essays*, ed. Blanchard Bates, trans Charles Cotton and W. Hazlitt, New York, 1949.

Payne, Olive, *The Libraries of Daniel Defoe and Phillips Farewall*, (1731), ed. Helmut Heidenreich, Berlin, 1970.

Pope, Alexander, *An Essay on Man* (1733-34), ed. Maynard Mack, London, 1951.

Rogers, Woodes, *A cruising voyage round the world: first to the South-Sea, thence to the East-Indies, and homewards by the Cape of Good Hope, begun in 1708 and finish'd in 1711*, London, 1712.

Rousseau, Jean Jacques, *Emile* (1762), trans. and ed. William Boyd, New York, 1956.

Sharp, (Captain), *Captain Sharp's Journal of His Expedition* in *A Collection of Voyages in Four Volumes*, London, 1729, IV.

Steele, Richard, *The Englishman*, XXVI/3 (December 1713), ed. Rae Blanchard, Oxford, 1955, 106-109.

Westminster Confession, Chapter 1: "Of the Holy Scripture" (1689) (http://www.vor.org/truth/1689/1689bc01.html).

SECONDARY

Alkon, Paul, "Defoe's Argument in *The Shortest Way with the Dissenters*", *Modern Philology*, XXXVII/2 (May 1976), S12-23.

Amussen, Susan, "Gender, Family, and the Social Order, 1560-1725", in *Order and Disorder in Early Modern England*, eds Anthony Fletcher and John Stevenson, Cambridge, 1985, 196-217.

Anderson, Benedict, *Imagined Communities*, 2nd edn, London, 1991.

Armstrong, Nancy and Leonard Tennenhouse, *The Imaginary Puritan: Literature, Intellectual Labor, and the Origins of Personal Life*, Berkeley: CA, 1992.

Austin, J.L., *How To Do Things With Words* (1955), eds J.O. Urmson and Mariana Sbisa, 2nd edn, Oxford, 1992.

Backscheider, Paula, *Daniel Defoe: Ambition and Innovation*, Lexington: KY, 1986.

---, *Daniel Defoe, His Life*, Baltimore: MD, 1989.

---, "The Verse Essay, John Locke and Defoe's *Jure Divino*", *English Literary History*, 55 (Spring 1988), 92-124.

Bonner, Willard Hallam, *Captain William Dampier, Buccaneer-Author*, Stanford: CA, 1934.

Burgess, Donald, *The Pirates' Pact: The Secret Alliances Between History's Most Notorious Buccaneers and Colonial America*, New York, 2009.

Castle, Terry, *Masquerade and Civilization*, Stanford: CA, 1986.

Clark, J.D.D., "Providence, Predestination, and Progress: Or Did the Enlightenment Fail?", *Albion*, XXXV/4 (Winter 2003), 559-89.

Clark, Sandra, *Elizabethan Pamphleteers: Popular Moralistic Pamphlets 1580-1640*, Rutherford: NJ, 1983.

Coetzee, J.M., *Foe*, New York, 1986.

Cordingly, David, *Under the Black Flag: The Romance and the Reality of Life Among the Pirates*, New York, 1995.

---, Introduction, to Captain Charles Johnson, *A General History of the Robberies and Murders of the Most Notorious Pirates* (1724), New York, 1998.

Crichton, Michael, *Pirate Latitudes*, New York, 2009.

Culler, Jonathan, *Framing the Sign: Criticism and Its Institutions*, Oxford, 1988.

Curtis, Laura, *The Elusive Daniel Defoe*, London, 1984.

Dahl, Erhard, *Die Kürzungen des "Robinson Crusoe" in England zwischen 1719 und 1819 vor dem Hintergrund des zeitgenössischen Druckgewerbes, Verlagswesens und Lesepublikums*, Frankfurt am Main, 1977.

Donovan, Bill M., Introduction, to Bartolome de las Casas, *The Devastation of the Indies* (1551), trans. Herman Briffaul, Baltimore: MD, 1992, 1-25.

Dottin, Paul, *The Life and Strange Surprising Adventures of Daniel Defoe*, trans. Louise Ragan, London, 1929.

---, *Robinson Crusoe Examin'd and Criticis'd: or A New Edition of Charles Gildon's famous Pamphlet now published with an Introduction and Explanatory Notes together with an Essay on Gildon's Life*, London, 1923.

Edwards, Philip, *The Story of the Voyage: Sea-narratives in Eighteenth-Century England*, Cambridge, 1994.

Eisenstein, Elizabeth L., *The Printing Revolution in Early Modern Europe* (1983), Cambridge, 1992.

Eitel, Keith E., Introduction, to William Carey, *An Enquiry into the Obligations of Christians to Use Means for the Conversion of the Heathen* (1792), ed. John Pretlov, Dallas: TX, 1988.

Engler, Balz, *Poetry and Community*, Tübingen, 1990.

Fausett, David, *The Strange Surprizing Sources of Robinson Crusoe*, Amsterdam, 1994.

Fuller, Mary C., *Voyages in Print: English Travel to America 1576-1624*, Cambridge: MA, 1995.

Furbank, P.N. and W.R. Owens, *A Critical Bibliography of Daniel Defoe*, London, 1998.

---, *The Canonisation of Daniel Defoe*, New Haven: CT, 1988.

---, *Defoe De-Attributions: A Critique of J.R. Moore's Checklist*, London, 1994.

Grabes, Herbert, *Das englische Pamphlet: Politische und religiöse Polemik am Begin Neuzeit*, Tübingen, 1990.

Greenblatt, Stephen, *Marvellous Possessions: The Wonder of the New World*, Chicago, 1991.

---, *Shakespearean Negotiations*, Berkeley: CA 1988.

Grice, H.P., *Studies in the Way of Words*, Cambridge: MA, 1989.

Habermas, Jürgen, *The Structural Transformation of the Public Sphere*, trans. Thomas Burger, Cambridge: MA, 1991.

Hakluyt, Richard, *The Original Writings and Correspondence of the Two Richard Hakluyts*, quoted in Helgerson, *Forms of Nationhood*.

Heidenreich, Helmut, ed. and introduction, *The Libraries of Daniel Defoe and Phillips Farewell (Olive Payne's Sales Catalogue)*, Berlin, 1970, vii-xlix.

Helgerson, Richard, *Forms of Nationhood: The Elizabethan Writing of England*, Chicago, 1992.

Hubbard, Lucius L.,"Text Changes in the Taylor Editions of Robinson Crusoe with Remarks on the Cox Edition", *Papers of the Bibliographical Society of America*, XX/1-2 (1926), 1-76.

Hulme, Peter, *Colonial Encounters: Europe and the Native Caribbean 1492-1797* (1986), New York, 1992.

Hunter, J. Paul, *Before Novels: The Cultural Contexts of Eighteenth Century English Fiction*, New York, 1990.

---, *The Reluctant Pilgrim: Defoe's Emblematic Method and Quest for Form in Robinson Crusoe*, Baltimore: MD, 1966.

---, "Friday as a Convert", *Review of English Studies*, New Series, XIV/55 (1963), 243-48.

Hutchins, Henry Clinton, *Robinson Crusoe and Its Printing 1719-1731*, New York, 1925.

---, "Two Previously Undisclosed Versions of Robinson Crusoe", The Library 4th Series, VIII (1927-28), 58-72.

Iser, Wolfgang, *Prospecting: From Reader Response to Literary Anthropology*, Baltimore: MD, 1989.

Jordan, Robert and Harold Love, Preface, to Aphra Behn, *Oroonoko*, ed. Joanna Lipking, Norton Critical Edition, New York, 1997.

Leeson, Peter, *The Invisible Hook: The Hidden Economics of Pirates*, Princeton: NJ, 2009.

Leranbaum, Miriam, "'An Irony Not Unusual': Defoe's Shortest Way with the Dissenters", *Huntington Library Quarterly*, LXXIII/3 (September 1974), 227-50.

Levine, Joseph M., *The Battle of the Books, History and Literature in the Augustan Age*, Ithaca: NY, 1991.

Lewin, Leonard, "The Guest Word: Report from Iron Mountain", *New York Times Book Review*, 19 March 1972.

Lindsay, Jack, *The Monster City: Defoe's London 1688-1730*, New York, 1978.

Linebaugh, Peter and Marcus Rediker, *The Many-Headed Hydra: Sailors, Slaves, Commoners, and the Hidden History of the Revolutionary Atlantic*, Boston, 2000.

Lipking, Joanna, ed., Aphra Behn, *Oroonoko*, Norton Critical Edition, New York, 1997.

Little, David, *Religion, Order, and Law: A Study in Pre-Revolutionary England*, New York, 1969.

Maddox Jr., James H., "Interpreter Crusoe", *English Literary History*, LI/1 (Spring 1984), 33-52.

Maltby, William S., *The Black Legend in England: The Development of Anti-Spanish Sentiment, 1558-1660*, Durham: NC, 1971.

Maslen, Keith I., "Edition Quantities for Robinson Crusoe, 1719", *The Library*, XXIV/2 (June 1969), 145-50.

---, "The Printers of Robinson Crusoe", *The Library*, VII/1 (June 1952), 124-31.

Mitchell, Joshuah, *Not By Reason Alone*, Princeton: NJ, 1992.

Moore, J.R., *A Checklist of the Writings of Daniel Defoe* (1960), 2nd edn, Hamden: CT, 1971.

---, *"Defoe in the Pillory" and Other Studies*, Bloomington: IN, 1939.

Morgan, Edmund S., *American Slavery American Freedom: The Ordeal of Colonial Virginia*, New York, 1975.

Neil, Stephen, *A History of Christian Missions*, London, 1964.

Nicholl, Charles, *The Creature in the Map: A Journey to El Dorado*, New York, 1995.

Ogg, David, *England in the Reigns of James II and William III*, Oxford, 1984.

Oxford, Robert Harley, 1st Earl of, *Encyclopedia Britannica*, 14th edn, 1929.

Partee, Charles, *The Theology of John Calvin*, Louisville: KY, 2008.

Patterson, Annabel, *Censorship and Interpretation: The Conditions of Writing and Reading in Early Modern England*, 1984, Madison: WI, 1990.

Pocock, J.G.A., *The Ancient Constitution and the Feudal Law* (1957), Cambridge, 1987.

---, *Virtue, Commerce, and History*, Cambridge, 1985.

---, "The Fourth English Civil War", in *The Revolution of 1688-1689: Changing Perspectives*, ed. Lois G. Schwoerer, Cambridge, 1992, 52-64.

Porter, David, "A Peculiar but Uninteresting Nation: China and the Discourse of Commerce in Eighteenth-Century England", *Eighteenth-Century Studies*, XXXIII/2 (Winter 2000), 181-99

Rediker, Maurice, *Between the Devil and the Deep Blue Sea: Merchant Seamen, Pirates, and the Anglo-American Maritime World*, Cambridge, 1987.

Richetti, John J., *Popular Fiction Before Richardson: Narrative Patterns: 1700-1739* (1969), Oxford, 1992.

Rodgers, N.A.M., *The Command of the Ocean: A Naval History of Britain 1649-1815*, New York, 2005.

Rogers, Pat, "Classics and Chapbooks", in *Books and Their Readers in Eighteenth-Century England*, ed. Isabel Rivers, New York, 1982.

Schwoerer, Lois G., "The Bill of Rights: Epitome of the Revolution of 1688-9", in *Three British Revolutions: 1641, 1688, 1776*, ed. J.G.A. Pocock, Princeton: NJ, 1980, 224-43.

Searle, John R., *Speech Acts: An Essay in the Philosophy of Language*, London, 1969.

Secord, Arthur Wellesley, *Studies in the Narrative Method of Defoe*, Urbana: IL, 1924.

Sherry, Frank, *Raiders and Rebels*, New York, 1986.

Shinagel, Michael, "Contexts", and "A Note on the Text", *Robinson Crusoe*, New York, 1994, 221-24.

Siebert, Fredrick Seaton, *Freedom of the Press in England 1476-1766: The Rise and Decline of Government Controls*, Urbana: IL, 1952.

Smith, Nigel, *Literature and Revolution in England, 1640-1660*, New Haven: CT, 1994.

Souhami, Diana, *Selkirk's Island: The True and Strange Adventures of the Real Robinson Crusoe*, New York, 2001.

Sperber, Dan and Dierdre Wilson, *Relevance: Communication and Cognition*, 2nd edn, Oxford, 1995.

---, "Irony and Relevance: A Reply to Seto, Hamamoto and Yamanaashi", in *Relevance Theory: Applications and Implications*, eds Robyn Carston and Seiji Uchia, Amsterdam, 1997.

Stamm, Rudolf, *Der aufgeklärte Puritanismus Daniel Defoes*, Zurich, 1936.

Starr, G.A., *Defoe and Spiritual Autobiography* (1965), New York, 1971.

---, *Defoe and Casuistry*, Princeton: NJ, 1971.

Stone, Lawrence, "The Results of the English revolutions of the Seventeenth Century", in *Three British Revolutions: 1641, 1688, 1776*, ed. J.G.A. Pocock, Princeton: NJ, 1980, 23-108.

Taylor, Charles, *Sources of the Self: The Making of the Modern Identity*, Cambridge: MA, 1989.

Texte, Joseph, *Jean Jacques Rousseau and the Cosmopolitan Spirit in Literature: A Study of the Literary Relations Between France and England in the Eighteenth Century*, trans. J.W. Matthews, London, 1899.

Tieken-Boon van Ostade, Ingrid, "Eighteenth-century Letters and Journals as Evidence: Studying Society through the Individual", in *Literature and the New Interdisciplinarity: Poetics, Linguistics, History*, eds Roger D. Sell and Peter Verdonk, Amsterdam, 1994,179-91.

Tournier, Michel, *Friday*, trans. Norman Denny, New York, 1969.

Traugott, Elizabeth and Mary Louise Pratt, *Linguistics for Students of Literature*, New York, 1980.

Walcott, Derek, "Pantomime", in *Remembrance and Pantomime: Two Plays*, New York, 1980.

Watt, Ian, *Myths of Modern Individualism: Faust, Don Quixote, Don Juan, Robinson Crusoe*, Cambridge, 1996.

---, *The Rise of the Novel* (1957), Berkeley: CA, 1962.

Youngs, Frederic A., Henry L. Snyder, E.A. Reitan, *The English Heritage*, 2nd edn, Arlington Heights: IL, 1988.

Zimmerman, Everett, "Defoe and Crusoe", *English Literary History*, XXXVIII/3 (September 1971), 396.

INDEX

Act of Settlement (1701), 79;
Act of Uniformity (1662), 79
Amsterdam Coffee House
    abridgement, 94-95, 97,
    131-54 *passim*; action focus,
    144, 153-54; claim to
    improve the book, 94, 131;
    date, 94; deliverance, 151-
    52; father Crusoe's
    character, 139; frame story,
    94-95, 129, 135; Friday's
    conversion, 150; moral, 133,
    154; quarrel with Defoe, 96,
    98-100; Robin's guilt, 154
Ancient Constitution (*see*
    Bloodless Revolution)
Anne, Queen, censorship
    attempts, 53-54; political
    appointments, 78; zeal for
    Anglican Church, 78
Annesley, Samuel, 12, 13
Astell, Mary, 68
Assiento, 123
Athenian Gazette, 47

Bacon, Sir Francis, 216
banter (*see also* irony),
    definitions by Locke and
    Swift, 73; Defoe's style of
    argument, 218; Defoe's use
    in *The Farther Adventures*,
169, 171; Defoe's use in
Serious Reflections, 205-
209; Defoe's use in *The
Shortest-Way with the
Dissenters*, 73-77, 81-82;
Defoe's use in *The True-
Born Englishman*, 36-37
battle of the books, 42
Behn, Aphra, 20, 108, 122;
    Oroonoco, novel and play,
    20, 108
black legend, 120
bloody flag, 65
Bloodless Revolution of 1688,
    24, 32n, 37-38, 111
Boyle, Robert (*see also*
    everyday writing), 45
buccaneers (*see also* pirates/
    privateers/buccaneers), 111-
    12

Calvin, John, 211
Calvinism, 45, 140
cannibalism, compared to
    European vigilante justice,
    182; Robin's discovery, 93
Carey, William, 203-204, 209
Cast Away, 3
censorship of print, by
    prosecution for sedition, 39,
    62; during Commonwealth

period, 23; during
Elizabethan and Stuart
periods, 23-24, 46; during
Queen Anne's reign, 53-54;
lapse of licensing act, 24;
relationship to pamphlet
numbers, 24, 41; under
parliament, 24, 41
chap books, 102, 193, 223
Coetzee, J.M., 4, 227
Cooke, Edward (*see also*
privateer *and* travel writing
in Defoe's time), 90, 116
Cox, Edward, publish
abridgement, 94; quarrel
with Defoe, 95-98; quarrel
with
Defoe's publisher, 98
Cruso, Timothy, 38

Dampier, William (*see also*
privateer *and* travel writing
in Defoe's time), 90, 107,
113, 116
Defoe, Daniel, **life:** bankruptcy
12-13; dissenter
connections, 52, 64, 68;
dissenter family, 11-12;
employment by government,
56, 59, 83; indictment,
arrest, and sentence for
sedition, 62-64, 83;
knowledge of American
colonies, 77, 208-209;
library, 89n, 114, 120, 215;
London merchant, 12-13,
188; loss of political role,
85; pillory, 68; proposal of

Orinoco colony, 13;
relationship to King
William, 13, 40;
biographers and canon,
15-16; **literary categories:**
allegoric history, 89; banter,
36, 81-82, 169, 201; fable,
99; honest reader, 198;
Quixotism, 100; parable, 89,
197, 202; reflections, 96,
201; romance, 20; satyr,
100; **Works:** *An Appeal to
Honour and Justice,* 14, 85;
*A Brief Explanation of A
Late Pamphlet,* 64-65; *The
Complete English
Tradesman,* 6; *An Essay
upon Projects,* 13, 31, 40;
The Family Instructor, 6,
56; *The Farther Adventures
of Robinson Crusoe,*
critique of privateer activity,
167, 180-83; flouting
conventions, 167, 178;
Friday's death, 159-60;
global trade as Providential,
171-73; iconoclasm in
Mongolia, 163-64; island
settlement, 158-59, 175-76;
massacre at Madagascar,
162-64, 182; publication,
95-96; Robin's
inconsistency, 179-80;
Robin's increasing
isolation, 186; trading
partnership, 162-66, 164;
universal morality, 168-71,
175; universal rationality,

165-66, 170; visit to China, 163, 176-78; *A Hymn to the Pillory*, 66-68; *Jure Divino*, 31, 38, 142, 200; *Legion's Memorial*, 13, 39-40; *The Life and Strange Surprising Adventures of Robinson Crusoe*, abridged versions, 88, 94; contemporary interpreta-tion, 129, 144, 154, 221; editions, 93-94; fatherhood, 131-33, 137-42 *passim*; frame story, 134-36, 142-44; Friday's conversion, 131, 151; island as kingdom, 92, 144-45, 153-55; names, 90-93; narration, 145-48; Providence, 131-32; publication, 89, 93-94; *More Reformation,* 65; *Prefaces* to the three volumes of the Robinson Crusoe Series, 222-23; interpretation as theme, 6-7, 216; *Review*, 55, 84, 173, 208, 216; *The Serious Reflections of Robinson Crusoe*, 5, 8, 9, 98-100; dialogue with providence, 199-200, 210-13; honesty as a code, 198-99; honesty of fathers, 196; honesty of readers, 198; moral of the series, 99-100, 195; recycled essay, 186; religious *crusado*, 205-209; religious reform, 201-205; solitude as

spiritual discipline, 192-93; solitude defined, 188-89; solitude in Locke, Pope, 188; solitude in London, 188; structure of volume, 186; world religion, 200; *The Shortest-Way with the Dissenters*, 7, 9, 59-85 *passim*; analysis by scholars, 69-70; banter, 37, 73, 169; Defoe's explanation, 64, 71-72; editions, 60, 65; pamphlet responses, 68; parallel cases, 62-63; prosecution, 62-66; text, 60-62; *The Shortest Way to Peace and Union*, 66; *A Tour thro' the Whole Island of Great Britain*, 6, 64; *The True-Born Englishman*, banter, 36; defense of King William, 32, 43; editions, 32-33; explanatory preface, 33-35, 37; public reaction, 35-36, 65-66, 91; *A True Collection of the Writings of the Author of the True Born Englishman*, 65

dissenters, civic roots and restrictions, 11-12; emigration, 77; relation to commerce, 45, 89, 140; schools, 12; support for Defoe, 68

Dublin piracy of Robinson Crusoe series, 96

Dunton, John, *Athenian Gazette*, 47; Athenian

Society, 47; autobiography, 52-53; connection to Defoe, 52; connection to Swift, 52-53; defense of Defoe, 52

Edict of Nantes, revocation, 64
English cultural shift, citizen ethic, 118-19, 198-99; social structure change, 141-42
English Exploration of the Americas (*see also* travel writing *and* Raleigh, Sir Walter), by buccaneers, 111-13; contrast with Spain, 120-22; Cromwell's attack on Hispaniola and Jamaica 111, 113-14; Drake's voyage 114; Elizabethan focus on Ireland, 114; Henry Morgan, 115; privateer explorers, 113-17; ship law, 113; trade epic of Hakluyt & Purchas, 115, 118-20
The Englishman, London newspaper, 47-48; Selkirk story, 48
everyday writing, 43-46; diaries, 44-45; ledgers, 45; letters, 44; occasional meditations, 45
The Examiner, 47

fatherhood, English social structure, 139-41; good fathers in Locke, 142; honest fathers in Defoe, 196
Friday, companionship, 149, 190; conversion, 150; death, 159-60; independence, 190; son/servant, 149

Gent, Thomas (*see also* Midwinter abridgement), 100-101, 224-26
Gildon, Charles, attacks on Defoe, 7, 97, 134, 190-92, 195-99; connection to Defoe, 193-95; witness to Defoe's success, 191-93
Glorious Revolution (*see* Bloodless Revolution)

Hakluyt, Richard and Samuel Purchase, 114, 118-19, 122
Harley, Lord, 14, 62, 83, 85, 123
Heathcot abridgement, alterations in text, 97, 142-44; co-opera-tion with Taylor, 96-97
honesty as civic code,119, 198-99
Hugenot refugees, 64

iconoclasm, 163-64
irony, as echoic speech, 27-28; banter, 81-82; Defoe's echo, 75-77; not seen in *The Shortest-Way*, 62; orthodox irony, 69

Kentish Petition incident, 39-40 (*see* Defoe, **Works:** *Legion's Memorial*)

Las Casas, Bartholome (*see also* Spanish exploration), 120

literacy, development, 43

literary revolution (*see also* travel writing), 42-43; criminal biography, 109; diaries, 45; family guide, 108-109; journalism, 46; letters, 44; novels, 44; novel readers, 49, 216; occasional meditations, 45; print capitalism, 43, 48, 50, 54; Providence, 9, 29; satire, 32, 42; spiritual guide, 108; travel, 47

Locke, John, on parental power, 142; on rational competence, 153-54, 166; on the term "banter", 74; social differences questioned, 160; use of travel narrative, 169, 200-201; **Works:** *Essay on Human Understanding*, 15, 89, 200; *Second Treatise on Government*, 144

London Coffee Houses, 51

Lost, 3

Mather, Cotton, 77

Masquerade culture, 32, 54-57, 82

Midwinter abridgement, abridgement's influence, 100-101, 215; addition to the text, 225-26; agreement with Defoe, 220-21; alterations to the text, action focus, 221-22; criticism of English sailors, 223-24; English virtue, 223; honesty as a civic code, 224-25; massacre, 223-24; submission to Providence, 225-26; world religion, 226

Montaigne, Michel de, 201

Morton, Charles (*see also* dissenter), 12

Newgate Prison, 63, 82

Newington Green Academy, 12

Noble, Francis, 19

"O" abridgement, 94-95

Oaths and sincerity, 79-80

Observator, 47

Orinooco colony, Defoe's proposal, 13; Sir Walter Raleigh's proposal, 107-108

pamphlet genre, anonymous, 32, 53-55; colloquial and dramatic, 20, 31, 41-42, 54; fictionalized, 42; stage as metaphor, 55-57

pillory, effect, 64, 83

privateer/pirate/buccaneer, buccaneer origins, 111-13; Cooke, 113, 117; Dampier, 90, 113, 116; Exquamelin, 112-13; Funnell, 116; "golden age", 123-24; Johnson, 123-24; Morgan, 115; pirate culture, 113-15; pirate political impact, 124-25; pirate rules, 111; pirate tales, 109-11, 124; privateer narrative conventions, 113-15, 128, 183-84; Rogers, 48, 90, 116-17, 122, 124; utopian myth, 125-27

Providence, Calvin, 211; contradiction of "hap", 210; Defoe on submission to Providence, 191, 210; dissenter theology, 201; not syllogistic, 204, 216; trade, 171-74; voice of Providence, 46, 171, 210-22, 216, 226

public sphere, coffee houses, 51-52; development, 6, 41, 44-47, 49, 216, 219-20

Purchase, Samuel (*see* Hakluyt, Richard)

Raleigh, Sir Walter, 107-108, 119, 120

Relevance theory, 25-28, 37, 71, 104-105

Review, 46-47; Defoe's use of the stage as a metaphor, 55-56, 84

Robinson Crusoe's character: bumbling and impetuous 20, 207; confused, 20-21,179; devout, 152-53, 210; evasive, 201-202, 206; foolish, 20; practical, 153; scholarly, 185; self-centered, 202-203; spiritually weak, 202

Robinson Crusoe's names: "Bob", 91; "Crusoe", 90-91;

"Mr Englishman", 92; "Robin", 3, 91

Robinson Crusoe's self mockery: describing his activity, 146; speaking of his island kingdom, 142, 152; writing his journal, 147-49

Rogers, Woodes (*see also* privateer), 47, 90, 116-17, 122, 124

Rousseau, Jean-Jacques, his version of The *Life and Strange Surprising Adventures of Robinson Crusoe*, 102-104

Sacheverell, Henry, 65, 76, 84

savages, European vigilantes, 161, 182; Robin's assumptions questioned, 169-70, 185

seditious libel, 39

Selkirk, Alexander, 4, 47-48, 117, 189

South Sea Company, 123

Spanish Exploitation of the Americas, black legend, 120; Las Casas, 120; treasure ships, 111

Spittalfield, 64

standing army dispute, 32, 34

Steele, Richard, 47-48

Souhami, Dana, 4

Swift, Jonathan, 19, 42, 52-53, 70, 73-74

Test Act of 1673, 40

Toleration Act of 1689, 12, 60-61
Tournier, Michael, 4, 227
trade development as theme, 138, 154, 171-76
travel writing in Elizabethan times: *see* Hakluyt, Richard *and* Purchase, Samuel; *and* Raleigh, Sir Walter
travel writing in Defoe's time, conventions, 115; conventions violated by Defoe, 167, 180-83; Cooke, Edward, 90, 116; Dampier, William, 6, 90, 107, 114, 116; Defoe's use, 169-71, 183-84; Raleigh, Sir Walter, 107-108; Rogers, Woodes, 47, 90, 116-17, 122, 124; Selkirk's story, 47-48, 117, 189; use by Locke and Montaigne, 114

Tutchin, John, 34, 52

universal values, China unnatural, 176-78; desire to trade, 170, 172-76; human nature, 165-68, 175, 188; rationality, 153-54; sense of justice, 170-71
Utrecht, Treaty of, 1713, 123

Westminster Confession, 211
William, King, accession to English throne, 32n; death, 59; European leader against Louis XIV, 32; link to Defoe, 40; Protestant succession, 61; standing army controversy, 32; toleration for dissenters, 32n.
Wolcott, Derek, 4